The ENTER*PRIZE* ORGANIZATION

Organizing Software Projects
for Accountability and Success

The ENTER*PRIZE* ORGANIZATION

Organizing Software Projects
for Accountability and Success

NEAL WHITTEN

PROJECT MANAGEMENT INSTITUTE

Library of Congress Cataloging-in-Publication Data

Whitten, Neal.
    The Enterprize organization : organizing software projects for
accountability and success / Neal Whitten.
        p.   cm.
    Includes bibliographical references and index.
    ISBN: 1–880410–79-6 (pbk. : alk. paper)
     1. Computer software industry ––Management.   2. Industrial project
management.   I. Title.
HD9696.63.A2W47   1999
005.3′068′4 – – dc21   99–41279
                                                CIP

ISBN: 1-880410-79-6

Published by: Project Management Institute, Inc.
               Four Campus Boulevard
               Newtown Square, Pennsylvania 19073-3299 USA
               Phone: 610-356-4600 or Visit our website: www.pmi.org

Copyright ©2000 Project Management Institute, Inc. All rights reserved.

PMI® books are available at quantity discounts. For more information, please
write to the Publisher, PMI Publishing, Four Campus Boulevard, Newtown Square,
PA 19073-3299 USA. Call: (610) 356-4600 or visit your local bookstore.

The paper used in this book complies with the Permanent Paper Standard issued by
the National Information Standards Organization (Z39.48-1984).

10 9 8 7 6 5 4 3

DEDICATION

With loving thoughts, to:
"Pop"
(Madison Neal Whitten Sr.)

In loving memory,
Cecil Richard "Rick" Grow Jr.
(1964–1998)

John Louis Whitten
(1961–1997)

William "Bill" Branch Whitten Jr.
(1950–1995)

CONTENTS

ILLUSTRATIONS

TABLES

PREFACE

This book addresses a serious problem that has plagued the software industry since its beginning: how to effectively organize software projects to significantly increase their success rate. A powerful tool that addresses this problem is the Enter*Prize* Organization, which is fully described in this book.

> **Enter*Prize* Organization** ***n.*** A method to organize software projects to appropriately drive and balance *responsibility, personal accountability,* and *authority* across the members of a project with the intent of optimizing their performance and produce a successful project.

The Enter*Prize* Organization takes advantage of the strengths of conventionally defined organizations such as the functional organization, projectized organization, and matrix organization, while eliminating or reducing their weaknesses. The Enter*Prize* Organization is a simple, yet versatile model that works.

Consider these questions:

◆ Do you have a clearly defined software project organizational structure?

◆ Are the roles and responsibilities easily understood across the project—especially for the lead positions?

◆ For what is the project manager held accountable? How about other members of the project?

◆ How do the project positions interrelate and complement one another?

◆ Is power and leadership shared? Should they be?

You can find the answers to these critical questions (and many more) with the Enter*Prize* Organization. Learn how this powerful approach drives *accountability* for day-to-day managing of the project to nonmanagers and to as low a level into the organization as reasonable. Learn why nonmanagers, not managers, should be *owners* of the project. Read these chapters with an open mind, and be prepared to rethink how projects should be organized.

This book is *not about theories or history.* It is a how-to, real-world, no-nonsense, practical guide to organizing software projects to maximize the commitment and accountability from all projects' members. It describes the roles and responsibilities of the key project leaders, as well as for other project members.

The book also discusses the *number-one reason why project managers—and all project members—fail* in meeting their commitments. It describes why so many of us choose to adopt *too-soft* behavior, provides many examples of too-soft behavior, and discusses what you can do to become more effective in your job.

This book also discusses the *project management office* (PMO) and the many tasks it can take on in a multiproject organization. The PMO discussions include how to organize one, the dangers of not having one, and whether your PMO is respected by other members of the organization.

Additionally, this book shows you *how to obtain closure on the most critical problems plaguing a project*. The *escalation process* is described, and examples are provided to help convey the concepts behind this highly effective and essential business tool.

The book collects the experiences and wisdom of thousands of people and hundreds of projects and reduces the *lessons learned* to a simple format from which you can immediately learn and apply to your projects.

It is my objective that your *investment* in acquiring this book and in learning about and using its recommendations will be rewarded many, many times over on your current or a future project.

Neal Whitten

ACKNOWLEDGMENTS

I have been fortunate to work alongside many talented, skilled, and seasoned professionals over the years. I continue to acquire valuable skills and knowledge from the thousands of people and dozens of companies, conferences, and organizations with whom and which I work with each year. Whatever a person sets out to achieve can become a greater accomplishment because of the participation and feedback from others. The evolution of the concepts discussed in this book and the refinement of the contents of this material by many of my colleagues are such examples. I am indeed grateful.

I am especially grateful to the following people for the dedicated, candid, and significant feedback and support they provided to me during the development of many of the book's concepts and/or reviews of the manuscript: Ray DeAngelo, Kathy Demery, Julie Griffin, Dan Lynes, Ray Morrison, Don Norton, Rodney Randall, Saul Thomashow, Jim Wooten, and Bob Wysocki.

I also would like to thank the following people for their respective comments, suggestions, and support as the manuscript evolved into the book: Chuck Achuff, Mary Blanchard, Kerry Brooks, Ernie Larger, Rick Klem, Jason Rupert, Mostafa Hashem Sherif, and the Book Review Advisory Board from the Project Management Institute.

And finally I am grateful to the highly professional staff at the PMI Publishing Division for their invaluable support and guidance during the manuscript development, editing, and production. I would especially like to acknowledge the special contributions of Toni Knott and Michelle Owen.

INTRODUCTION

I have worked with many hundreds of projects over the years. These projects have varied in size from a handful of project members or less to over five hundred. The duration of these projects has ranged from several weeks to several years. Most of them focused on developing new software products or developing enhancements to existing products. Some of these projects were maintenance releases where existing products are repaired and sustained to satisfy clients.

I have personally managed some of these projects and have performed project management consulting on the other projects. Having been in the software and project management professions for nearly thirty years, I have seen some well-run projects and many more not-so-well-run projects. I have learned a plethora of lessons from my own successes and failures and from association with thousands of people on hundreds of projects over the years.

I will share many of these lessons with you, lessons that can have a profound impact on the success of your projects. Moreover, these lessons can have a profound impact on drawing out and realizing the potential of the members of a project, as well as helping you realize your own potential.

This book describes how to most effectively organize a software project to maximize the commitment and accountability from members across a project. The projects can be small (e.g., ten or less members), medium-sized, or large (e.g., hundreds of members). The roles and responsibilities of the various project leaders, as well as the roles and responsibilities of the other project members, are clearly defined.

Haunting Questions Are Answered

This book addresses questions whose answers haunt many—perhaps most—project leaders and their projects. You have probably wondered about the answers to many of these questions yourself. Here are some examples of questions that are answered in this book:

◆ What is the primary reason why projects fail?

◆ What is the primary reason why a project manager fails?

◆ How technical should managers be?

◆ When should a project manager be assigned to a project?

◆ Is it okay for a person to assume multiple key project roles such as manager, project manager, and product architect?

◆ Who owns the profit and loss responsibility of a product?

◆ Who champions the client's cause? Who is the client's primary advocate?

◆ Who owns the product requirements?

◆ Who owns the product specifications?

◆ Who is responsible for the technical outcome of the product?

◆ What project leaders perform as miniproject managers?

◆ Is it reasonable to expect projects formed from matrix organizations to be run effectively?

◆ Which management style is usually most effective: consensus management, democratic rule, micro-management, or benevolent dictatorship?

◆ Who is responsible for hiring and firing project members?

◆ Who is responsible for looking out for the professional development of project members?

◆ Who is responsible for evaluating the performance of project members?

◆ Who is responsible for ensuring that people remain employed as long as they perform satisfactorily?

◆ Who is responsible for ensuring good project management practices are followed?

◆ Who is responsible for ensuring an acceptable software development process is defined and followed on a project?

◆ Who is primarily responsible for resource planning and allocation?

◆ Who has the authority to make job assignments?

◆ Who has the responsibility to escalate issues that require help to resolve?

◆ What is the process to follow to escalate issues?

◆ To whom should project members turn when they don't know where else to turn?

◆ Who owns project documentation?

◆ Who approves project documentation?

◆ How should projects be organized if they are large? Medium-sized? Small?

- Can a maintenance organization effectively run its releases as projects?
- Should maintenance and new development work be performed by the same group?
- What are the duties of a project management office (PMO)?
- When should an organization create a PMO?

The Enter*Prize* Organization

This book describes the Enter*Prize* Organization, which takes advantage of the strengths of conventionally defined organizations such as the functional organization, projectized organization, and matrix organization, while eliminating or reducing their weaknesses. The Enter*Prize* Organization is a method for organizing software projects to appropriately drive and balance responsibility, personal accountability, and authority across the members of a project with the intent of optimizing their performance and produce a successful project. This is a simple, yet powerful model that works.

I have named this organizational approach the Enter*Prize* Organization for two primary reasons. The first is that this organizational approach for a project does not just focus on the project manager or the resource managers but also focuses on all of the key project leaders, as well as the other project members. In other words, the major roles across the *enterprise* are clearly defined and assigned. The second reason for the name is that this organizational approach offers so much value to those projects adopting it that these organizations will be viewed as *prized* assets within their companies.

Who Should Read This Book

Every member and stakeholder of a software project should read this book. It describes the roles and responsibilities of the major project leadership positions of:

- product manager
- project manager
- business architect
- product architect
- process architect
- resource managers
- team leaders.

The book also describes the roles and responsibilities of *team members*. All of these project positions represent virtually all members of a project. Said another way, this book is intended for project managers, product managers, functional managers, team leaders, quality assurance personnel, planners, developers, testers, writers, trainers, and support personnel—anyone and everyone involved in a project. If clients, contractors, and vendors are part of a project, then this book applies to them as well.

It's a book for seasoned employees, as well as those just entering the workforce. However, the more experience the reader has with software organizations, the greater the benefit that will be realized. This is so because an experienced project person can more readily identify with the many concepts and lessons upon which the Enter*Prize* Organization has been built.

Helpful Information to Know Before You Read This Book

Key lessons are highlighted. Many lessons are revealed throughout the chapters, but the key lessons are designated as **Lesson** and are highlighted by a shaded box. This technique helps you to focus quickly on the most notable points being made.

Q & A sections. Most chapters end with a question-and-answer section, *Q & A*. The questions are commonly asked by members of organizations or workshops while learning about these concepts and how to adopt them to their organizations and projects. These questions are not already answered in the main body of text.

*Read first: Overview of the Enter*Prize* Organization.* Before you skip to later chapters, you will find it helpful to read Chapter 1, Overview of the Enter*Prize* Organization. This chapter defines many concepts and terms that will be used in later chapters.

Terminology and concepts. Many of you likely will encounter terminology used in this book that is different from terminology to which you are accustomed. Although the terminology I use "gets the job done," I am not here to lobby that you necessarily adopt my terms. I am, however, advocating that you carefully study and understand the *concepts* behind the terms. I had to create some terms, so *things* can be labeled and discussed.

A reference book. Many topics discussed in this book are treated in more detail in an earlier book by the author. The book, *Managing Software Development Projects: Formula for Success, Second Edition*, published by John Wiley & Sons, 1995, is available through the Project Management Institute's online bookstore (www.pmibookstore.org), as well as through other booksellers. The topics that are treated in more detail include:

- definition and documentation of a software development process
- attributes of successful leaders
- people communications
- project planning
- project tracking
- product requirements
- product objectives
- product specifications
- change-control board/process
- vendor relationships
- project reviews
- postproject reviews.

Client versus customer. I have used the term *client* also to mean *customer*. Many software organizations produce products for a single client, who can be either internal or external to the company. However, many other software organizations produce products for many clients, ranging from dozens to hundreds or more. For simplicity of illustration, I have chosen to refer to clients in the singular: *client*.

An open mind. As you read through the many points and lessons throughout the chapters, I ask that you keep an open mind. It is difficult for most of us to change the way we have been doing our jobs and truly engage in the thoughtful thinking that must occur before significant positive change can be achieved. You are likely to recognize some familiar ways to define the key project roles and responsibilities. But, I trust you also will discover some new ideas in organizing a software project.

How This Book Is Organized

Figure I.1 shows the physical layout of the book's seventeen chapters; a glossary follows the last chapter. The following sections briefly describe the book's chapters.

Chapter 1. Overview of the EnterPrize Organization. This chapter introduces many of the basic concepts that make up the Enter*Prize* Organization. An overview of the roles and responsibilities of the project leaders and the other project members is described. Also, both functional- and project-reporting views are shown for a thirty-member project. This project is used as the perspective from which many of the basic concepts of the Enter*Prize* Organization are introduced. However, as you will find from chapters 10–13, the Enter*Prize* Organization applies to projects of *all* sizes.

FIGURE I.1

Book Layout

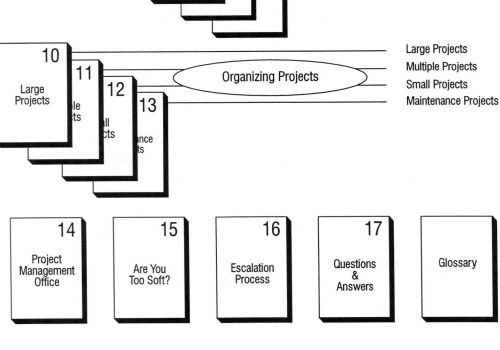

Chapters 2–9. Roles and responsibilities. These chapters describe the roles and responsibilities of the project positions defined by the Enter*Prize* Organization. The project positions are product manager, project manager, business architect, product architect, process architect, resource manager, team leader, and team member. A separate chapter is dedicated to each of these project positions.

Chapters 10–13. Organizing projects. The first of these chapters shows how a large project of about two hundred members can be organized. The next chapter illustrates how an organization comprising many projects—eight in this example—can be organized. Another chapter shows how small projects can be organized and uses examples that focus on projects of two different sizes: four members and ten members. The last chapter focuses on how projects can be organized for maintenance releases.

Chapter 14. The Project Management Office. This chapter describes the many tasks that a PMO can take on in a multiproject organization. It also discusses how to organize a PMO, the dangers of not having one, and whether your PMO is respected by other members of the organization.

Chapter 15. Are You Too Soft? This chapter discusses the number-one reason why project managers—and all project members—fail in meeting their commitments. It describes why so many of us choose to adopt *too-soft* behavior, provides many examples of such behavior, and discusses what you can do to become more effective in your job.

Chapter 16. The Escalation Process. This chapter discusses how to obtain closure on the most critical problems plaguing a project. The *escalation process* is described and two examples are provided to help convey the concepts behind this highly effective and essential process.

Chapter 17. Additional Questions and Answers. This chapter addresses questions and answers regarding the Enter*Prize* Organization that do not necessarily fit into the context of earlier chapters. Some questions address the Enter*Prize* Organization in general, and some address a specific aspect of it. These questions have been asked at workshops and consulting engagements; they are included here because of their general interest.

Glossary. A glossary of terms has been included for quick reference.

CHAPTER 1

OVERVIEW OF THE ENTER*PRIZE* ORGANIZATION

There are numerous ways to organize software development projects; obviously some are more effective than others. Many organizations embrace conventional methods such as the *functional organization*, *projectized organization*, or *matrix organization*. The EnterPrize Organization captures the strengths of conventionally defined organizations, while eliminating or reducing their weaknesses.

The EnterPrize Organization is a method for organizing software projects to appropriately drive and balance responsibility, personal accountability, and authority across the members of a project. The EnterPrize Organization defines the roles and responsibilities of the eight positions that make up a project:

1. Product manager
2. Project manager
3. Business architect
4. Product architect
5. Process architect
6. Resource manager
7. Team leader
8. Team member.

The objective of the EnterPrize Organization is to optimize the performance of the project members while yielding a successful project.

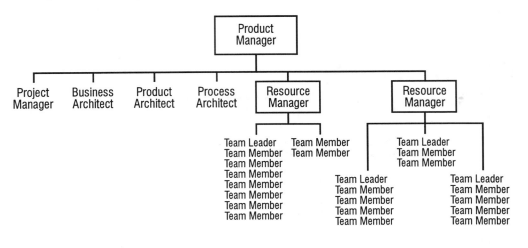

FIGURE 1.1

The Enter*Prize* Organization: Functional-Reporting View of a
Thirty-Member Project

Figure 1.1 shows the Enter*Prize* Organization applied to an organization of a single project—the simplest case chosen for illustration purposes where there is only one project under way. Let's assume that this project is made up of thirty members.

Product Manager

The *product manager* typically is an executive or senior manager. This person has the overall responsibility for the success of the *product*. The product manager is held accountable for the product—which includes profit and loss—from cradle to grave. There can be multiple *projects* occurring simultaneously, such as different versions of the product in various stages of development and maintenance, or there can be only one project under way for the product at any given time. Typically, the most critical project positions—and the most influential—report directly to the product manager: project manager, business architect, product architect, process architect, and resource managers. (See Chapter 2, The Product Manager, for more about the product manager.)

Project Manager

The *project manager* holds the most important position on a project. He directs the planning and execution of the project and is held personally accountable for the success of the project—as with the captain of a ship or a military general in the field. As problems arise, the project manager ensures that the right people are assigned to work the problems and track them to closure. The project manager behaves as if this project is a business that he owns. Working on behalf of the product manager, the project manager has considerable latitude to make decisions relating to managing the project. The project manager works closely with the business architect, product architect, process architect, resource managers, and the team leaders. As needed, the project manager also will work with various project members (in this case, also called team members) that work under the direction of team leaders. (See Chapter 3, The Project Manager, for more about the project manager.)

Business Architect

The *business architect* is the client's advocate. She is charged with ensuring that the right set of requirements are documented and understood. A requirements document typically is a small, concise document that focuses on the problems to be solved, not on the solution to those problems. In so doing, the business architect makes sure that the development community doesn't lose sight of the client's problems as the solution is being developed and readied for implementation. The business architect has approval rights on project documents that have a direct bearing on solving the client's problems (e.g., product specifications, test plans, and so on). The business architect is also charged with managing client expectations. Unfortunately, many projects do not have a single project member assigned and held accountable to watch client's interests. (See Chapter 4, The Business Architect, for more about the business architect.)

Product Architect

The *product architect* is accountable for the technical solution to the client's problems. He owns the product specifications and the overall design (architecture) of the product. The product architect ensures that the product is being *built right*, in contrast to the business architect who ensures that the *right product* is built. This person typically chairs the design- and specifications-change-control boards. As odd as it may seem, many projects do not have a single project member who is held accountable for the technical aspects of the product. (See Chapter 5, The Product Architect, for more about the product architect.)

Process Architect

The *process architect* is the *process champion* for the project. She is charged with ensuring that effective processes are defined, documented, and followed so that high productivity, high quality, and minimal cycle times are achieved. Many problems that surface on a project have their roots in weak or missing processes. The process architect begins by defining or tailoring the development process to be followed on the project. The process architect then works with project members to ensure that the processes they require for their success are put into place. Process definition can be highly specialized work, and many project members are not sufficiently trained to do it well or simply don't have the time. Furthermore, some processes require being integrated with one another and can impact many project members across a project. The process architect is continually focused on helping project members perform their duties "faster, better, and cheaper." (See Chapter 6, The Process Architect, for more about the process architect.)

Resource Manager

Resource managers hire, fire, make job assignments, coach, counsel, evaluate, award, promote, and secure future work opportunities for their direct reports. Said another way, the primary role of resource managers is to nurture their direct reports; that is, to support their direct reports in helping them be successful in two key areas: meeting their project commitments and helping them discover and achieve their potential in the organization and company. Every project member is a *direct report* to a resource manager. While the resource manager is arguably one of the most important positions in a company or organization, that is not the case on a project. However, the resource manager does play a critical role on a project. (See Chapter 7, The Resource Manager, for more about the resource manager.)

Team Leader

Each functional group (e.g., development, test, publications, training, and others) assigned to the project requires a person to lead its team. This person is called the *team leader*. Team leaders work closely with their teams (team members) in building plans and executing those plans. They perform roles and responsibilities similar to those of the project manager, only on a smaller scale. Depending on the size of the team, team leaders can take on some of the actual tasks of the team. Team leaders report directly to a resource manager and take career and professional direction from a resource manager, technical direction from the product architect, and project direction from the project manager. If this sounds confusing, it's not when the full scope of responsibilities is taken into account by all of these project positions.

In some cases, a team leader may have no team members. Examples of a one-person *team* include when there is only one tester or one writer on a project, or a project member who is providing the liaison role to a vendor. (See Chapter 8, The Team Leader, for more about the team leader.)

Team Member

The *team members* include all of the other members on a project. They report to a resource manager and mostly take technical direction for their assigned tasks from their team leader or someone else within their assigned team. Team members can also take technical direction from their resource manager or a person outside of their department such as the project manager, business architect, product architect, or process architect. In these cases, the team member might bypass working under the direction of a team leader. Figure 1.1 shows such a case with the leftmost resource manager; note that two team members work apart from a designated team leader. (See Chapter 9, The Team Member, for more about the team member.)

Working Relationships

There is considerable communication among all of the key project players. They work together in strengthening a project and helping the project manager drive the project to a successful completion. Later chapters describe in more detail the roles and responsibilities of each of these positions.

The project manager, business architect, product architect, and process architect typically do not also perform as resource managers. In rare cases, they might be resource managers to a small support staff. However, it is strongly preferred that a support staff member report to a full-time resource manager, and take technical direction from the person she supports.

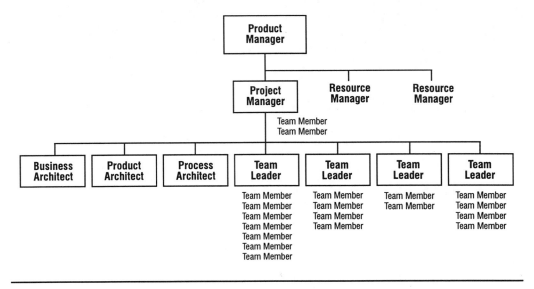

FIGURE 1.2

The Enter*Prize* Organization: Project-Reporting View of a Thirty-Member Project

The project members who attend the routine project-tracking meetings (typically conducted weekly) are the project manager, business architect, product architect, process architect, and team leaders. The project manager conducts the meeting. Resource managers are invited but typically are not required to attend. Other project members may be required to attend from time to time.

Functional-Reporting View

Figure 1.1 shows a view of the Enter*Prize* Organization from a functional-reporting perspective. It identifies who actually reports to whom from a personnel administrative point of view. Said another way, Figure 1.1 shows who has the responsibility to make job assignments, coach and counsel, write and administer performance evaluations, give salary increases and promotions, and search for future work opportunities for their direct reports. The team leader and all of his corresponding team members report directly to a resource manager.

Project-Reporting View

Figure 1.2 shows a view of the Enter*Prize* Organization from a project-reporting perspective. In the functional-reporting view (Figure 1.1), everyone is seen working for a resource manager. (Note that the product manager is a resource manager for the project manager, business architect, product architect, process architect, and resource managers.) But in the project-reporting view (Figure 1.2), the responsibility and authority that the project manager has over a project is more easily seen. This perspective clearly shows the project members who attend the routine project-tracking meetings: business architect, product architect, process architect, and the team leaders.

Notice in Figure 1.2 that the resource managers are shown as peers of the project manager. The resource managers work in a strong support role assisting their direct reports in any way necessary, but virtually all of the project work is owned and performed by other than resource managers.

Organizing for Large, Multiple, Small, and Maintenance Projects

In the purest case of the Enter*Prize* Organization, a project member does not perform the roles and responsibilities of more than one of the project positions of product manager, project manager, business architect, product architect, process architect, team leader, or resource manager. They are all full-time positions. To do so would be to dilute the attention—and therefore, the resulting effectiveness—that performing each of these roles demands. If a project cannot justify a person in one of these roles full time (e.g., the business architect), it is preferable that the person be a business architect on one or more other projects, so the person is *full time* in performing and developing the skill of a business architect. On small projects of, say, ten or less members, multiple roles can be performed satisfactorily by one project member. (See Chapter 12, Organizing for Small Projects.)

Figures 1.1 and 1.2 show a simple example of the Enter*Prize* Organization from a perspective of thirty people on a project, and that project is the only project in the organization. What if the project was much larger, say over one hundred people? How then might the Enter*Prize* Organization look? This is discussed in Chapter 10, Organizing for Large Projects.

But what if there are many projects occurring simultaneously in an organization? And what if project managers must contend for resources in this multi-project environment? What would the Enter*Prize* Organization look like? See Chapter 11, Organizing for Multiple Projects, for this discussion.

What about a support or sustaining organization one that is responsible for maintenance activities to correct problems discovered by the client, and keep applications or systems up and running? Perhaps this organization would develop some product enhancements, as well. This discussion can be found in Chapter 13, Organizing for Maintenance Projects.

You are now armed with a fundamental overview of the Enter*Prize* Organization. The chapters that follow will expand upon this view, according to your specific interest and needs.

CHAPTER 2

THE PRODUCT MANAGER

The *product manager* is the business owner. This person has overall responsibility for the success of the *product*. (The project manager has responsibility for the success of a *project*.) This means that the product manager has a vested interest in the full life cycle of the product from conception to the end-of-life. The product manager obtains product funding, has profit-and-loss responsibility, and typically performs as the product sponsor. The product manager often holds an executive-level position within the company. The product manager is also a resource manager. Therefore, most of the roles and responsibilities defined for the resource manager in Chapter 7, The Resource Manager, also apply to the product manager.

Figure 2.1 lists the major roles and responsibilities of the product manager. Let's take a closer look at each of these items.

Obtains Product Funding

The product manager is responsible for obtaining funding for the project. Before the funding can be made, a business case typically is developed. The business case substantiates the need for the product (and, therefore, the project) and discusses such critical subjects as business objectives, return on investment (ROI), market penetration, competitive pressures, legal issues, sourcing options, and so on. If the product to be developed is for in-house use, the business case development can be minimal but must include a business-objectives perspective that ties into the company's (or division's or organization's) business strategy.

FIGURE 2.1

Roles and Responsibilities of the Product Manager

◆ Obtains product funding
◆ Owns profit and loss responsibility for the product
◆ Approves product plans affecting overall product success
◆ Performs as resource manager for direct reports
◆ Performs as product sponsor
◆ Provides final point of escalation

Owns Profit and Loss Responsibility for the Product

A key area of focus for the product manager is ensuring that the product is achieving a satisfactory ROI. For those organizations producing a product to be sold outside the company, this means making a profit and achieving customer satisfaction. For organizations that build products for clients that are internal to the company, it means achieving customer satisfaction while remaining within the budgeted costs and schedules and achieving the desired quality.

It is curious that in the free-enterprise system, which so many countries throughout the world have embraced today or are moving to adopt, so many project members do not appreciate what it means to make a profit—or suffer a loss. Just as it is a mistake for parents not to teach their children how to manage budgets, expenses, savings, and the like, it is a mistake for managers at all levels to not include these concepts in the work culture of their employees. Making a profit is good business—not something about which to be timid or ashamed. Losing money is bad business; if it occurs, we need to understand what went wrong and how we can learn from the experience. We all behave according to the measurements we are being held accountable to achieve. Financial-related measurements should be included as part of the measurement system of a project to help drive a higher level of awareness and importance for making a profit (if applicable) and working within budget constraints.

LESSON 2.1

Financial-related measurements must be part of a project's measurement system to raise the project members' awareness, as well as the importance, of working within budget constraints.

Approves Product Plans Affecting Overall Product Success

The product manager, as the business owner, approves all plans that have a direct impact on the overall success of the product. This includes plans with titles such as the product plan, project plan, marketing plan, communications plan, pricing plan, rollout plan, and the like. The product manager can be closely involved in approving the details of these plans, or delegate key project members (e.g., business architect, project manager, and so on) to be involved with the creation and/or approval of these plans.

Let's look at an example of the product manager's involvement in a plan: the project plan. The project manager leads the development of the project plan. Virtually every project member is involved with the project planning process. After the project plan is constructed and approved by the project members, the product manager must approve it. Even if the plan was well constructed, the product manager can ask that it be changed to accommodate a more aggressive delivery date.

Performs as Resource Manager for Direct Reports

The project manager, business architect, product architect, process architect, and resource managers associated with a project are all highly influential project positions. The people who hold these project positions work closely with one another. Having them all report directly to the product manager (see Figure 1.1) encourages communication among themselves, and sends an organizationwide message that these are important and empowered positions. The referent power that these positions broadcast, because of their connection to the position of the product manager, has a real impact on the immediate respect that project members in these positions receive when accomplishing their tasks. Keeping that respect is a matter of earning it every day thereafter.

LESSON 2.2

The most influential project positions should report directly to the product manager—or as close as is practical.

There are times, however, when it is not practical to have all, or even most, of these positions report to the product manager. For example, if many projects are active under the same product manager, the product manager can carry the burden of too many direct reports. This situation can cause communications between the direct reports and the product manager to severely suffer. In this case, a remedy could be to insert one or more layers of reporting structure between these positions and the product manager. The goal, however, should be to have as flat an organizational structure as possible, and have these positions report as close to the product manager as is practical.

Performs as Product Sponsor

The product manager could also be called the *product sponsor* or *project sponsor*. Other labels used include *product director, project director, account manager*, and *business unit manager*. It is important for every project or product to have a sponsor who will champion its cause from a business perspective, and help remove obstacles that might harm its overall success. If a project has no apparent sponsor, or has a weak sponsor, the project will suffer a severe handicap whenever senior management support needs to be obtained. The product manager can assign a resource manager to be the product sponsor, which can help distribute responsibilities away from a very busy product manager who may have many products. It also can help prepare a resource manager who is aspiring to become a product manager.

LESSON 2.3

A project with no apparent sponsor, or a weak sponsor, will suffer at those times when senior management support is needed most.

Provides Final Point of Escalation

When a project- or product-related problem arises, and its solution requires higher levels of management to intervene, an escalation may be required. If the problem and its solution are contained within the product manager's domain, the product manager is the final point of escalation. If the domain expands outside of the product manager's control (e.g., vendor, client, or other organizational areas), the product manager might not be the final point of escalation. In either case, an escalation process should be defined at the start of the project, not after a problem arises that requires escalating. The escalation process should include the escalation paths for all potentially affected organizations. (See Chapter 16, The Escalation Process, for more information on the subject of escalations.)

LESSON 2.4

The escalation paths should be defined for every project.

Q & A

Q2.1   If the product manager has the overall responsibility for the success of the product from conception to end-of-life, doesn't that mean that a product manager likely is juggling more than one project at a time?

A2.1   A product manager can be responsible for multiple products or multiple projects related to a single product, or both—all at the same time. For purposes of illustration, let's look at a case where the product manager has multiple ongoing projects focusing on a single product.

Figure 2.2 shows the version activity of a product; the first appearance of the product is called Version 1.0 in the figure. There are three additional versions shown: Version 2.0, Version 3.0, and Version 4.0. A version is considered the first offering of the product or follow-on offerings with significant enhancements added. Each version is a project and, in this example, requires one full year to develop. A new version is started every six months, and a version is shipped (e.g., delivered to a client or placed into production) every six months.

Figure 2.2 also shows maintenance *releases* for each new version. A maintenance release contains fixes to problems discovered in the released product and could also contain some minor enhancements. (Maintenance releases typically are made available at no charge if you already have purchased the version.) The new version, Version 1.0, has five maintenance releases: V1.1, V1.2, V1.3, V1.4, and V1.5. Each maintenance release in the figure is a project and requires four months to prepare. A maintenance release is begun every two months, and a maintenance release is shipped every two months.

FIGURE 2.2

Versions and Maintenance Releases of a Product

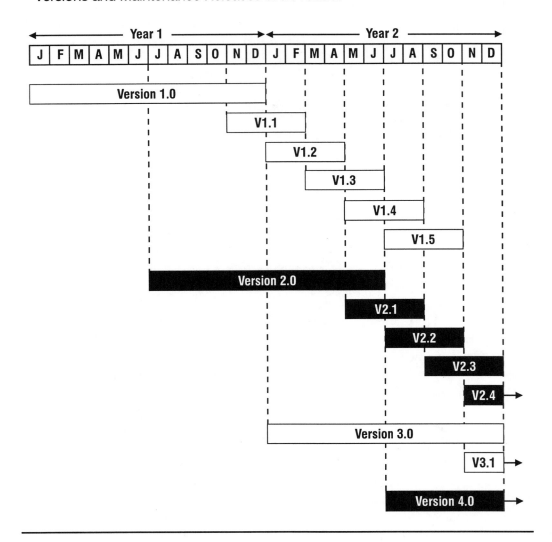

Looking again at Figure 2.2, notice that in the month of January of the second year, there are four projects under way. The projects are V1.1, V1.2, Version 2.0, and Version 3.0. There could be a different project manager assigned to each of these projects. However, V1.1 and V1.2 may be run by the same project manager if the two projects are relatively small in effort. (See Chapter 13, Organizing for Maintenance Projects, for more on managing maintenance projects.)

Q2.2   Referring to the last answer and Figure 2.2, is there something significant about the versions shipping every *six months* and maintenance releases every *two months*?

A2.2   Figure 2.2 is intended to show the broad responsibility of a product manager and that there can be many projects under way at the same time. The durations shown for the new versions and maintenance releases have been created for illustrative purposes and might not apply to your situation. However, it is important to establish routine deliveries of new versions and maintenance releases for reasons discussed in Chapter 13, Organizing for Maintenance Projects.

Q2.3   How important is it that the product manager be held responsible for the profit and loss of the product (or for meeting budget constraints for products that are for internal company use)?

A2.3   Very important—it is the difference between the mindset one has when owning a company versus being a worker in that company. The product manager is in a position of great authority and influence. The product manager will work smarter, be more creative, and feel more commitment if her performance is measured, in part, by the profit earned from the product and the overall client satisfaction with the product. If someone other than the product manager is responsible for making a profit, the product manager is at least one position removed from feeling the full accountability for the product's success. This one position removed can make all the difference when tapping into the product manager's full potential for excelling and achieving. Furthermore, if the product manager is not held responsible for the product's profit and loss, then a power struggle, big or small, will likely be felt between the product manager and the *real* owner of the product. Power struggles generally are very unproductive.

LESSON 2.5

Having one person—the product manager—be responsible for profit and loss unleashes the motivation and passion required for the product manager to want to perform at her very best.

Q2.4 What are some examples of financial-related measurements that a product manager should track?

A2.4 The product manager can choose to track many different types of financial-related measurements. For example, there are *point-in-time* measurements such as performance against the project budget, estimated budget at completion, and release of funds for new stages of development work. Another category of measurements can be called *trend* measurements such as cost per effort hours, cost per function point over time, or cost per thousands of lines of code. There are also *externally focused* measurements such as maintenance costs and product net income.

Q2.5 Is it okay for a marketing or sales group to set—without the product manager's participation—commitments that the product manager and his organization must meet?

A2.5 Of course not, but it commonly happens. Marketing and sales groups and the product manager must work closely to ensure that commitments made are realistic and can be fulfilled. Client deals should never be cut without the product manager's participation in reviewing the proposals and assessing the effort, costs, and rewards that can be expected.

LESSON 2.6

All product commitments require the authorization of the product manager.

Q2.6 Does everyone on the project have to report into the product manager's organization?

A2.6 No, it may be preferred, but this situation is not always realistic. It is unlikely that all of the needed skills would be found within a product manager's organization. A project can have members from vendors, clients, and other areas of the company. What is important, however, is that once the members of a project are identified, they all take direction from the project manager or other key positions within the product manager's domain. For a project to be optimally managed, it must have clearly defined roles, responsibilities, and lines of authority.

LESSON 2.7

To have an effectively run project, there is no requirement that all members of a project come from within the product manager's organization.

Q2.7   What if the product manager is not completely in charge?

A2.7   Some*one* should always be in charge. If it is not the product manager, it should be an executive who works for the product manager's company. For example, let's look at a software installation project. Many of the resources assigned to the project may be client employees or employees of a vendor. These *noncompany* employees may be performing activities such as training, software environment upgrades, acceptance testing, security registration, data preparation and clean-up, and so on. This can create special problems for the project manager, and they cannot all be solved by the product manager.

One approach is to designate executive-level project sponsors consisting of the product manager, a key executive from the product manager's company (if the product manager cannot fill the position), a key executive from the client, and from each key vendor. These executives serve as an executive support board (ESB) for the project manager. When a project manager must escalate an issue across company boundaries, it is expected that the issue will never go higher than the ESB. The goal is to secure agreement for an acceptable resolution. However, in lieu of an agreement, the executive from the product manager's company has the final say. Why? Because the project manager and product manager are charged with driving the project (in this case, a product installation) to a successful completion. The project manager cannot be held accountable for the project, nor the product manager for the *profit and loss*, if they are not in control of the project and then remain in control. Any deviation by the client or vendor from the original scope must be properly sized; that is, its impact must be stated in terms of schedules, costs, and quality—and allow the business drivers to prevail.

A note of caution: If the product manager *does not* insist on maintaining control over the product and project—even if that means escalating to the highest levels of the executive leadership—you can bet that when the *dam bursts*, the product manager will be the first to feel the pain. Clients want the product manager (and her designate, the project manager) to assertively drive the project to a successful closure, even if that means upsetting the client's apple cart from time to time.

LESSON 2.8

The client, in spite of commonly giving mixed signals, *wants* to rely on the product manager (and project manager) to drive the project to a successful conclusion. *No wimps need apply!*

CHAPTER 3

THE PROJECT MANAGER

*T*he project manager has the single most important position on a project with overall responsibility for the success of that project. This high-profile position comes with a tremendous amount of responsibility, accountability, ownership, and authority. Because of the criticality of the role, project managers must be carefully selected, trained, and nurtured to give them every opportunity to be successful—for themselves, their projects, their organizations, and their companies. The project manager is sometimes referred to with different labels, such as *engagement manager*, *project coordinator*, or *project architect*. However, in the Enter*Prize* Organization, as with generally accepted practice, the term is *project manager*.

Figure 3.1 lists the roles and responsibilities of the project manager. Let's examine each of these items.

Has Full Responsibility and Accountability for the Project

The project manager is not merely a coordinator of project activities. She is the glue that holds the project and its members together. The project manager accepts and welcomes full responsibility for the project, and recognizes that she is the primary focal point for the accountability of the project. This is where the buck stops.

LESSON 3.1

The project manager is fully accountable for the outcome of the project and must be trained and encouraged to behave accordingly.

If there is a problem anywhere on the project, the project manager is ultimately responsible for ensuring that the problem is appropriately addressed. You may be thinking, "How can one person be responsible for every problem on a project? That's not fair—nor is it reasonable."

LESSON 3.2

The project manager cares about the resolution of any project problem that can negatively affect the outcome of the project.

Each project member has responsibilities that are his own to address. However, all of us, at one time or another, need help from others before we can make needed progress, or we are not sure of the priorities we should be working or simply are not sure what we need to do next. It is the responsibility of the project manager to maintain open and timely communications across the project, especially with key project leaders. This is accomplished in a number of ways when the project is being planned or with weekly project-tracking meetings, one-on-one discussions, work meetings as appropriate, escalation meetings, and others. Once a project manager becomes aware of a potential or real problem, she works with those involved to ensure that an acceptable solution is planned, worked, and tracked to closure.

Owns the Business of Running the Project

The most effective project managers demonstrate a passion for driving the project to a successful completion as if the project represented his *own* business—with ten or less employees. Why so few? Because most of us more easily can relate to a business that is small and that we personally own. The small business model helps us better comprehend the potential impact of our choices and behaviors. If it is the right thing to do for *our* business, then it is almost always the right thing for the project that we are driving.

LESSON 3.3

The project manager leads the project as if it was his *own* business.

FIGURE 3.1

Roles and Responsibilities of the Project Manager

- ◆ Has full responsibility and accountability for the project
- ◆ Owns the business of running the project
- ◆ Demonstrates leadership; makes things happen
- ◆ Has no direct reports
- ◆ Applies lessons learned from recent projects
- ◆ Defines project roles and responsibilities
- ◆ Leads the project planning activities
- ◆ Performs project tracking
- ◆ Adopts project management best practices
- ◆ Manages to project priorities; performs risk management
- ◆ Communicates project status upward and to the client
- ◆ Drives decision making to lowest level reasonable
- ◆ Promotes client involvement
- ◆ Encourages and supports escalations
- ◆ Enforces effective change control
- ◆ Challenges conventional thinking
- ◆ Mentors project members
- ◆ Promotes good working relationships
- ◆ Preserves key project documentation

Demonstrates Leadership; Makes Things Happen

It is not enough to be a project head. Someone needs to actually take charge of the project and instill the needed day-to-day discipline required to drive the project to a successful completion. The project members expect the project manager to satisfy this crucial need.

LESSON 3.4

"Leadership is action, not position."

Donald McGannon, American broadcasting executive

We all want to follow a leader who will take us down a path that achieves *success*. Even if we are leaders ourselves, we cherish following someone in whom we believe and a cause in which we believe. The project manager has this very important mission. She is the person to whom anyone on the project should be able to turn when there is nowhere else to turn or when a project member is uncertain where to turn.

LESSON 3.5

The project manager is the person to turn to when there is no where else to turn, or it is uncertain where to turn.

You don't have to be the smartest, most knowledgeable person on the project to be the leader, the project manager. You do, however, need to have the knowledge, skills, and experience to be able to recognize when problems surface or when potential problems are looming. You must be able to articulate those problems, bring the right people together to solve them, and know when problems have been properly addressed and closed—all this with the proper sense of urgency that the problem requires.

A project manager believes in her ability to make a difference. She recognizes the important role that she serves and uses this position to drive the needed change and behavior across a project. The project manager is an always visible force on a project that project members become conditioned to trust and interact with as needed.

The single most influential person on a project or in a project-oriented organization is the project manager. Some people believe that it is someone in management or an executive position; almost always this is not true. The project manager works with the troops in the trenches—where the real day-to-day work is performed. The leadership exhibited by the project manager will more directly influence and impact more people than any other position. If the culture must be changed, the project manager is typically in the best position to affect that change—more than anyone else.

LESSON 3.6

The project manager occupies the most influential position on a project.

Has No Direct Reports

The project manager must be focused on driving the project to a successful completion, which is almost always a full-time job. If it's not, the project manager can lead several small project teams at once. The project manager must not also be a resource manager with other responsibilities for people and assignments. Another way to say this is that the project manager should not have *direct reports*; only resource managers have direct reports. Having direct reports means that you also have *administrative* responsibilities, performing such duties as hiring and firing employees; evaluating performance; providing salary increases, promotions and awards; and working with employees to help them achieve long-term training and job assignment goals. These resource manager responsibilities address manager-employee issues.

If a project manager requires support staff (e.g., project analysts) to help him with day-to-day project management responsibilities, that staff should report directly to a resource manager for manager-employee issues but be *dotted line* to the project manager to take direction for assigned tasks. (Chapter 7, The Resource Manager, Section *Q&A7.1*, discusses why a project member holding a key Enter*Prize* Organization position should not also take on the roles and responsibilities of another key Enter*Prize* Organization position.)

Applies Lessons Learned from Recent Projects

A practice of great value is performing postproject reviews to identify lessons learned that can be applied to future projects. The project manager is responsible for ensuring that time is set aside to perform this activity. He is also responsible for ensuring that the most important lessons learned from the most recent postproject reviews are carefully studied and applied to his future projects.

> **LESSON 3.7**
>
> The project manager must show that he has reviewed the lessons learned from the most recent projects and applied the most important lessons to the new project.

Many projects don't require high-priced consultants to determine what the most important problems are. Project managers need only to listen to the wealth of wisdom and experience bottled within the project team—and then take appropriate action. Consultants may be useful, however, in helping to address specific identified problems.

Defines Project Roles and Responsibilities

Many projects fail to have clearly defined roles and responsibilities for core leaders, not to mention all project members. The resource managers are responsible for defining the roles and responsibilities of their employees. However, when that has been neglected or has been weakly defined, the project manager must get involved. She must insist that all project members know what is expected of them—particularly the key project positions identified in the Enter*Prize* Organization.

> **LESSON 3.8**
>
> The project manager is ultimately responsible for ensuring that project members understand what is expected of them.

Leads Project Planning Activities

The project manager drives the most important plan of a project—the project plan. The project manager trains the project members—or ensures that they are properly trained—to prepare an effective plan for their assigned areas. Plans should address items such as scope, schedules, resources, costs, assumptions, dependencies, and risks.

> **LESSON 3.9**
>
> The project manager directs the creation, approval, and ongoing change control of the project plan.

The project manager personally and thoroughly reviews, at a minimum, the more important parts of the overall project plan but is accountable for all of it. Depending on the size and complexity of the project, he might review all parts of the project plan. The project manager's support staff must review any areas not personally reviewed by the project manager.

The project manager ensures that the proper approvals are obtained for the project plan. He then ensures that the proper change-control steps are followed to keep the project plan current.

Performs Project Tracking

The project manager is responsible for the effective, routine tracking of the project's progress. This is intended to be a proactive exercise; that is, discover potential problems *before* they occur. This is the number-one reason for tracking a project. The second reason is to put recovery plans in place before unrecoverable harm occurs.

> **LESSON 3.10**
>
> The number-one reason for tracking a project is to discover potential problems *before* they occur.

The participants of a project-tracking meeting include the business architect, product architect, process architect, team leaders, and the project manager, who runs the meeting. Resource managers are invited, but their attendance is optional. However, resource managers can learn a lot about the project and how their team's commitments are progressing, as seen through the eyes of other project members, by attending these meetings. Resource managers also show their support for their direct reports by attending. Other project members may attend as needed.

To have an effective project-tracking meeting, there must be an approved project plan; otherwise, what are project members being tracked against? Even a project that is only days or weeks old should have a short-term plan from which to track the progress being made by project members. The plan might only be two to four weeks in duration until another miniplan or the real project plan can be developed, but it is important to have some plan against which the project members can pace themselves.

The best-run projects provide an environment that makes it easy for project members to communicate problems. It is the problems that are hidden from view that have the greatest potential for harm, because they are not properly confronted and addressed. The project manager must ensure that problems are being reported in a penalty-free environment and are deliberately being resolved as needed. The discipline that the project manager demonstrates in running the project-tracking meetings will have a direct influence on the discipline demonstrated throughout the project.

> **LESSON 3.11**
>
> Effectively run projects require effectively run project-tracking meetings.

If a project manager demonstrates behavior that consistently allows the tracking-meeting participants to exhibit a lack of professional behavior, then what is being created, one day at a time, is a "failed project waiting to happen." Examples of poor professional behavior are evident when the project manager or project members come to the tracking meetings late, skip meetings, or come to meetings ill prepared. Other examples of poor behavior are when the project manager doesn't insist on recovery plans for potentially or already late tasks, nor works closely with project members who are in trouble and need help. The project manager must lead by example.

Adopts Project Management Best Practices

The project manager is responsible for understanding acceptable project management *best practices*. The project manager serves as the primary catalyst to ensure that these practices are deployed throughout the project's life cycle.

LESSON 3.12

The project manager, not management, is responsible for defining, teaching, and enforcing the use of good project management practices.

A frequent occurrence for me is to ask the project manager of a project in trouble, "What are the project management practices being followed?" I commonly get the response, "We don't follow many accepted project management practices. Management has done a poor job of institutionalizing such practices." The reality is that the project manager has the responsibility for defining, teaching, and enforcing the use of good project management practices; it is not the responsibility of the project or organization's resource managers to perform this role.

Manages to Project Priorities; Performs Risk Management

The top problem on all projects in trouble is that the priorities—the most important project-related problems—are not being worked and closed with the sense of urgency they require. Instead, they linger for weeks or even months. The project manager must ensure that the project's most important problems are identified, assigned to the appropriate project members, and mitigated with the sense of urgency they deserve.

LESSON 3.13

The number one problem on all projects in trouble is that the most important problems are not being worked to a swift closure.

The project manager, as well as every project member, should always identify the top three to five priorities that need to be worked. Furthermore, they should demonstrate discipline to focus most of their daily energies on resolving these priorities.

LESSON 3.14

The most effective project managers spend most of their time each day appropriately addressing the project's top three to five priorities.

The term *top three to five priorities* can include problems that are highest risk for adversely affecting the project. It can also include problems that are not risks; that is, they are problems already known to adversely affect the project. Whether or note the top three to five priorities are problems that are still categorized as risks, they all need to have plans put in place to mitigate the damage they can or might cause. These plans could be called *priority management plans* or *risk management plans*. (See Q3.5 of the Q&A section of this chapter for more information on managing priorities.)

Communicates Project Status Upward and to the Client

The project manager is responsible for all project status being reported outside the project. He may or may not personally report this status, depending on the size of the project and the full duties being performed by the project manager. However, all significant project status reported outside of the project must be personally reviewed and approved by the project manager.

LESSON 3.15

No significant project status leaves the boundaries of the project without the approval of the project manager.

Drives Decision-Making to Lowest Level Reasonable

The project manager ensures that the project members understand the notion of empowerment. *Empowerment* means understanding your job, taking ownership of it, and doing whatever is necessary to accomplish that job, providing that it is within legal and ethical parameters. The ownership for the work being performed must be driven to the lowest reasonable level—the level where the *accountability* for the decision lies. In so doing, project members—with proper training and coaching—will almost always rise to the expectations placed on them.

Promotes Client Involvement

The project manager, working with the business architect, ensures that the proper level of client involvement with the project is occurring. Although the business architect is directly charged with being the client's advocate, the project manager verifies that the client is well represented.

Quality can be defined simply as *satisfying the client*. It is not enough for the project manager, working with the product architect and process architect, to ensure that the product is built *right*. It is equally important that the *right* product is developed. Client involvement in the development process helps ensure a satisfied customer. It is up to the project manager, working with all of the project's leaders, to ensure that the client is sufficiently involved throughout the project life cycle.

Encourages and Supports Escalations

When two parties are at an impasse in resolving an important issue, someone must make sure that the issue is driven to an acceptable closure in a timely manner. The project manager creates (if needed) and supports the culture that utilizes escalations as a healthy and important business tool. If the project manager determines that these issues are not being urgently addressed and closed with the attention that they require, the project manager serves as a catalyst to help drive the issue to an acceptable closure.

> **LESSON 3.16**
>
> The project manager is responsible for creating and maintaining a project culture where escalations, when needed, are viewed as good business and are not viewed as being personal.

Escalations should be initiated within *two* days of knowing that involved parties are at an impasse in resolving an issue. An earnest attempt at resolving the issue should have occurred before an escalation is started. (See Chapter 16, The Escalation Process, for more on the subject of escalations.)

Enforces Effective Change Control

The project manager ensures that the proper level of change control is in place for key project items, so scope creep, communications, and quality are carefully managed. These items can include product requirements, product specifications, project plan, contracts, product code, and documentation.

Change-control teams can be an effective tool in enforcing effective change control. Change-control teams should not be vote or consensus driven; instead, the chairperson should serve as the only person with a vote. The chairperson is responsible for making the right *business* decision after listening and discussing the input from team members. Consensus or majority-vote teams frequently compromise issues to the extent that the best business decision gets diluted, and a less-than-optimal solution is implemented. An individual needs to be held accountable for the outcome. The notion of accountability often gets weakened and impersonal when applied to teams.

Challenges Conventional Thinking

A project manager doesn't follow traditional practices unless those practices prove to be of suitable value. Instead, the project manager serves as a catalyst for change, practicing the *right thing* to do rather than the traditional or standard practice. This *forward thinking* can have a profound effect on driving positive change through a project or organization.

> **LESSON 3.17**
>
> The most effective project managers do not adhere simply to past traditions but to being a catalyst to ensure that the *right thing* is done.

You will not recognize your organization three years from now. The technology will have changed, processes will have changed, the tools you use will have changed, and even many of the faces around you will be different. Your organization may have downsized, upsized, been sold off, or been outsourced, or a plethora of other actions may have occurred. Even one year from now, your organization will undergo significant change. Here's the golden question: "Will *you* be the catalyst for those changes?" Someone will; a small number of people in an organization will be the primary catalysts for the change. It could be you. Will it?

Mentors Project Members

All project members need some degree of mentoring from time to time—some encouragement, pointers, or a sounding board. To the extent necessary, the project manager fills this often overlooked but critical role. Furthermore, if a project member is floundering and the project could become at risk—and the project member is not receiving the needed coaching and counseling from his resource manager, team leader, or other designate—the project manager must make a business decision to appropriately intervene. Whether the project manager works alongside those in an authority position with the project member, gets personally involved one on one, or does both is a matter of choice. However, in all cases, the project manager makes himself "present and accounted for."

LESSON 3.18
The most effective project managers are teachers and helpers.

Promotes Good Working Relationships

The project manager encourages good working relationships among all project members, as well as with the client. People associated with the project will take a cue from the project manager regarding the behavior to embrace when working with others. The project manager is in a unique position of influence across the project team. When a project member or team has a problem, it's up to the project manager to step in and help if that problem is not getting the attention it requires, or if the project manager can add value to the problem resolution process. The example the project manager demonstrates in working with others is a powerful influence across all project players.

LESSON 3.19
The project manager is the most influential person to promote good working relationships across a project.

Project managing is not about punishing, inflicting pain or embarrassment, belittling, and the like. These behaviors are *always* unacceptable. Instead, the project manager gives help and ensures that the knowledge, skills, and experiences found across the project are shared when needed. The project manager understands that a successful project requires that all project members be successful and sincerely work as a cohesive team.

Preserves Key Project Documentation

The project manager ensures that important or potentially important project documentation is preserved for audit, review, historical, template, and legal purposes. For example, using documents from past projects as starting points or templates for related documents on new projects can be a big time and productivity saver. Also, when starting a project, always assume that the project will wind up in litigation. Although only a small number of projects do, the project manager should assume the worst case and plan appropriately.

LESSON 3.20

Preserving project documentation can be of great benefit to the current project, as well as to future projects.

Q & A

Q3.1   How does a project manager, or any other project member, perform successfully when the responsibility and accountability is given to her, but the authority is not.

A3.1   It is a copout in almost all cases to believe that you do not have the authority that goes along with your responsibility and accountability. When was the last time you were reprimanded for exceeding your authority? Most of us cannot recall a time. Be a doer. Be bold. Take charge of your assigned duties. (See Chapter 15, Are You *Too Soft?* for more on making things happen.)

LESSON 3.21

You already have the authority, but do you take it?

Q3.2 Who is responsible for deciding the process to follow on a new project if there is no defined software development process for the organization?

A3.2 The process architect is responsible for ensuring that an acceptable software development process is defined and followed. Without such a process, it is futile to prepare a project plan. However, the project manager works closely with the process architect and other project members on this process and also has approval rights. (See Chapter 6, The Process Architect, for more on this subject.)

Q3.3 What if a project is made up of vendors, contractors, and client personnel in addition to the company's personnel? How should the project manager relate to each of these diverse groups?

A3.3 This is a common problem on many projects; yet the answer is simple. Once people are assigned to a project, regardless of where they are from, they are all treated the same—*no exceptions.* Figure 3.2 shows a project that consists of all of these groups. For purposes of illustration, each team is led by a team leader and made up of a different group of project members: company personnel, vendor personnel, contractors, and client personnel. Note that it is possible for a team leader to have a mixture of people from these different groups. (The product manager and resource managers are intentionally not shown for simplicity of illustration.)

LESSON 3.22

Every member of the project is treated the same, regardless of his origin: company, vendor, contractor, or client.

The project manager, for the most part, is blind to their origins. The project manager sees everyone as a project member and will work with each group and person as if all were company personnel. Each group is expected to have plans, commit to them, and track according to them. If any area is in trouble or headed that way, the project manager initiates the attention required to help the group get back on plan. Every group is held just as accountable for its commitments as any other group. I commonly see project managers treat the client's people assigned to the project with kid gloves, and I often see vendors treated as if they are a tamperproof black box. The project manager must treat each project member the same and hold each accountable for his commitments. The project is sure to suffer if preferential treatment is given to any person or group.

FIGURE 3.2

A Project-Reporting View of a Project That Includes Personnel from Company, Vendor, Contractors, and Client

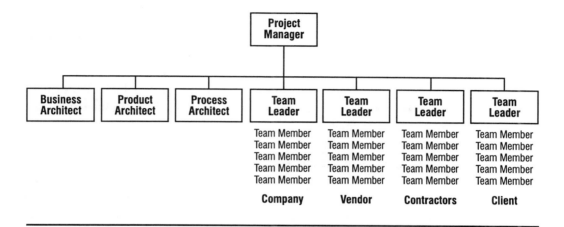

Q3.4   Referring to the previous question, what if each of these different groups were accustomed to using different processes, standards, and tools before they all came together as a project team? Can they continue to use them?

A3.4   The answer is strictly up to the project manager and the process architect; however, other project members may get involved as well. If the project manager and process architect view that the *outside* methods are not as effective as the *in-house* methods—or perhaps are even counterproductive—the in-house methods will prevail. The right *business* decision must be made.

Q3.5   If managing priorities is so important, do you have any special tips to share?

A3.5   All project members should manage to their top three to five priorities to make the most effective use of their time. Let's look at an example of how this is performed by a project manager.

LESSON 3.23

The project's top three to five priorities must be tracked daily and resolved as quickly as reasonably possible.

First, identify the top three to five priorities. You probably already know what they are, but if you aren't certain, you can do the following. Assemble a small team consisting of project members holding key project positions, such as those defined in the EnterPrize Organization. (If the project team is very small, then assemble the entire team.) Brainstorm and generate a list of project problems; now prioritize the list of problems based on the importance of them being solved. Clip the list after the top three to five items, and focus only on these. Now assign a person to own each problem, preferably a different owner per problem. The assigned person puts together a plan to resolve the problem, which can be called a *priority management plan* or a *risk management plan*. The plan identifies, at a minimum, the following items:

◆ who owns the problem
◆ activities to be performed to resolve the problem
◆ owner of each activity (if different from the owner of the problem to be resolved)
◆ dependencies that each of the activities have on other activities
◆ duration of each activity
◆ special items of note, if any, such as the likelihood of this problem occurring (if it is a risk)
◆ persons who must sign off (approve) the plan; these are people with whom the plan has a dependency for it to be successful
◆ how the plan can be tracked daily.

Each plan must be trackable on a *daily* basis. (All other project problems are tracked on a weekly basis.) The owner of each of the top three to five problems meets with the project manager at a designated time each day. For example, one problem owner meets in the project manager's office from 4 to 4:15 P.M. each day, another meets from 4:15 to 4:30 P.M., and so on. Meeting each day, even if only for five or ten minutes, shows the sense of urgency that is placed on resolving the problems. Each problem should be closed as soon as reasonably possible. It is expected that an owner of a top problem is spending most of her time each day in solving the problem. If this is not the case, the person's time is not being used effectively on the project. As the top three to five problems are worked off the priority list, the next level of priority problems are assigned, addressed, and so on throughout the project.

Q3.6   We do postproject reviews on most of our projects, but we don't do a good job of applying lessons learned to new projects. Any ideas?

A3.6   See the section, *Ensuring That New Projects Apply Lessons Learned*, in Chapter 14, The Project Management Office, for an approach that can help.

Q3.7   Because you recommend that the chairperson of a change control team is the only person with a vote that counts, what if that person does the following: The chairperson makes a decision that has a harmful effect on some aspect of the project, such as causing the product delivery schedule to slip or the project budget to overrun? Does the chairperson have authority to do this?

A3.7   Only the product manager can approve changing items that have been externally committed, such as product delivery dates and budgets, and sometimes only with the support of the client. However, the chairperson does have the responsibility to *propose* the best business solution. If that solution breaks product commitments, it cannot be committed without also obtaining support from the product manager. In all cases, the project manager must be involved to ensure that the impact of such decisions is understood and appropriately implemented if approved.

LESSON 3.24

Both the project manager and the product manager must be involved before a commitment that has been promised to someone outside of the project can change.

Q3.8   It is common in our organization to be given the end date for a new project, and then we work backwards to put a project plan in place to attempt to meet the end date. Isn't this a bad practice?

A3.8   This not only is a common practice; it can also be an effective practice. For example, if the desired end date is not given, the project members will likely spend a lot of time putting a plan in place that will *not* be desirable or acceptable. To avoid rework and wasting precious people resources, every attempt should be made to do it right the first time. Not only is it often desirable for a project team to be given an end date, it should also be given target dates for when major phases or key activities (e.g., product specifications, design, code, unit test, function test, and system test, to name a few) should complete. These target dates help the project members to understand how much they need to stretch themselves in developing an acceptable plan.

It is a bad practice, however, to challenge a project team to build a project plan based on an end date, and then ignore feedback that the end date is not achievable. When this occurs, the project manager can bring in someone from outside the project to act as a sanity check to see if the project plan is reasonable and achievable. This outsider should preferably be from inside the company but be independent of the project being reviewed. It should be a person that has credibility or can earn credibility among the management team members.

LESSON 3.25

Creating a project plan based on being given the preferred project end date and/or intermediate target dates for completing major phases of the project can be an effective planning practice, providing that only achievable plans are committed.

Q3.9 As a follow-up to the last Q&A, what can be done when the project members are expected to commit to something that they haven't even defined in detail yet?

A3.9 Software projects often get a bum rap for missing schedules and commitments to clients and executives. Think about it: Who in their right mind would commit to dates and costs to produce something, when that something is not even clearly defined or understood? Moreover, who would expect someone to commit to them under these circumstances?

An answer lies in the following. When building a project plan, the project manager and project members are committing to achieve the first major phase. Although the project plan should include activities and estimated schedules and costs for work that must be performed throughout the project, stretching far beyond the first major phase, the far-reaching estimates should not be interpreted as firm commitments. Instead, at the end of every major phase of the software development process or project cycle, there should be an activity—called, for example, *resize project*—that is part of the project plan. The project is then optionally resized, if this activity is judged by the project manager as being required. If the resizing activity is not a planned event included in the project plan, the project manager will appear *out of control* in calling for a resize exercise. But, if the resize project activity is made part of the project plan, the project manager is following the plan.

An exception to firmly committing to only one major phase at a time is when a contract is being signed that commits the schedules and costs for the entire project. Although not desirable, sometimes this is necessary. In these cases, the contract must be carefully reviewed by the appropriate project members (e.g., project manager, business architect, and product architect) to ensure that the project is not being overcommitted or under funded. Even in the case of contracts, it is often wise to resize the project at the completion of major phases so that the *new news* can be appropriately addressed.

LESSON 3.26

Project plans should include a *resize project* activity at the end of each major phase of the project.

Q3.10   How often should a project formally be tracked?

A3.10   Project-tracking meetings should occur once a week (The exceptions are small projects that are only several weeks or less in duration, in which case, project-tracking meetings could occur more frequently.) Meeting less often than each week can allow the discovery or discussion of serious problems to be delayed, which can result in harming the successful outcome of the project. Meeting more frequently than weekly can be quite unproductive by wasting valuable time, because it requires members of the project-tracking meeting to spend additional time preparing more than one progress status per week. It also requires the project-tracking members to spend additional time in meetings rather than being free to work their plans.

LESSON 3.27

Project-tracking meetings should occur weekly.

Q3.11   Does it matter what day of the week one conducts the project-tracking meeting?

A3.11   Yes, routine project-tracking meetings are very important to the health of a project, and require participants to attend—on time and prepared. Therefore, avoid having meetings on Mondays or Fridays; these days are often used as holidays or personal days for extended weekends. Furthermore, meeting participants use Mondays to catch up on progress that may have occurred over the weekend. This leaves Tuesdays, Wednesdays, and Thursdays for the meeting. My favorites are Tuesdays and Wednesdays, because I like to reserve the day after the project-tracking meeting for work and escalation meetings. This means that Thursday would be used as the reserved day if the project-tracking meeting were held on Wednesday.

LESSON 3.28

Reserve the work day immediately following the project-tracking meeting to work unresolved issues or new issues identified from the meeting.

Q3.12   Referring to the answer to the previous question, what if there are multiple ongoing projects across an organization, and project members find themselves assigned to more than one project? If all project-tracking meetings were held on a Tuesday or Wednesday, it seems that there would be too many meeting conflicts.

A3.12   Most organizations seldom would experience this problem. However, in those cases where it does occur, the project managers need to meet among themselves, and carefully coordinate their project-tracking meetings to avoid such conflicts.

Q3.13   Is it overkill for the project-tracking meeting participants to meet briefly every day?

A3.13   The weekly, formal project-tracking meeting is a must. However, an additional technique that can work surprisingly well follows. The project manager can meet with participants of the project-tracking team for fifteen to thirty minutes at the start of each work day to ensure that the top priority problems are receiving the attention they require. This mostly is an informal meeting that requires little preparation, if any, from the participants.

LESSON 3.29

A fifteen- to thirty-minute meeting at the start of each day can help ensure that the most important project problems are receiving required attention.

Q3.14   Who is responsible for tracking the planned budget versus the actual costs of a project?

A3.14   The project manager is responsible for including budgets as part of the tracking process. This activity has its beginnings during the development of the project plan, when the team leaders propose their budgets, usually with direction from the project manager and by working closely with the resource managers. Once the budgets have been approved, team leaders compare their actual costs against their planned budgets, and report this data at the project-tracking meetings. The project manager rolls this information up to the project level, and typically reports it, along with other project status to the product manager, other senior management, and the client, if appropriate.

Q3.15   What is *earned value*, and who decides if this approach is used in tracking a project?

A3.15   Briefly, *earned value* is defined as "a method for measuring project performance. It compares the amount of work that was planned with what was actually accomplished to determine if cost and schedule performance is as planned." (This definition was extracted from the book, *A Guide to the Project Management Body of*

Knowledge, by the Project Management Institute, 1996.) The earned value concept integrates cost, schedule, and work performed usually by ascribing monetary values to each. Although the product manager has the final say, the project manager usually is the person charged with deciding if this approach, or a modified version, will be adopted.

Q3.16 Who controls the monies on a project?

A3.16 After a project plan is created and approved, the budget is set. From this point on, each project member or project team is expected to work within the committed budgets. When needed, additional funds can be released by the project manager from the *management reserve* (discussed in a later question in this chapter).

Software development projects of six months or longer should be divided into smaller pieces such as increments or iterations. Another approach is to divide the project into major phases such as design, build, test, beta test, and the like. When an increment or phase has completed, an assessment is performed (project review) to determine if the project should be continued as is, altered, or stopped. After the decision is made, and it is other than *stopped*, funds are released by management (a review board) to allow the project to continue on until the next increment or phase, and so on, until the product is completed and readied for delivery to the client. If more monies are required than that held in management reserve, the product manager must make the decision.

Q3.17 How technical must a project manager be?

A3.17 The answer was partially addressed earlier in this chapter in the section, *Demonstrates Leadership; Makes Things Happen*. Nonetheless, to expand further, if a project manager is well versed and experienced in the application of project management principles, yet relatively new to the industry (e.g., ship building, missile construction, auto assembly, aircraft development, software development, and others) where the principles will be applied, she can expect to experience a very real handicap. She likely will have difficulty with the terminology, the technology, and knowing when and what questions to ask and being able to sufficiently understand the responses. Can the project manager learn? Yes. Can the project manager be highly effective on her first project with this technical handicap? This is not likely.

Q3.18 How important are soft skills for a project manager?

A3.18 Critically important; see Chapter 15, Are You *Too Soft*?, for a treatment of this subject.

Q3.19   Where do the best project managers come from?

A3.19   This question is difficult to answer because effective project managers can be developed from very different career paths. However, let's look at several jobs that can help develop a person for the role of project manager. Because this book is specifically targeted to software projects, we'll put our focus there. A software development project manager, for example, would find it highly beneficial to come from a background of development programmer, team leader, and resource manager, three areas which help develop the technical, organizational, and leadership skills that are essential to being an effective project manager. A project manager would be further served by assisting (i.e., as a deputy project manager) an experienced project manager for at least the first project. The last significant aid is for a new project manager to be assigned a mentor. The mentor should be a seasoned project manager with project successes (and failures) in his experience bank. The mentor's primary role is to help the new project manager learn how to do things right the first time. A qualified mentor can be an extremely powerful tool in cultivating successful project managers.

Q3.20   When should a project manager be assigned to a new project and begin working that project?

A3.20   A project manager should be assigned to a new project when the business architect has been assigned to create the product-requirements document. Many projects lose valuable time in the early phases of the product cycle primarily because no one (i.e., a project manager) is around to act as a catalyst to ensure that the requirements phase is planned and tracked, and problems that arise are quickly and appropriately addressed.

Q3.21   Is it okay for a project manager to be a contractor instead of a regular full-time employee of the company owning the project?

A3.21   Whenever possible, a position as important as project manager should be filled by employees from within the company. But if a qualified person is not available, you are better off with a qualified contractor than with an inexperienced and untested company employee. Contracting for an effective project manager can work, but be careful. It's all about how you plan to measure the performance of the project manager contractor. For example, if the contractor is eligible for a bonus for delivering the product by a certain date and within a specified budget, she probably will achieve the objective. However, the price can be more than you bargained, with poor product quality, excessive overtime by project members, lack of adherence to documented processes, low morale, high employee attrition, and more. In other words, the contractor will likely rise to the expectation of whatever she is being measured against and very possibly will sacrifice other coveted parameters. Therefore, it is important to create a contract that clearly specifies the measurements that must be met before paying a bonus—and yes, I am a great fan of the power of incentives to obtain the best from people.

LESSON 3.30

If a qualified project manager is not available from within a company to lead an important project, then a qualified contractor should be obtained.

A possible advantage to hiring a contractor is that she *might* be less prone to engage in company politics and will experience less company nonproject distractions. These conditions could allow the project manager contractor to be more focused on the project. A downside to hiring a contractor is that when the project ends, the experience gained by the contractor is no longer retained within the organization.

Q3.22   Should the project manager have the authority to manage management reserves of schedule and budget, or should some other person?

A3.22   *Management reserve* is a term that can apply to schedules, costs, or both. After a project has been planned, schedule reserves and/or budget reserves can be set aside to be used, if needed, at the discretion of the project manager. The project manager should have control over the use of management reserves and not have to seek approval each time they are needed.

Q3.23   Should the project manager be in the loop when negotiating contracts with vendors and then be the primary liaison to the vendors for the duration of the project?

A3.23   The project manager should always have rights in reviewing and approving all vendor contracts as they pertain to areas such as statement of work, schedules, quality of work delivered, planning and tracking, and the escalation process. Because the project manager is fully accountable for the outcome of the project, he needs this level of involvement. However, on medium to large-sized projects, the project manager will have limited time to focus on this area and might have a designee define and work most of the details. Also, for medium to large projects, the project manager will not have time to be the primary liaison working with the vendor. This responsibility could be a full-time or near full-time role and should be assigned to someone else. In all cases, the project manager must be involved in weekly tracking of the vendors' performance and be in the loop relating to important vendor issues.

> ### LESSON 3.31
> The project manager controls the use and distribution of management reserves.

> ### LESSON 3.32
> The project manager must have approval over all vendor contracts that can impact the project and must be informed weekly on the performance of the vendors.

Q3.24 Can the project manager reject a resource (person) that a resource manager has assigned to the project?

A3.24 Only a resource manager can make job assignments. (See Chapter 7, The Resource Manager, for why this is the case.) If a project manager does not want an assigned person on her project, the project manager must have a valid, specific reason for requesting that the person be barred from the project. A valid reason might be that the employee is a disruptive project member who consistently comes to required meetings late or not at all, is habitually late on commitments, produces low quality work that frequently requires rework, impacting schedules and budgets, and the like. If the resource manager does not think that the project manager's argument is valid, the employee remains on the project. However, the project manager can escalate this issue to higher management in an attempt to convince a higher authority. It could be that the resource manager is the primary problem, because the resource manager is not working closely with the employee to ensure that the employee is given every reasonable opportunity to be trained, coached, and nurtured. Whether the problem is the employee, the resource manager, or both, the project manager must drive this issue to closure while working through the proper channel of the resource management structure. Remember that the project manager is ultimately accountable for the outcome of the project, so problems must be addressed head on.

Q3.25 How can a project manager be held accountable for project members that do not report directly to him? Won't these project members do whatever they choose, whether or not it is in the best interest of the project and the project manager?

A3.25 Project members make commitments to the project manager via the project plan near the start of a project. Project members are then held accountable for meeting their commitments. Anytime throughout the project that the project manager discovers potential or actual problems, the project manager immediately works to get a recovery plan in place that is both reasonable and trackable. If a project member is neglecting, intentionally or otherwise, her commitments, the project manager constructively escalates that issue to the project member's resource manager to help resolve the issue. In most cases, the issue will be satisfactorily addressed. In the exception cases, the project manager escalates the issue to higher levels of resource management, and the escalation continues until the problem is satisfactorily resolved, or the resource manager making the decision is also in the project manager's line of command. In other words, the resource manager making the decision represents the point in the management structure where both the resource management of the poor performing project member and the resource management of the project manager come together.

It is common for a project member on a project to also be working on other commitments outside of that project. If the project member is no longer able to meet her commitments in all areas, one or more of those commitments can suffer. Here is a good example of the escalation process helping resource management decide the appropriate priorities for the project member. (See Chapter 16, The Escalation Process, for a discussion of the escalation process.) If the project manager does not accept the priorities, the issue again is escalated to higher levels of resource management. Most issues do not get escalated; they are resolved at the ground level. But a project manager must not hesitate to escalate, to ensure that the impact to his project is understood and factored into the decision. By the way, 95+ percent of project members want to do the right thing; they want to contribute positively to their projects and organization. The problem is that they may not know how to get help or decide on the priorities to work. The project manager can help.

LESSON 3.33

Project members want to do the right thing on a project, but they need to understand what is expected of them.

Q3.26 Can a person learn to become an effective project manager? Or are effective project managers mostly born that way and others "need not apply"?

A3.26 You can learn to become an effective project manager. Although the skills necessary to become an effective project manager come easier to some than to others, I believe that anyone with an interest—a passion—for this profession can work at acquiring the skills and experience to become quite proficient.

CHAPTER 4

THE BUSINESS ARCHITECT

It is unreasonable—and perhaps even arrogant—to believe that a development organization knows what is best for the client. The developers are expected to be experts in application of the latest technology, not necessarily experts in understanding the problems that the client needs to solve. What often is missing during the development of a product is someone—one project member—who is accountable for ensuring that the proposed solution does indeed address the client's problems. The *business architect* serves this role and works closely with both the client and the development organization.

Figure 4.1 lists the roles and responsibilities of the business architect. Let's examine each item.

Defines the Client's Problems (Requirements) to Be Solved

The business architect works closely with the client to understand the problems that need to be solved. She ensures that these problems are defined and written in a document commonly called the *product-requirements* document. This document is approved by, at least, both the client and the development organization but could also be approved by other interested groups such as one or more testing organizations, product planning and marketing organizations, the training organization, and the quality assurance organization.

The product-requirements document is a relatively thin document that focuses strictly on the client's problems that must be solved in easily understandable terms. The product-requirements document should not intentionally

FIGURE 4.1

Roles and Responsibilities of the Business Architect

◆ Defines the client's problems (requirements) to be solved

◆ Owns the business process direction designed into the product

◆ Has no direct reports

◆ Manages client expectations

◆ Drives "meets minimum requirements" for product content

◆ Works closely with the product architect, team leaders and project manager

◆ Is a catalyst in resolving business-related problems

◆ Performs business process-related mentoring to project members

focus on solutions to those problems. Unfortunately, most dedicate very little space, if any, to defining the problems to be solved, and utilize most of the product-requirements document for defining the perceived solution that should be built.

If the product-requirements document does not focus on the client's problems, it is likely that the client's true wants and needs will not be fully considered or even understood by the development organization. Why? Because there is a strong tendency for a development organization to want to get moving—show progress—on developing a product as soon as possible. Therefore, the development organization often jumps to make assumptions on *behalf* of the client, resulting in the development organization becoming consumed by its own vision and desires of what it *perceives* the product should be. The business architect insists on a product-requirements document as defined here and insists that the appropriate groups understand and approve the document.

LESSON 4.1

The product-requirements document focuses strictly on the client's problems that must be solved—not the solutions to those problems.

Owns the Business Process Direction Designed into the Product

The business architect must ensure that the solutions to the client's problems are, indeed, appropriate to the client's business. In other words, will the solutions complement the business process model that the client now embraces or plans to adopt? What might seem like the neatest whiz-bang, state-of-the-art technology product by the development organization could be seen as a business nightmare by the client. The business architect ensures that the client's needs are being fulfilled satisfactorily as the product undergoes definition and development. Said another way, the business architect continually focuses on the need to build the *right* product. This mindset contrasts to that of most of the project members, who are focusing on building the product *right*.

LESSON 4.2

The business architect ensures that the *right* product is being built, while most of the other project members focus on building the product *right*.

Has No Direct Reports

The business architect has a demanding and critical job in being the client's advocate; it can be a full-time job. If it's not, the business architect can perform this role for several small products or project teams at once. As with the project manager (discussed in Chapter 3, The Project Manager), the business architect must not also be a resource manager with other responsibilities for people and assignments. In other words, the business architect should not have direct reports; only resource managers have direct reports.

If the business architect requires support staff to help him in day-to-day business-architect responsibilities, that staff should report directly to a resource manager for manager-employee issues but be *dotted lined* to take direction from the business architect for assigned tasks. Chapter 7, The Resource Manager, Section Q&A7.1, discusses why a project member holding a key Enter*Prize* Organization position should not also take on the roles and responsibilities of another key Enter*Prize* Organization position.

Manages Client Expectations

You may have heard the saying: "It's all about managing expectations." Managing client expectations is a huge and critical responsibility. For example, no matter how well the development organization performs when building and delivering the product to the client, if the client expected anything different from what is delivered, the client will not be satisfied.

> **LESSON 4.3**
>
> Effectively managing client expectations has a major impact on client satisfaction.

The business architect has responsibility for managing the client's expectations. Managing expectations is not only about listening to the client; it is also about *setting* expectations with and for the client. Expectations for the product comprise a myriad of subjects, including the following:

◆ content
◆ usability
◆ cost
◆ schedules
◆ quality
◆ flexibility with changes
◆ status communications
◆ issue escalation process
◆ support services.

As difficult as it is, it's always better to set somewhat lower expectations with a client than to set expectations that are too lofty and exceed reality. It's important that the project scope is realistic. An effective business architect must work closely with both the client and the development organization to fully comprehend what is needed, possible, and likely.

> **LESSON 4.4**
>
> When working with a client, it is always better to set somewhat lower expectations than that which will likely be achieved and *hit* the achieved level, than to set expectations too high and *miss*.

Drives *Meets Minimum Requirements* for Product Content

A common problem that software development shops have with clients is over-commitment—taking on too much work with too little time available to accomplish the work. This contributes to a plethora of ill effects including late deliveries, budget overruns, low morale, and poor quality. Attempting to cram the proverbial ten pounds into a five-pound sack is a common occurrence, with disastrous results.

Part of the solution is to build products that meet minimum requirements. You may be thinking that such a product would have low appeal to your client or customers, but it's not what you think. *Meets minimum requirements* means giving the client what she needs to be successful, but not committing to unessential function. Additional function is what future releases and future business opportunities are all about. It is important to earn a reputation for being reliable in meeting customer commitments and then be trusted to continue to upgrade on a routine, predictable basis. This is good business.

The business architect leads the charge in working with the client in identifying what constitutes meeting minimum requirements. A client almost always will want more than what is essential to be successful. The business architect must ensure that the list of needs delivered to the development shop has been pared to reflect minimum requirements.

LESSON 4.5

Meets minimum requirements is giving the client the *essentials* of what is needed to be successful; anything more is too much.

Works Closely with the Product Architect, Team Leaders, and Project Manager

The business architect must work closely with the product architect and team leaders to ensure that the product evolves according to the client's best interests. To help make this happen, the business architect has approval rights over key deliverables that can have a direct bearing on the client's satisfaction with the product and project. Examples of these deliverables include the:

- product specifications that are owned by the product architect
- test plans owned by the team leaders responsible for development test, independent test, and client acceptance test
- user documentation owned by the team leader of such documentation
- performance and usability plans that are owned by the team leaders for those areas.

The business architect also works closely with the project manager. The business architect approves the overall project plan on behalf of the client. In doing so, the business architect ensures that the proper level of client involvement has been planned as the product is being defined, built, and tested. The business architect also is a required member of the project-tracking team run by the project manager.

LESSON 4.6

The business architect ensures the proper level of client involvement as the product is being defined, built, and tested.

Is a Catalyst for Resolving Business-Related Problems

The business architect is a catalyst to resolve or facilitate the resolution of business-related problems and conflicts. When a problem arises—and the outcome can have an impact on the client's satisfaction of the product—the business architect is involved in influencing that outcome on behalf of the client. Most projects suffer from too little advocacy for the client. The business architect helps bring the client's perspective to the day-to-day decisions that must be made during product development. The addition of a business architect on a project can result in better business decisions being made on the project.

LESSON 4.7

The business architect brings the client's perspective to the day-to-day decisions that must be made during the development of the product.

Performs Business Process-Related Mentoring to Project Members

The developers of a product need to understand the client's problems. They need to place themselves in the client's shoes when making product-related decisions. This is not easy to do; nor typically is there a relatively expedient manner to acquire this perspective. In steps the business architect who provides the important function of mentoring project members with regard to the impact that their product decisions can have on the client's overall satisfaction with the product.

LESSON 4.8

Without the influence of the business architect, products often err, being insensitive to satisfying the client.

Q & A

Q4.1   Must the business architect report directly to (be an employee of) the product manager and be an *in-house* member of the development organization?

A4.1   This is preferred but is not a *must have*. For example, the business architect could be an employee of the client or work in a marketing organization within the company developing the product. However, if the business architect does not report directly to the product manager, the business architect must be *dotted line* to the product manager and assume the role defined in this chapter. The development organization must accept this *outsider* (someone temporarily assigned from the client or another organization from within the company) as one of the project members and work accordingly with that person.

Caution: If the business architect is an employee of the client (instead of being an employee of the product manager), he may be consumed with a different set of priorities and agendas—one that may not be beneficial to the project. For example, the business architect may be separated geographically, consumed with political bias/issues, or distracted by local issues. The project manager must ensure that the business architect understands his roles and responsibilities and that the business architect is held appropriately accountable.

Q4.2   Referring to the previous question, if the business architect is also the client, doesn't this mean that the business architect and the product manager are equivalents?

A4.2   Absolutely not; the business architect is a project member and takes direction from the project manager and, at times, the product manager. The project manager runs the project. The business architect performs the duties defined for the business architect regardless of where the business architect is from (e.g., client, vendor, contractor, or company).

Q4.3   You say that only essential function should be committed to a client. That's what my projects always do, so what's new here?

A4.3   For most of us, most times, we set out to provide *more* than essential function. Have you ever faced slipped delivery dates and chosen to remove some of the function originally planned? When the project began, everyone swore that all of the planned function was essential. Yet, as the project progressed—and got further behind schedule—some of the essential function no longer looked so essential.

LESSON 4.9

If you can remove function from a product during its development cycle, yet insist that the product can be delivered to the client, the product contained nonessential function from the start.

Q4.4   Okay, you might have a point, but shouldn't the client get what he wants? If that turns out to be more than meets minimum requirements, so be it.

A4.4   Promising more to a client than is essential and then failing to deliver even the essential functions is a huge disservice to the client. This technique of building a product to achieve meets minimum requirements is not just good business for the development shop, but for the client as well. The client should have a commitment to receiving *essential function*. If more function is delivered, it is a bonus, but should not be part of the basic commitment. Let's look at an example to help make this point, a Y2K project because many people have worked on these projects. Here's what should occur.

Let's say you have identified one hundred functions (enhancements or changes) that need to be made in your company's programs. You categorize these functions as high, medium, or low, based on a priority that you assign. You know that all one hundred functions are desirable, but you recognize that your limited resources won't allow all of the functions to be ready by the hoped-for date. You find that forty functions fall within the high-priority category, thirty in medium, and thirty in low. You build a project plan to implement only the forty high priorities. Why? Because you don't want to jeopardize these forty from being completed on time by building a plan to include the other sixty functions—all of lesser importance and, for purposes of illustration, deemed *nonessential*.

You might be thinking that you should build a plan with all one hundred functions and later, if (actually, *when*) the project gets into trouble, you can always back out lesser-priority function. This plan sets false expectations for the client. Don't go there! This foolish plan requires that valuable time, dollars, and resources be spent working on other than the most important functions. Moreover, when you back function out, it costs again. Build a plan that significantly reduces rework; this means that the original plan only must address essential function.

What about the other sixty functions? You carefully look these over and put workarounds in place that, although not optimal, can get you through the business until more substantial actions can occur—actions that would occur in some future release.

But there is something else to do. You decide the most important of the sixty functions—maybe its all of the thirty medium functions or some subset thereof—and you create multiple, independent small projects with any and all of the resources that you can muster. I call these small projects, collectively, a *closet plan*. They are managed with the same care and attention to quality as the primary project. If any of these small projects can be completed by a predetermined date (e.g., system test), and the risk to the primary project is judged to be acceptable, the completed small projects are merged with the primary project. There are many advantages to this technique such as reducing risk to the primary project, motivating the members of the small projects to complete by a predetermined date, and setting customer expectations that are most likely to be met or exceeded.

It seems that most of us have been conditioned to believe that meets minimum requirements is unexciting and noncompetitive; I believe it to be the opposite. Deliberately practicing meets minimum requirements helps an organization or company be first to market, earn increasing credibility from its client, and strongly posture its enterprise for taking on new business opportunities. Adopting the concept of meets minimum requirements can set up your organization for exceptional performance and client satisfaction.

LESSON 4.10

Practicing meets minimum requirements helps an organization or company to be first to market, earn increasing credibility from its client, and strongly posture its enterprise for taking on new business opportunities.

Q4.5   Doesn't the product architect also have a responsibility for ensuring that the solution to the client's problems meets minimum requirements?

A4.5   Yes, in fact, all project members have a responsibility to build to the agreed-to meets minimum requirements. However, the business architect leads in this effort by working closely with the client to ensure that the requirements have been properly prioritized early in the project, so the essential requirements receive top billing. The business architect then has approval rights over the product specifications to ensure that the solution addresses only the essential function.

Q4.6   In the roles and responsibilities of the Enter*Prize* Organization, who is responsible for business- and marketing-related activities such as creating a business case for new projects, creating marketing plans, forecast and sales plans, competitive analysis plans, manufacturing and distribution plans, evangelizing the product and performing public relations, and the like?

A4.6   Depending on the clients and marketplace for your products, these activities can be significant or minimal. Many organizations have marketing and business groups that focus on these areas. However, at a minimum, the business architect is the primary liaison to them and has approval rights over the plans that address these areas. The product manager and project manager also can have approval rights. For companies that have small or weak business and marketing areas, the business architect plays a more dominant role in the creation and rollout of these plans.

CHAPTER 5

THE PRODUCT ARCHITECT

*W*ho's in charge of the technical outcome of a product? On many projects, it is a shared responsibility, depending on the number of developers, development team leaders, and managers who have their hands in the pie. Unfortunately, many products take on the look and feel of being developed by many different people, which is bad for the client, bad for the developers, and bad for enhancing the product later.

One person—one leader—should be held accountable for the technical aspects of the product; it is not a shared position. This person is the *product architect*.

Figure 5.1 lists the roles and responsibilities of the product architect. The upcoming sections discuss these items.

Owns the Technical Solution to the Client's Problems—the *What* and the *How*

The product architect is responsible for the creation and approval of the *product specifications*. Product specifications can be called by many different names, but it is a document that defines *what is to be built*—the product as the client will see and use it. It defines solutions to the client's problems that were identified in the product-requirements document.

FIGURE 5.1

Roles and Responsibilities of the Product Architect

◆ Owns the technical solution to the client's problems: the "what" and the "how"
◆ Chairs the change-control board
◆ Has no direct reports
◆ Works closely with the business architect, team leaders and project manager
◆ Ensures acceptable technical processes and methodologies are defined and followed
◆ Is a catalyst in resolving technical-related problems
◆ Performs technical-related mentoring to project members

The product architect also is responsible for the overall architecture of the product; that is, *the how*—how the components of the product work with one another and with the hardware and software environment with which they must operate. Simply stated, the product architect provides the primary role for ensuring the consistency, completeness, and appropriateness of the definition and design of the product. In so doing, the product architect is the visionary for *what* the product looks like, *how* it should be built, and *how* it might evolve through future releases or upgrades.

LESSON 5.1

The product architect is responsible for defining the solution to the client's problems.

LESSON 5.2

The product architect is the visionary for what the product looks like, how it should be built, and how it might evolve through future releases or upgrades.

Chairs the Change-Control Board

The product architect chairs the change-control board(s) that controls the product specifications and product architecture. These boards typically are composed of people who represent various groups that make up what is commonly called the *development* organization. Examples of teams typically represented at the change-control board meetings include:

- design and code
- development test
- independent test
- client acceptance test
- product documentation
- education and training
- quality assurance.

Of course, the business architect also participates. Resource managers are not required participants but attend as desired. Representatives from operations and support teams may also participate.

LESSON 5.3

The product architect performs as a *benevolent dictator* in running a change control board and does not adopt the democratic rule or consensus approaches to decision-making. Instead, she solicits input from all parties, considers all information, makes the best *business* decision, and then is held accountable for that decision.

Change-control boards should not operate as democracies where every participant gets a vote and every vote counts; nor should they operate as consensus teams. Instead, the chairperson is the only one with a vote that counts—in effect, the chairperson performs as a *benevolent dictator*. What do I mean? One person is held accountable for the outcome of the technical aspects of the product. Therefore, that person makes the best *business-related* technical decisions—but not alone. Let's look at an example of how this can work.

The owner of a product component, Julie, wants to change the design interface to that component. Because several other components, each owned by different people, must change their design and code to accommodate the proposed interface change, Julie must propose the change before the change-control board, and lobby support for that change. The chairperson (product architect) of the change-control board solicits a position from each participant. Let's say that 75 percent of the participants agree that the change is the right thing to do. The chairperson considers all the information discussed at the meeting and makes what he believes to be the right business decision. If the chairperson took a vote or waited until the group could reach a consensus, the interface change might not be made, and the right business decision might be lost. If the chairperson's decision will negatively impact the product's scope, cost, schedule, or quality, the decision cannot be made until the project manager—and possibly the product manager—is consulted. The project manager must be involved in any decisions that can impact the overall project.

Has No Direct Reports

The product architect has a critical role in the project and must always be accessible to the project members who need her support. This is almost always a full-time job. If it's not, then the product architect can perform this role for several small products or project teams at once. Like the project manager and the business architect discussed in earlier chapters, the product architect must not be a resource manager with other responsibilities of people and assignments. In other words, the product architect should not have direct reports; only resource managers have direct reports.

If the product architect requires support staff, to help him in day-to-day product architect responsibilities, that staff should report directly to a resource manager for manager-employee issues but be *dotted line* to the product architect for directions on assigned tasks. (Chapter 7, The Resource Manager, Section *Q&A7.1*, discusses why a project member holding a key Enter*Prize* Organization position should not also take on the roles and responsibilities of another key Enter*Prize* Organization position.)

Works Closely with the Business Architect, Team Leaders, and Project Manager

The product architect must work closely with the business architect to ensure that the right product is being defined and built, and she must work closely with the team leaders to ensure that the product is being built right. The product architect creates the product specifications, based on input from the product-requirements document, and obtains required approvals for the product specifications from the business architect, team leaders, and others, as needed. The product architect personally inspects, at a minimum, the design of the key components of the product. She has approval rights over many of the project's deliverables, such as the product documentation and test plans. As you can see, the product architect has significant influence in the overall development of the product.

The product architect also works closely with the project manager. The product architect approves the overall project plan and ensures that time, cost, and quality have been sufficiently accounted as the product is being defined, built, and tested. She also is a required member of the project-tracking team run by the project manager.

LESSON 5.4

The product architect ensures that the product is being built *right*, while the business architect ensures that the *right* product is being built.

Ensures Acceptable Technical Processes and Methodologies Are Defined and Followed

The product architect ensures that acceptable technical processes and methodologies are being used for construction of the product. For example, if object-oriented design and coding is to be implemented, the product architect ensures that people are properly trained (working with the resource managers and the project manager) to appropriately implement and support the technology, and that the design and coding is performed properly. The product architect works closely with the process architect, as needed, to define, document, and implement required processes.

LESSON 5.5

The product architect ensures that an acceptable approach is adopted for the development of the product.

Is a Catalyst for Resolving Technical-Related Problems

The product architect is a catalyst for resolving or facilitating the resolution of technical-related problems and conflicts. When a problem arises—and the outcome can have an impact on the technical direction or integrity of the product—the product architect is involved, as required, in influencing the outcome. Many projects suffer from "Who's in charge technically?" as inconsistent, inadequate, or misguided technical solutions spring up around the project. The product architect helps ensure that the most important technical problems are getting the attention they need and are being solved.

LESSON 5.6

The product architect ensures that the most important technical problems are being solved with the urgency required.

Performs Technical-Related Mentoring to Project Members

The product architect is an expert on software development and the application of software technology. Although the product architect is, of course, not expected to know everything there is to know in this rapidly changing field, he should know how to obtain information when it is needed. This is also a person who possesses far more knowledge and experience than most technologists on the project team. The product architect is expected to share his skills across the team, and make himself accessible to help strengthen the individual contributors.

LESSON 5.7

The product architect shares his skills across the project and helps strengthen the contributions of project members.

Q & A

Q5.1   Does the product architect personally write the product specifications and design the product?

A5.1   Not necessarily; on very small teams, the product architect might do the lion's share of this work. However, on other than very small teams, it is often not feasible for the product architect to perform this work. Instead, the product architect leads the effort to write the product specifications and design the product. This includes conducting work meetings, reviews and inspections, as well as being available to participate in discussions and questions.

Q5.2   Are the product specifications always the vehicle for describing the solution to the client's problems, or the only vehicle?

A5.2   No and no; depending on the software development process or methodology that you choose to follow, other documents, templates, or tools could be used. For example, for large projects, it is recommended that a product-objectives document be created before writing the product specifications. Why? Think about it. If your project is so large that it can take months to develop product specifications, what happens when that document is distributed for approval and a lot of changes are required? A lot of rework—a major problem on most projects—can affect schedules, costs, quality, and client satisfaction.

　　　　To help reduce rework, you can spend less time and resources by first developing a product-objectives document. The product objectives are about one-tenth the size of product specifications. They define solutions to the client's problems, but don't go into detail until agreement has been reached on the high-level solution. After the product objectives have passed muster on solving the client's problems, albeit at a high level, the detailed product specifications are developed.

LESSON 5.8

On large projects, a *high-level* product-specifications document, sometimes called a *product-objectives* document, should be written and approved before expending time, resources, and monies to write detailed product specifications.

Q5.3   Is there a conflict between the roles of the product architect and the process architect?

A5.3   No, the process architect owns the software development process; she supports the use of this process. If the product architect wants to deviate from the process, the product architect works with the process architect and project manager to obtain approval to deviate. If a process is unique to the roles and responsibilities of the product architect (e.g., processes used to control changes to the product specifications or the product architecture), the product architect most likely will own those processes. If a technology is being introduced to the project to, say, design the product, the product architect will also likely own the processes required to support that technology.

Q5.4   Does the product architect have any responsibility for defining the design and code standards?

A5.4   Yes, this is within the product architect's domain of responsibility. If these standards have not already been defined across an organization, for use with its projects, the product architect must declare them for his project. The process architect may be of great assistance; if the product architect neglects to define standards, the process architect should flag the matter as an issue requiring resolution. If needed, the project manager will become involved to ensure that the issue is satisfactorily resolved.

Q5.5   In Chapter 4, The Business Architect, the concept of *meets minimum requirements* was discussed. How much responsibility does the product architect have in enforcing this concept?

A5.5   As stated in Chapter 4, the business architect leads the effort in ensuring that only *meets minimum requirements*—that is, essential—functions are planned and developed. However, the product architect plays a significant role in enforcing this concept, because the product architect owns the product specifications and architecture of the product.

Q5.6   Is the product architect accountable for such issues as proof of concept, scalability, performance, reliability and serviceability?

A5.6   Absolutely—these are product specifications and product architecture issues.

Q5.7   Is the product architect ever expected to interface with other product architects?

A5.7   Yes, it should be a relatively common occurrence. For example, design and code reuse is an issue that should be of interest to all product architects. That is, a product architect should be asking what design and code already exists from other products across the organization that can be used on her project. Also, the product architect should be open to designing and coding in a manner that allows other product architects to benefit from its reuse.

Another example of product architects conferring is for advice on technical issues and processes. Yet another example is when two product architects are building products that must integrate with one another, or one product is the follow-on version of another.

CHAPTER 6

THE PROCESS ARCHITECT

*W*hen you think about the many roles and responsibilities that must be addressed on a project, who comes to mind as the process champion? Who do you think is the person charged with ensuring that effective processes are followed so that high productivity, high quality, and minimal cycle times are achieved? The project manager? The business architect? The product architect? The team leaders? Others? All of the above?

For many projects, no one project position or person owns this role; all project members are expected to address processes as they relate to their pieces of the project pie. The function is too important for the responsibility to be diffused across a project. Although project members are responsible for the processes that directly affect their performance, there is a strong need to define a project position that focuses on the increasingly critical area of project processes, whether those processes are isolated or integrated across a project.

In the Enter*Prize* Organization, the *process architect* is the process champion on a project. He is charged with ensuring that the appropriate processes are defined, documented, and followed. Process definition can be highly specialized work, and many project members are either not sufficiently trained to do it well or simply don't have the time. Furthermore, the need to integrate many of the processes argues that one project member be accountable for working across the project to ensure that the overall integrity of the processes is achieved. The process architect can be regarded as the person continually focused on helping project members perform their duties more productively.

FIGURE 6.1

Roles and Responsibilities of the Process Architect

- Defines/tailors the software development process
- Has no direct reports
- Leads the effort in designing, documenting, and measuring project processes
- Ensures the appropriate processes are being followed
- Is the catalyst in resolving process-related problems
- Performs process-related mentoring to project members
- Recommends/approves the metrics to be tracked for selected activities

---

Figure 6.1 lists the roles and responsibilities of the project architect. Let's look at them more closely.

LESSON 6.1

The process architect helps the project members perform their duties "faster, better, and cheaper."

Defines/Tailors the Software Development Process

In the early stages of a project, there is a need to define the software development process to be used. The process architect, working closely with the project manager and other project members, defines this process. If a software development process already exists across the organization, it needs to be tailored. If a software development process does not exist, one needs to be defined for the project. The software development process is essential to creating a project plan. The major activities that will be addressed in the project plan will be derived from the defined software development process. Furthermore, the process identifies the sequence of major activities to be performed and the dependencies that these activities have with one another.

Every project is different. If an organization has a defined and documented software development process, it must be tailored to fit the needs of each project within the organization. For example, a fifty-person project should not be expected to follow the exact same detailed software development process as a three-person project. The larger project has more need for formality in terms of documentation, change control, planning, and tracking, to name a few. This doesn't mean that small projects can ignore these areas; all projects need structure, order, and discipline. However, smaller projects can reduce the time and energy required for performing some of these activities because the team is so small, and the members have a greater degree of instant communication and control.

LESSON 6.2

The software development process must be flexible to fit the unique needs of each project in an organization.

Has No Direct Reports

The process architect has a demanding role in the project and must always be accessible to the project members who need her support. As project members recognize the great benefit that a process architect can add to a project, she will be sought all the more. This can be a full-time job. If it's not, the process architect can perform this role for several small project teams at once. As with the project manager, business architect, and product architect discussed in earlier chapters, the process architect must not be a resource manager with other responsibilities of people and assignments. In other words, the process architect should not have direct reports; only resource managers have direct reports.

If the process architect requires support staff to help him in day-to-day process-architect responsibilities, that staff should report directly to a resource manager for manager-employee issues but be *dotted line* to the process architect to take direction for assigned tasks. (Chapter 7, The Resource Manager, Section Q&A7.1, discusses why a project member holding a key EnterPrize Organization position should not also take on the roles and responsibilities of another key EnterPrize Organization position.)

Leads the Effort in Designing, Documenting, and Measuring Project Processes

The overall software development process is typically the single largest process on a project. However, many of its activities utilize processes of their own. For example, processes can be defined to:

◆ gather, validate, and change product requirements

◆ create, obtain approval, and maintain the project plan

◆ track the project plan

◆ plan for, implement, and validate product design and code

◆ perform unit and function testing

◆ allow orderly and deliberate control over product code and documentation changes

◆ record project problems, assign them to project members, and track the problems to closure

◆ correct defects discovered in the product and validate that the defects were appropriately fixed

◆ review and approve project documentation.

The process architect works with the members across a project to help them, as needed, define and document their processes. After processes are defined and in use, there is a need to continually monitor and improve them for efficiency. The process architect ensures that improvement is addressed in the processes that have the most impact to both the product's and the project's success.

The process architect, along with the project manager and others, as appropriate, has approval rights in reviewing and agreeing to the processes that are used across the project. If a process is considered to be weak or ineffective, it must be corrected.

LESSON 6.3

The most important project processes must be continually monitored and improved.

Ensures that Appropriate Processes Are Being Followed

The process architect can audit processes when desired to ensure that the processes are well defined, documented, and being followed. A great point in the project that sets the stage for process use is when the project plan is created. The project plan is created in pieces where the pieces are owned by project members (e.g., product architect, team leaders, and selected team members). The project-plan pieces are reviewed and, when found acceptable, included in the overall project plan. As the plan pieces are being reviewed, the process architect can assist the project manager in ensuring that the use of required processes is being planned appropriately.

Is the Catalyst for Resolving Process-Related Problems

When process-related problems arise, the process architect serves as the catalyst for ensuring that the problems are appropriately resolved. For example, if a project is well into its testing phase and far more product problems are being discovered than were expected, the process architect may become involved. The process architect may propose to the project manager what actions to take to accelerate the discovery and correction of latent defects. The process architect also may choose to review many of the identified problems, and determine what earlier phase in the software development process should have or could have caught the problems. This information will be helpful to improve various processes to prevent this situation from occurring in future development increments of the project.

LESSON 6.4

It is not enough to fix problems; the processes that allowed those problems to occur must also be fixed.

Performs Process-Related Mentoring to Project Members

The process architect is an expert, or on the way to becoming an expert, at defining, implementing, tracking, and improving processes. The process architect is expected to share her process skills when called upon by project members. My experience shows that more project members would become more active in defining and improving their processes if they had a knowledgeable and willing process person accessible to them to assist when needed.

Recommends/Approves the Metrics to Be Tracked for Selected Activities

A process architect requires the use of methodical and investigative approaches to perform many of his duties. These developed skills have a great benefit in another area of a project: metrics for use in tracking the progress of project activities.

Many project activities require metrics to be recorded and analyzed, so their progress can be sufficiently monitored. The process architect defines the metrics to be used for key activities if they have not already been defined. If metrics have been defined, the process architect, along with the project manager and appropriate others, has approval rights in reviewing and agreeing to the metrics.

LESSON 6.5

The use of metrics is the only way to know if your project and its associated activities are proceeding according to plan.

An example of an activity that requires metrics is the execution of a formal test, such as a system test. The metrics that can be recorded and analyzed can vary widely, but can include the:

- planned number of test scripts that were expected to be attempted each week
- actual number of test scripts that were attempted each week
- planned number of test scripts that were expected to successfully run
- actual number of test cases that were successfully run
- planned number of problems that were expected to be discovered each week
- actual number of problems that were discovered each week
- planned number of problems discovered that are high, medium, and low severity
- actual number of problems discovered that are high, medium, and low severity
- planned time required to fix high and medium severity problems
- actual time required to fix high and medium severity problems.

The identification of metrics that should be tracked for key activities can be a big help to the project members who own those activities; it is also a great help to the project manager. Many projects suffer from too little or too weak metrics. The result is uncertainty about the real progress being made in these activities and/or across the project.

Q & A

Q6.1 When you talk about processes, are you only referring to the text in a document that describes a process, such as the process to perform code reviews, or do you also include the creation and use of templates and other tools?

A6.1 All of the above—the process architect is charged with helping project members do things "faster, better, and cheaper." If this means using templates, tools, mentors, or whatever, it is within the domain of the process architect's job.

Q6.2   Does the process architect own any processes?

A6.2   Yes, the process architect owns the software development process. The process architect optionally can own other processes; however, as a general rule, processes should be owned by the project member who has the most at stake for using that process. For example, the test team leader should own the processes required for the test team to operate effectively.

Q6.3   I am concerned that the process architect can be obsessive in requiring that an overly burdensome software development process be used on a project? What is the check and balance to keep the process architect in toe?

A6.3   The project manager has the final call on the use of processes and metrics. The process architect works process-related issues and assists the project manager when and where needed. He does, however, carry weight over other project members in ensuring that they comply with process-related directives.

Q6.4   What about the opposite occurring? What about the project manager insisting on what many would see as an unacceptable software development process that potentially could place the project at risk? Where's the check and balance here?

A6.4   This is a more difficult case to mitigate because the project manager has considerable authority on her project. However, the process architect can escalate the issue to the project manager's boss, the product manager (or the manager of project managers for larger organizations). The product manager should be sufficiently motivated to ensure that the project is not placed in harm's way and that only reasonable risks are taken.

Q6.5   Does the process architect own any documents on a project?

A6.5   Yes, but for small projects, the document(s) can simply be a memo(s). For example, the process architect must document what the software development process will be. If the software development process is already defined, the process architect will document the tailoring to be applied to the existing process to accommodate the needs of the new project. The project manager must approve this document, as well as any other project members that can be affected (e.g., business architect, product architect, and team leaders).

     Another document that can be created by the process architect identifies the key processes required on a project and identifies the owner of each process. Yet another document that can be created identifies the metrics to be recorded and evaluated for the key project activities. Here again, the project manager, as well as any other project members that can be affected, must approve these documents.

Q6.6   What role, if any, does the process architect have with a *software engineering process group* (SEPG)?

A6.6   The process architect supports the processes defined and documented by the SEPG, should such a group exist in your organization. An SEPG is typically a group of people who serve as representatives from the varied functional groups across an organization. The primary roles of the group are to define, document, maintain, and improve the processes comprising the underpinnings of the software development process that is used across the organization and its projects.

The process architect is in a position to help enforce the use of the many processes that make up the software development process. An SEPG or SEPG-like function is recommended and can add considerable value to the continual improvement of an organization's software development process. The process architect typically would be the representative on the SEPG from the project.

Q6.7   If an organization has defined a software development process for use across its projects, how does a project that is under way cope with changes that an SEPG makes that have a direct impact on the project?

A6.7   Moving targets can be difficult or impossible to hit. For this reason, the process architect and project manager can freeze the state of the software development process at a point in time, and work off of that version for the remainder of the project (or until the start of the next major phase of the project). If changes to that version occur, the process architect recommends to the project manager whether or not those changes should be applied to the project. The final decision rests with the project manager.

Q6.8   When a software development process is defined for use by all the projects of an organization, should the corresponding metrics also be defined as part of the overall software development process?

A6.8   The metrics can be recommended; however, every project is different. Large or very complex projects can require more metrics to track than simpler and smaller projects. It would be helpful if a set of metrics are defined, and the process architect, project manager, and others can choose from that list those metrics that best serve their needs.

Q6.9   Is the process architect a good candidate to help an organization achieve certification with its processes, such as reaching capability maturity model level 2 or 3, or ISO 9001?

A6.9   Assuming that the process architect understands the requirements that must be met to achieve the targeted certification, the process architect may very well be a person with the interest and skills to drive the certification effort. However, a process architect, by definition, is there to serve the needs of one or more projects, not the needs of an organization. If the process architect moonlights to fulfill the needs of the organization, so be it.

Q6.10   Does the process architect attend the project-tracking meetings that typically occur weekly, run by the project manager?

A6.10   Yes, project-tracking meetings are loaded with process-related issues and discussions of metrics. Furthermore, many project problems require new or improved processes as part of their solutions. The process architect can be quite beneficial when working with project members to help them become more process efficient.

CHAPTER 7

The Resource Manager

By the time you read this section, you may be wondering what roles and responsibilities are left for the *resource manager*. Plenty! Resource managers are responsible for a lot and have the most diverse set of roles and responsibilities. For example, they:

◆ perform a support role in helping their direct reports meet their commitments
◆ evaluate their direct reports, and reward them appropriately
◆ work with their direct reports in performing professional and career counseling
◆ seek future work opportunities for their direct reports
◆ a whole lot more.

Figure 7.1 lists the roles and responsibilities of the resource manager. Let's take a closer look at each of these items.

Has Direct Reports

Only resource managers have *direct reports*. Having direct reports means that you have *personnel* or *administrative* responsibilities for employees, performing such duties as hiring and firing; evaluating performance; providing salary increases, promotions, and awards, and looking out for their professional development and careers. In other words, resource managers address what is typically called *manager-employee issues*.

FIGURE 7.1

Roles and Responsibilities of the Resource Manager

◆ Has direct reports
◆ Hires and fires
◆ Performs resource planning and allocation
◆ Defines roles and responsibilities for direct reports
◆ Supports direct reports in meeting their commitments
◆ Drives decision making to lowest level reasonable
◆ Is a catalyst to resolve domain-related problems
◆ Evaluates performance of direct reports
◆ Compensates and awards direct reports
◆ Provides career counseling and development
◆ Promotes a productive work environment
◆ Procures and manages logistics for direct reports
◆ Serves as channel for company communications
◆ Executes company policies and practices
◆ Secures future work opportunities

Everyone reports to a resource manager. Even if a project member is assigned or is on loan from a different department to work with a project manager, team leader, or whoever, everyone has a resource manager that looks out for his wellbeing and best interests.

Resource managers typically have up to fifteen people working for them. Less-experienced resource managers might have up to ten direct reports, and more seasoned resource managers could have fifteen. If resource managers have more than fifteen direct reports, their effectiveness to continuously perform their duties as defined in this chapter can be seriously eroded.

LESSON 7.1

If a resource manager has too many direct reports, then she cannot be effective, and the entire organization and its component projects will suffer.

Hires and Fires

The resource manager has the distinct role of being responsible for hiring new people into the organization. The time and care that the resource manager provides to this *highly important* activity will have a direct impact on the long-term success of the organization and the projects that are undertaken. As part of the hiring process, people who are not resource managers also can—and should—participate in the selection process, even though the final decision always rests with resource managers.

LESSON 7.2

A resource manager must invest the time required to hire qualified people who can help the projects and organizations achieve their goals.

But what about firing a poor performer? Or, preferably, working to turn around a poor performer to become a satisfactory contributor? The resource manager is responsible for these actions. We have all seen instances of a resource manager ignoring the obvious signs that a project member is not pulling her weight, and the resource manager does little or nothing, offering lip service instead of action. Taking too long to address this situation can have a devastating effect on a project and the morale of the project members.

LESSON 7.3

Resource managers have the responsibility to appropriately work with and, as occasionally might be necessary, terminate direct reports for poor performance.

Performs Resource Planning and Allocation

Only a resource manager can make major job assignments (e.g., assign a person to be a designer, coder, tester, writer, trainer, or support person) for project members. They may ask for guidance from team leaders, the project manager, and others regarding who might be qualified or the best candidate for a given assignment, but only the resource manager can make such an assignment. Why? Because the resource manager is responsible for the professional and career development of her direct reports. If anyone other than the resource manager is making job assignments, who's looking out for the employee (direct report)? Those other than the resource manager would make job assignments based on what's best for the team or project, with little interest for what's best for the direct report.

LESSON 7.4

Only resource managers make job (versus task) assignments.

If a project manager, team leader, or anyone else is looking for available resources to perform a task, these commitments of people can only be obtained from a resource manager. Resource managers *own* the people resource in an organization and have the responsibility of managing that resource.

Once a project member has been assigned (e.g., given a major job assignment by his resource manager) to a project, that person can take on day-to-day assignments (tasks) from others that relate to the overall job assignment made by the resource manager. For example, the team leader or project manager can make specific task assignments (e.g., write the test scripts to test a new feature) that are within the domain of the project member's major job assignment (tester).

In addition to being responsible for the allocation of human resource, resource managers must also anticipate future resource needs. They do so by obtaining resource projections from the product managers, project managers, team leaders, and others. When resources are required, resource managers are expected to have the resource on hand or accessible on relatively short notice. Moreover, they are expected to put the right people in the right positions in response to every request. (You thought your job was tough!)

Resource managers must fill a very difficult and demanding responsibility. It also requires frequently resizing staff (direct reports) and/or looking again at staff assignments to enable priorities and future commitments to be met.

LESSON 7.5

Resource managers must plan for and anticipate future demands for their resources (direct reports).

Defines Roles and Responsibilities for Direct Reports

The resource manager is responsible for ensuring that the roles and responsibilities for her direct reports are well defined. This means that each of the direct reports should not only know the tasks for which they are responsible but also how their performance will be measured against those tasks. As stated earlier, project members want to contribute; they want to be respected for pulling their own weight; they want to be needed. But they need to know how they will be measured, so they can focus on those areas. Resource managers who neglect defining and communicating measurements are overlooking a powerful tool for obtaining the best performance from their direct reports.

LESSON 7.6

Direct reports need to know what is expected of them if they are to consistently perform well.

Supports Direct Reports in Meeting Their Commitments

One of the primary roles of a resource manager is to work with their direct reports to help them be successful. There are many ways to achieve this. For example, when a resource manager's team leaders are developing their plans, the resource manager should be supporting this activity to the degree necessary. Many team leaders have difficulty developing plans that are complete, well thought out, and easily tracked. If the resource manager doesn't have the skills to teach his team leaders or team members how to develop good plans, the resource manager should be a catalyst for finding someone who can.

LESSON 7.7

The most effective resource managers provide the support necessary to help their direct reports achieve success.

After a team's plan is developed—but before it is thoroughly reviewed by the project manager—the resource manager should have already reviewed and blessed the plan. After all, once the team's plan is committed, the resource manager is on the hook to ante up the resources required to execute the plan successfully. If the resource manager reviews the team plan before the project manager reviews the plan, there should be fewer problems discovered by the project manager that might cause the team plan to be reworked.

The resource manager should not expect the project manager to manage his team plans or direct reports. The real catalyst behind smooth-running team plans should be the ever-present resource manager working with and nurturing the team leaders and their team members toward implementing their approved plans. This requires the continuous monitoring of the team plans by the resource manager. A test to see how effective the communications are between the resource manager and a team leader is the following question: In most cases, does the resource manager learn about problems with a team plan *before* the project manager learns of them, or *afterward?* If the answer is "afterward," the resource manager is not as active and involved in the day-to-day running of the team as he needs to be.

It should be noted that seasoned team leaders will require—and rightfully desire—less interference from the resource manager in developing and implementing their plans. But even with veteran team leaders, there need to be good, ongoing, channels of communications between the team leader and the resource manager.

Drives Decision-Making to Lowest Level Reasonable

A characteristic of a good resource manager is encouraging decision-making to be driven to the lowest level reasonable within the department or team. The last thing that a direct report wants is to be held accountable for a task while not being allowed to make decisions that will influence the outcome of that task. Micromanaging, for example, zaps a project member's sense of commitment and accountability. That person will lack the passion that inspires one to perform at her highest. Instead, a person will almost always underachieve her potential.

Most of us can look back at the job assignments that were the most enriching to our professional and personal growth, and recall assignments in which we were given great freedom to take control and make decisions. We didn't always make the best decisions, but we felt personally accountable and gave *110 percent* to successfully completing the assignment. If a resource manager wants the absolute best from her direct reports, she will give them authority with responsibility and accountability—and watch them blossom.

> **LESSON 7.8**
>
> Accountability must be placed at the lowest level reasonable in order to secure commitments that you can take to the bank.

Is a Catalyst for Resolving Domain-Related Problems

The resource manager occupies a leadership position within an organization or project, which means that he should demonstrate the desired behavior not only to ensure that the right action is taken, but also to act as a role model for his direct reports. If a problem or conflict within the *responsibility domain* of the resource manager is not being resolved—say, by a team leader or team member—with the required sense of urgency, the resource manager should serve as a catalyst for ensuring that the situation gets the attention it needs. The responsibility domain includes all commitments and responsibilities that fall within the scope of the resource manager's responsibility, as well as the responsibilities of his direct reports.

Sometimes escalating the issue to a higher authority is the right thing to do. Please note that I am not advocating that the resource manager suddenly take on and own the problem—don't go there. The person who owns the problem—is accountable for resolving the problem—should keep the responsibility. But the resource manager should work with that person to help her take the right actions to achieve an acceptable resolution of the problem.

Evaluates Performance of Direct Reports

The resource manager is responsible for evaluating the performance of his direct reports; it is not anyone else's responsibility. In performing this duty, it is okay to ask others who worked with the subject employee to provide feedback about the employee's effectiveness. But it is not okay to require or ask someone else to write the evaluation—even a portion of it. Why? Because it is not anyone else's job! All have full-time jobs; if they wanted to write evaluations, they would have become resource managers. Furthermore, a resource manager cannot possibly provide his direct report with a fair evaluation unless the resource manager is involved with the direct report's job assignments to the extent discussed in this chapter.

LESSON 7.9

Unless a resource manager is working closely with his direct reports, the resource manager is handicapped when it comes to fairly evaluating the performance of the direct reports.

Compensates and Awards Direct Reports

The resource manager has a responsibility to properly compensate and award her direct reports when it is justified. No wimpy resource managers, please! The case study logs are filled with resource managers who perform miserably; common *excuses* include:

- ◆ I don't want to upset other direct reports, who may feel that they are being overlooked.
- ◆ My boss doesn't compensate or award me well. Why should I do so for my direct reports?
- ◆ They will make more money than I do.
- ◆ I am afraid to set precedents.
- ◆ I don't have time to work on this.

Proper compensation and awards are very important areas of responsibility for a resource manager—if you want to have a consistently successful organization. If you choose not to pay and reward well, then you *choose* not to retain many of your best people. And the cost of losing a good performer is much higher than most people realize. It can cost *tens of thousands of dollars* in schedule slips, lost revenues, retraining costs, and so on.

And what about those awards! It is so inexpensive to award people for exceptional behavior, compared to not awarding them and losing their passion, loyalty, and dedication to their work—and maybe even losing them to another company. If a resource manager errs with awards, it is better to err on the side of too many or too large. Money is certainly not the only motivator for direct reports, but it sure can send the signal that the resource manager either cares—or doesn't—about your contributions.

> **LESSON 7.10**
>
> Better to err on the side of too many and too large awards, than too few and too small.

Provides Career Counseling and Development

The resource manager has the duty of providing career counseling and professional development to all direct reports. Some need it more than others; some want it more than others, but all have the right to receive it. If the human resource is of paramount importance to an organization or project, isn't there something wrong with not developing her, so she can approach her true potential? Isn't that a win for everyone?

The resource manager also has a responsibility to inform the direct reports when they perform well, as well as when they show difficulty in assigned areas. The resource manager must be available and accessible to work and help develop the direct reports in both the best and the worst of times—and in between.

> **LESSON 7.11**
>
> Each human resource needs to be nurtured to reach his potential.

Promotes a Productive Work Environment

More than any other position in the EnterPrize Organization, the resource manager has responsibility for ensuring the continual improvement in the productivity of his direct reports. The resource manager cares about the organization being stronger today than it was yesterday—and even stronger tomorrow than today. The resource manager initiates programs and activities that contribute to the improvement of productivity; some examples include:

- defining and measuring productivity-related areas for improvement
- reviewing, acquiring, and replacing productivity-enhancing tools
- creating or requesting training classes
- performing postproject reviews on department-related work to acquire lessons learned
- establishing a suggestion award process for productivity-improvement ideas that are accepted.

The process architect can be called upon to help in process-related areas.

LESSON 7.12

The processes and human resource productivity within a resource manager's area of responsibility should show improvement from project to project.

Serves as Channel for Company Communications

The resource manager serves as a conduit for the dissemination of company-related information to the direct reports. The information can originate from the corporate, divisional, organizational, or departmental levels. It can relate to a wide range of subject areas such as policies, business strategies, business initiatives, company products, financial reports, legal issues, tax issues, personnel benefits, employee recognition, job opportunities, and general news items. Although some of this information will be communicated to employees through media such as direct mailings, postings, and intranets, the resource manager represents the company on the front lines working directly with its employees.

LESSON 7.13

A resource manager puts a *face* on the corporation with which direct reports can communicate.

Executes Company Policies and Practices

Resource managers are the *enforcement* arms of the company executives. They are charged with putting into practice the policies and directives that define the company's corporate image to the direct reports and the communities that they populate. Resource managers ensure the appropriate enforcement of legal issues with such areas of products and services, workplace safety, and contractor relationships.

As an example, let's look more closely at workplace safety. The resource manager is responsible for ensuring the safety of all direct reports and others who work alongside her. This includes safety issues relating to fires, building structures, building equipment, office and lab environments, electrical facilities, sanitation, chemicals, parking areas, smoking, drugs, alcohol, and weapons—to name a few. The resource manager's safety duties also include areas such as harassment and other civil or criminal activity.

Although most companies have departments that specialize in many of the areas mentioned above, resource managers are ultimately accountable for ensuring that they are in compliance for their domain of responsibility.

Procures and Manages Logistics for Direct Reports

Resource managers are always looking for ways to help improve the productivity and success of their direct reports, which, in turn, benefits the organization and the company. An example of the implementation of this philosophy is the myriad of administrative tasks that resource managers perform on behalf of their direct reports. For example, resource managers are responsible for ensuring that *space planning* is performed, so future building space is available when needed for offices, meeting and training rooms, test labs, production areas, and storage areas, to name a few. Resource managers assign workspace areas to direct reports and procure office and lab computers, pagers, office furniture, and general supplies. Resource managers deal with issues such as telecommuting from home, for their direct reports, as well as ensuring ample parking spaces for office workers.

Once again, although many companies have departments that specialize in many of the tasks mentioned above, resource managers are ultimately accountable for ensuring that these areas are appropriately addressed.

Secures Future Work Opportunities

The resource manager is responsible for performing a visionary role in securing future work opportunities for his direct reports. The best resource managers do not resort to *downsizing* as a standard or convenient method of managing the business. Instead, they accept responsibility for seeking and developing new business opportunities, while the direct reports focus full time on driving the day-to-day operations. The fundamental importance of this role in providing job security for their direct reports—assuming that they continue to perform satisfactorily—cannot be overstated. Consider the following scenario.

> You work in an organization where there is uncertainty about having a job after your current job assignment completes. The workers—including members of management—are continuously looking over their shoulders in anticipation of bad news. Each time there is a hint of bad news, there seems to be another wave of workers leaving the company unwilling to work under the stress and strain of not knowing if or when the ax will fall.

Each time this happens, the workers that remain question their actions and behaviors for staying. This highly unproductive environment causes many of the workers to update their résumés and troll them on the outside market for tempting hits. There is an atmosphere afoot that encourages workers not to be totally committed to their assignments and not to work as smart or as hard as they can. It is becoming increasingly more difficult to fully concentrate on doing the best job possible. Even overtime work—particularly if it comes with no additional pay—seems a foolish use of personal time.

How productive do you think this scenario is for the workers and the business? It has a disastrous effect. This is but one of the fallouts of an organization or company that doesn't look out for its people. Don't let this happen to your organization or project.

LESSON 7.14

Resource managers are responsible for securing future work opportunities for their direct reports whose performance is satisfactory.

Q & A

Q7.1 Can a resource manager be effective as a resource manager if she also takes on one or more other positions defined by the Enter*Prize* Organization?

A7.1 Being a resource manager is a full-time job. There is no time to also fill one of the other Enter*Prize* Organization positions we have discussed, or will discuss in upcoming chapters (e.g., The Team Leader, The Team Member). If resource managers take on key positions in a project in addition to their own, they are negatively compromising their contribution to the project and organization. Let's look at an example.

Ahmed is both a resource manager and a product architect on a project. He has twelve people reporting directly to him. He is on a project that consists of about fifty people. Ahmed is an experienced developer and mostly enjoys focusing on the technical (versus organizational or people) side of projects. He was offered a promotion into management about a year ago and, after some thought, chose to accept the resource manager assignment. Ahmed never really had any strong desire to be in management. The primary reason for accepting the promotion was that it seemed to be where the money was; after all, the technical career ladder had serious limitations.

Ahmed is viewed by all the project members as the chief technologist on the project. He is consulted by almost every one at one time or another, and is the owner of the product specifications. Ahmed also chairs the change-control board for specifications and design issues. When Ahmed is not performing as product architect, he assumes his duties as a resource manager. Because he likes the technical side of his job the most, he spends 80 percent of his time with it. Of course, this means that he only gives 20 percent of his time to the resource manager duties—not nearly enough time to be effective.

What's happening in this example? Several things: Ahmed is not available 100 percent of the time as a product architect, which means that he is not accessible to the project members whenever they need him. Nor is he able to work technical issues with the sense of urgency that many require. Moreover, Ahmed is not able to look out for his twelve direct reports; he just doesn't have the time for his required resource manager duties. Therefore, his direct reports are getting short-changed in their career development and with professional opportunities. When a person takes on two or more key positions, she gravitates toward the position where most comfort is felt while sacrificing other duties of lesser interest—but not necessarily of lesser importance. It is dead wrong to take on two or more of the critical Enter*Prize* Organization positions. (See a discussion of an *exception* in Chapter 12, Organizing for Small Projects.) The project, the product, the people, and the organization will suffer.

One more example: If a resource manager were also to be a project manager, the resource manager could find himself in a no-win situation. That is, there will be many times when decisions must be made, weighing what's best for the project versus what's best for one or more direct reports. If there is no one championing the direct reports, the decision will almost always be made in favor of the project. Such decisions may not always be in the best long-term interest of the company, not to mention the employee.

LESSON 7.15

Resource managers should not take on other positions of the Enter*Prize* Organization at the sacrifice of effectively performing their own duties.

Q7.2 Referring to the previous Q&A, are you suggesting that it is wrong for a person to take on a job with which they have considerably less interest than the one they now hold, even though the new job pays more and has better long-term financial potential?

A7.2 Let's be careful here—this is a sensitive issue for a lot of people, and circumstances vary widely among all of us. Each person must weigh all of the factors, both personal and professional, that pertain to her own situation. Now, having said that, let's cut to the quick with a warning flag here: Ahmed, from the scenario, accepted a new job for the wrong reason. He's not really as happy in his new job; nor is he as effective. Ahmed was not true to himself. Thus, his quality of life has taken a downturn; he knows this but is unable (unwilling is more like it) to follow what his instincts are telling him.

But Ahmed is not the only culprit; his senior management is also to blame. Why? Because it doesn't have an adequate technical career path for folks like Ahmed. In the long run, Ahmed, and many like him, may leave the organization or company for more personally rewarding jobs. Many of us behave at one time or another as Ahmed did in the scenario, but some people make choices that cause them to be unhappy for years.

> **LESSON 7.16**
>
> Management must provide the means for employees who wish to pursue a technical career ladder (as opposed to managerial or project management); otherwise, technical talent will leave the company or become less effective while taking on higher-paying, nontechnical jobs.

Q7.3 Are group interviews an effective method for selecting qualified candidates to hire?

A7.3 Group interviews can be very effective. What do I mean by a group interview? It is when a candidate for hire is interviewed by two or more people at the same time. There are many reasons for taking this interview approach, and they all center around selecting the best people to hire. Résumés cannot be trusted to be complete or accurate and must be presumed to be self-serving. If you hire the wrong person, here is a brief look at some of the consequences:

- ◆ It may take several months to discover that an unqualified person was hired.
- ◆ Both parties experience a painful and costly process in terminating the unqualified employee (or attempting to find a better skills fit elsewhere in the company).
- ◆ Several months can be needed to find and obtain a qualified replacement.
- ◆ Additional time can be necessary to get the replacement up to a productive speed.

So what do you do? You invest a fraction more of your hiring dollars into beefing up the hiring process to help weed out people who are not a good fit. You owe this to both your organization and the hiring candidate.

A group interview can last anywhere from one hour to the better part of a day. It is important that certain categories of questions are asked to determine:

◆ the validity of the person's background skills and experience
◆ how well the candidate can work with people in general and the potentially assigned team in particular
◆ how the candidate goes about planning work, meeting commitments, and performing problem solving
◆ the person's career interests
◆ the work ethic of the candidate, and how long the candidate might be expected to remain with the company, assuming that certain opportunities can be fulfilled.

Group interviews allow the interviewers to work off of each other's questions and observe the candidate's responses together. There almost always will be no dead time during the interview while questions are being considered or notes are being taken. This keeps the candidate on her toes. In fact, some people believe this interview process is unfair to the candidate because of the stress it may place on her. But that's the idea; we are trying to run a successful business. We want the best-fit candidates. It is wasteful to *both* the candidate and the company to hire an ill-fit candidate. After the group interview has been completed, the group gathers to compare notes and recommend whether or not the candidate is a good fit and a hiring offer should be made.

LESSON 7.17

Group interviews can be an effective candidate-selection technique.

Q7.4   If only resource managers can make job assignments, does this mean that a project manager cannot assign *action items* to project members?

A7.4   A project manager *can* assign action items. An *action item* is defined as a project problem that is logged, assigned to an owner to resolve, and then tracked until it is closed. When a resource manager makes a job assignment, he is assigning a direct report to work on a given project. Moreover, the resource manager makes the decision as to what the direct report is responsible for, such as developing code, writing user documentation, or testing the product. If the actual use of the direct employee on the project was decided by the project manager, the employee can find herself assigned to perform tasks that are inappropriate, based on the direct report's level and skills. Moreover, the assignment might not be in the best interest of the direct report's long-term aspirations. Therefore, the resource manager and the direct report work closely when these assignments are made. Once made, the project manager (or team leader, if applicable) works with the direct report, as needed, to ensure that her work is planned and tracked, and relevant problems are resolved accordingly.

Q7.5 The job of a resource manager is a challenging one. Wouldn't you say that a resource manager's direct reports are there to support their boss?

A7.5 Resource managers are in a unique and powerful position in a company. They are the only employees who can disperse funds and hire and fire. Their power is needed to ensure orderly control of company resources and that the overall wellbeing of the company is and remains satisfied. Resource managers are in place to support their direct reports, so the direct reports are successful in achieving their commitments. The day-to-day operations of a company should be run by the direct reports with the full support of the resource managers.

While this concept is not new, it is not commonly embraced or practiced. Resource managers who practice this approach tend to be the most cherished by those who work for them. Think about the jobs you have held over the years and the jobs from which you derived the most satisfaction. The likelihood is high that they were jobs where you worked for a resource manager who expected a lot from you, gave the support you needed, and *gave* the authority you needed to fully own and be accountable for your assignments. The most effective resource managers behave as if the successes of their direct reports matter—because they do.

LESSON 7.18

Resource managers are there to support the troops, not the other way around.

Q7.6 It seems that resource managers work more overtime than many of their direct reports. Should it be this way?

A7.6 It is common for resource managers in an organization to work more overtime, on average, than their direct reports. However, resource managers should have the *same* relative overtime habits as their direct reports. The primary reason why many resource managers work more hours (on average) is that they don't *let go*. There is a strong tendency for a resource manager, especially one relatively new to management, to attempt to do the work alongside the troops, rather than support the troops in performing the work. The result is that the department's work doesn't get done as timely or as completely, accountability wanes across the department, and the resource manager is negligent in performing many of the resource manager duties described in this chapter.

LESSON 7.19

Resource managers should have the same relative overtime habits as their direct reports.

Q7.7   Is it ever appropriate for a resource manager to have more than fifteen direct reports? Is there a minimum number?

A7.7   As stated in an earlier section of this chapter, less-experienced resource managers might have up to ten direct reports, and more seasoned resource managers could have as many as fifteen. Of course, when a resource manager is staffing a department, there can be a very small number of direct reports for a time, or even more than fifteen, until an unusually large department can be broken into smaller departments. What should be avoided are permanent departments of a handful or less of people or departments that are so large, they are viewed to be resource pools. Both scenarios can be ineffective, unproductive, and cost burdens to an organization.

Q7.8   Is it okay for a resource manager to be a contractor instead of a full-time employee of the company?

A7.8   Whenever possible, a position as important as resource manager should be filled by employees within the company. Although this also is true for project managers, there is an additional complication that can apply. Resource managers must be fully accepted by their management peers and privy to mounds of sensitive information about the company and its employees—information that a project manager does not need to know in order to do his job. Most companies find it difficult to open their arms this wide to embrace a resource manager who is *only* a contractor.

If this is the case, the resource manager contractor will experience a handicap and so be less effective than the company resource managers. Another complication is that the direct reports to the resource manager contractor can be handicapped in having their boss champion their salary increases, promotions, and awards. Furthermore, the troops might view the resource manager as a short-timer who, therefore, only focuses on short-term decisions. It should be noted, however, that, for limited periods of time, it can be better to have a qualified resource manager contractor than an unqualified company employee as a resource manager.

LESSON 7.20

If at all possible, resource managers should be full-time employees of the company.

Q7.9   How often should a resource manager provide feedback to a direct report regarding his performance?

A7.9   Every attempt should be made to provide feedback on a direct report's performance at the time the behavior is observed. However, formal performance evaluations should occur somewhere in the range from monthly to quarterly and summarized annually. Many companies evaluate their employees annually with little or no substantive feedback to the employees throughout the performance period. This sloppy behavior on the part of a resource manager causes direct reports to be surprised during the performance review and, worse, have to wait up to a year before they can begin to take positive action on the lessons they learn. How would you like someone to inform you up to a year later that your performance needs to change in order for you to be more effective? Me neither. If you are a resource manager reading this and saying, "I don't have time to give monthly or quarterly reviews," then you are saying, in effect, "I don't have time to be an effective resource manager."

LESSON 7.21

Performance feedback is best when delivered at the time the behavior is observed, independent of the behavior being praiseworthy or not.

Q7.10   During a formal performance review of a direct report, is it best for the resource manager to focus mostly on areas for improvement or areas of strengths?

A7.10   More time, by far, should be spent on helping the direct report understand her strong suits and helping her exploit these areas. A person's value to a company will be defined by her strengths, not weaknesses. We all have strengths we bring to bear. If we focus on maximizing these talents and skills, we can considerably boost our potential to make a mark in the company and our careers. It's a mistake to focus significantly on a person's weaknesses. Most weaknesses will have little impact on a person's overall contributions compared to the person's strengths. This doesn't mean that a resource manager should gloss over areas for improvement. There are useful lessons; just don't get stuck there.

LESSON 7.22

A person's *strengths* and potential strengths are far more important to a company and the person's career than the person's *weaknesses*.

Q7.11   Is a resource manager responsible for mentoring his direct reports?

A7.11   No, resource managers are not in the best position to mentor their direct reports. Preferably, mentors should be people who are *not* an employee's resource manager or in his direct line of management. Mentors can be more effective if they do not also engage in performance evaluations of the mentee or are in a power position that can affect the employee's next assignment, promotions, or awards. However, resource managers should work with their direct reports to help them find suitable mentors. (See the first several Q&A's in Chapter 14, The Project Management Office, for more on mentoring.)

Q7.12   Are certificates of appreciation an adequate award for showing employees that you appreciate their contributions?

A7.12   Certificates of appreciation can be very effective to an employee if they are accompanied with cash or something tangible. The flip side also applies: avoid giving a cash or value award without a certificate. Why? Think about this.

>   Mark has been performing unusually well for months at his level and receives a certificate of appreciation—and no cash—for his good work. He mounts the certificate on his office wall where he can appreciate it daily, and it can remind his peers of his acknowledged contributions. Although Mark appreciates his certificate, he feels that it would have been more sincere had it come with a bit of cash, even a paltry $100. Mark feels privately that he has gotten the short end of the award stick.

>   Dorothy, Mark's office mate, receives a cash award of $1,000 for achieving something more notable than Mark but receives no certificate. Dorothy would rather have the $1,000 than a certificate and has the money spent in short order. As the weeks and months pass by, Dorothy becomes increasingly—but privately—annoyed that Mark's certificate remains on the wall for others to view with respect. New people continue to come into the organization and see Mark's certificate without a clue that Dorothy has received a more substantial award. Dorothy appreciates the $1,000 but wishes her resource manager had cared enough to also give her a certificate as a more lasting memento of appreciation.

If you believe that both Mark and Dorothy are being a bit immature, perhaps this is so; however, their actions are typical. Their stories represent classic human nature and the real world. If we are to live in the real world, why not factor in the human element accordingly? A certificate is an award that keeps on giving over the months and years. The money or tangible item that is given with the certificate amplifies the message of appreciation at the time that the certificate is awarded.

LESSON 7.23

Do not give an employee a certificate award without accompanying cash or an item of tangible value, nor give a cash award without also presenting a certificate of appreciation.

Q7.13   I believe that awards are good things, but we have a difficult time finding the money for awards. Any ideas?

A7.13   Yes, but first another story.

> Rick has been working ten to fifteen hours of overtime a week for a two-to-three-month period. He is a salaried programmer and doesn't usually receive additional compensation for working overtime. Rick has finished his assignment and has done a praiseworthy job, not just for the extra effort but also for the results he has attained. Ann, Rick's resource manager, believes this is a valid awardable situation and presents Rick with a certificate of appreciation and a check for $150, saying that it's for him and someone special to have a night out at the company's expense. Rick is quite pleased. He didn't expect this but is thankful that his boss appreciates his contributions.

What just happened? Ann *bought* Rick for about $1 an hour for all of the extra time he sacrificed. Where can you buy an employee with Rick's skill for only $1 an hour? Nowhere! The alternative is to award nothing and, over time, have Rick become disenchanted with working at this company when he then moves to "greener pastures." Should Rick choose to leave, it could cost the company tens of thousands of dollars in lost work, time to find a qualified replacement, and time to get that new hire up to speed. These cash awards are *pocket change* to a company. They are practically nothing compared to the value they bring to retaining and getting the most from employees.

An idea: set aside at least $2,000 per direct report for awards that can be given throughout the year. ($2,000 is an arbitrary amount; it could be anywhere from $2,000 to $5,000 or more, depending on your department's value to the company.) Not everyone will receive an award; awards have to be earned. Many awards will be $250 or less. Some people will receive more than one award per year. Some will receive an award of several thousand dollars. Budget now and disperse appropriately throughout the fiscal year. You might not make a better investment in showing your direct reports that you care. By the way, the troops have no need to know the budget that has been set aside for awards.

LESSON 7.24

Set aside at least $2,000 per direct report per year.

CHAPTER 8

THE TEAM LEADER

A project is typically made up of several teams, each performing its craft. For example, one team might design and write the code for the product, another might write the user documentation including online help, while another team might perform a big portion of the testing of the product to ensure that it is ready for the client. In the Enter*Prize* Organization, these team lead positions are called *team leaders*. Team leaders can be thought of as miniproject managers and take on many of the characteristics of a project manager, only with a smaller domain of responsibility—their teams.

A team leader reports directly to and takes career and professional direction from a resource manager. This is represented from a functional-reporting view of a project, as shown in Figure 1.1. The team leader receives project-related direction from the project manager, as represented in Figure 1.2. Moreover, technical direction often is taken from the product architect (not shown).

Figure 8.1 lists the roles and responsibilities of a team leader. Notice some similarities to those of a project manager. Let's examine each of these items.

Has Full Responsibility and Accountability for a Team

The team leader has overall responsibility and accountability for the success of his team and its plan. He leads the charge in putting together a sound team plan, obtaining commitments for the required resources, tracking the plan, being a catalyst in identifying and resolving plan problems, and working across the team and project to help make that plan successful.

FIGURE 8.1

Roles and Responsibilities of the Team Leader

◆ Has full responsibility and accountability for a team
◆ Has no direct reports
◆ Assists resource manager with job assignments
◆ Leads the creation and tracking of the team's plan
◆ Identifies and tracks interplan dependencies
◆ Works with business architect and product architect
◆ Supports team members
◆ Monitors quality of the team's deliverables
◆ Informs resource manager
◆ Supports project tracking meetings
◆ Approves project documentation that affects the team
◆ Ensures acceptable processes, methodologies, and tools are defined and used

The team leader ensures that all problems related to the team's plan are getting the attention that they need. These problems also are being closed on a timely basis. Although team members other than the team leader own most of the team's problems, the team leader acts as a catalyst for ensuring that the most important problems are receiving the most immediate attention.

LESSON 8.1

The team leader is fully accountable for the results produced by his team.

Has No Direct Reports

The team leader should not also be a resource manager and therefore should not have direct reports. Being an effective team leader is a full-time job, whether the team leader has to lead one large team, several small teams, or one large team with people assigned across several projects. Mixing these two very different roles and responsibilities of team leader and resource manager undermines the importance and compromises the effectiveness of both of these roles. (See Chapter 7, The Resource Manager, Section Q&A7.1, for a discussion as to why a project member holding a key Enter*Prize* Organization position should not also take on the roles and responsibilities of another key Enter*Prize* Organization position. For an exception, see Chapter 12, Organizing for Small Projects.)

Assists Resource Manager with Job Assignments

Only the resource manager can make job assignments, as discussed in Chapter 7, The Resource Manager. However, the team leader works closely with the resource manager in recommending team members for specific assignments. Because the team leader probably has a close working knowledge of the capabilities of many of the direct reports to the resource manager, she can be an invaluable asset to the resource manager as a team is being formed, or whenever team member assignments are being made.

Leads the Creation and Tracking of the Team's Plan

The project manager is accountable for the project plan; a team leader is accountable for his team's plan. The project plan comprises all of the collected team plans on a project. Therefore, each team's plan plays an important role in the overall success of a project.

When creating a project plan, the project manager directs each team leader to build his team plan according to certain rules and guidelines (e.g., account for training, vacations, and holidays; work first shift only; build into your plan a contingency buffer of x percent; and so on). Each team leader builds the team plan with the participation of all available team members. The team leader has the plan reviewed for completeness and reasonableness by the team members who contributed to its creation. The team plan is then reviewed by the team leader's resource manager, who must approve it and commit to obtaining required resources. Afterward, the project manager thoroughly reviews the plan. Once the team plan is approved, the project manager uplifts portions or all of it into the overall project plan.

The team leader tracks the team plan with the team members as frequently as needed (at least once per week but often more frequently). The resulting tracking information is reported to the project manager in the weekly (typically) project-tracking meetings. The team leader's resource manager is always kept informed of plan progress, problems, and actions being taken. The team leader ensures that his team appropriately handles all team-related issues. This responsibility includes identifying, communicating, tracking, escalating, and resolving these issues.

LESSON 8.2

The team leader directs the creation, approval, and tracking of the team's plan.

Identifies and Tracks Interplan Dependencies

The team leader is responsible for identifying any and all dependencies that her team plan has on other team plans. Furthermore, she obtains needed commitments from team leaders with whom there is a dependency. These interplan dependencies are tracked in two places to minimize problems that can arise from interplan surprises. The dependencies are tracked by each team leader, while working closely day to day and week to week with their counterpart team leaders. The dependencies are again tracked more formally at the project-tracking meeting run by the project manager. These interplan dependencies appear as trackable tasks in the project plan.

LESSON 8.3

The team leader identifies all interplan dependencies, obtains the appropriate commitments, and tracks the dependencies to closure.

Works with Business Architect and Product Architect

The team leader works closely with the business architect to help ensure that the team is sensitive to building the *right* product, and he works closely with the product architect to help ensure that the product is being built *right*. Most team leaders will produce deliverables that require review and/or approval from the business architect and the product architect. Examples are design inspections, test plans, and drafts of user documentation, to name a few. A team leader also is required to review and/or approve deliverables from the business architect and the product architect. Examples are the product-requirements document and the product specifications, respectively. Review and approval rights serve as a necessary check and balance tool to ensure that the needed communications are occurring across the project.

LESSON 8.4

The team leader works closely with the business architect and the product architect in both a support and a check-and-balance relationship.

Supports Team Members

The team leader champions the team and leads—drives—the team to success. Whenever obstacles appear, the team leader works to ensure that the obstacles are being addressed and mitigated. He may personally take on resolving some of the problems or assign them to team members. If a team member is having a serious or potentially serious problem related to the plan, the team leader should always be involved to constructively ensure that the problem is receiving required attention, so it can be appropriately closed. The team leader can initiate escalations, if needed, to speed up the resolution of a problem.

A team typically may be made up of anywhere from one to ten members. Is a one-member team a legitimate team? Yes, a team leader could have only himself on the *team*. For example, this could be the person who is the liaison to a vendor. Or it could be the only representative of a particular functional or skill group, such as the only person on a project who is responsible for writing user documentation.

LESSON 8.5

A team leader can lead a team of only one member (himself) or a team of ten members.

Although the team leader may be the most technical or skilled individual on the team, this does not necessarily need to be the case. When there are many members on a team, it is likely that some of them are highly skilled specialists, and one might serve as the technical team leader. Although not necessarily the most technical member of the team, the team leader does need to lead the team in planning the work, tracking the plan, identifying problems, ensuring that the problems are being driven to closure, and communicating effectively across the team and project.

LESSON 8.6

The team leader may or may not also be the technical team leader.

Monitors Quality of the Team's Deliverables

The team leader is responsible for monitoring the quality of all team deliverables. The team leader reviews all deliverables before they are distributed and ensures that the appropriate level of quality has been achieved. The deliverables may be of the type that is distributed only within the team, or they may be distributed outside of the team. If a deliverable does not meet the proper level of quality, the team leader works with the appropriate team members, and ensures a recovery plan is put into place to remedy the situation. Of course, any potential impact to the project is communicated to the resource manager and the project manager at the earliest possible time. Others may also be informed (e.g., product architect or client) as needed.

Informs Resource Manager

The team leader keeps her resource manager informed of the progress being made on the team's plan on a timely basis. This includes communicating the status of the team's problems and corresponding actions. In most cases, the resource manager should know about a problem that the team is experiencing before the project manager becomes aware of it. If this typically is not the case, the communications between the team leader and the resource manager may be too weak to be effective. Caution: A team leader should not excessively delay communicating problems to the project manager because her resource manager is not reasonably accessible.

LESSON 8.7

The team leader should ensure that her resource manager is aware of most problems before the project manager is informed.

Supports Project-Tracking Meetings

The team leader is a member of the project manager's project-tracking meeting and represents his team at these meetings. He reports plan progress, based on the format that the project manager requires. This typically will include metric charts to show actual progress being made compared to the progress that was expected. For example, how many modules were to be coded this week versus how many were actually coded? Or how many test scripts were to be written this week versus how many were actually written? Or how many defects were planned to be discovered and fixed this week versus—you get the idea.

The team leader also may report status on other items such as open problems and action items, the top three to five priorities/risks, and the plan outlook for the next thirty days—that is, what is the likelihood of being ahead, on, or behind schedule thirty days from now? And, oh yes, whether or not any help is required from outside the team leader's team.

> **LESSON 8.8**
>
> The team leader represents his team at project-tracking meetings.

Approves Project Documentation That Affects the Team

The team leader approves all project documentation on which her plan is dependent to be successfully implemented. This is a critical responsibility that frequently but *wrongly* is left to resource managers to approve. Team leaders need their own approval rights on dependent project documents if they are to be held personally accountable for the outcome of their plans.

> **LESSON 8.9**
>
> A team leader must have approval rights on project documents that can impact the success of her team's plan.

Ensures That Acceptable Processes, Methodologies, and Tools Are Defined and Used

The team leader is responsible for the required processes, methodologies, and tools to successfully implement the team's plan. For example, let's say that a team is responsible for performing designing, coding, and unit testing. There needs to be defined processes and/or tools for, say, performing the design, inspecting the design, writing the code, inspecting the code, writing the unit test plans, inspecting unit test plans, and performing the unit tests. The team leader must ensure that these processes are in place. The team leader can choose to personally define some of these processes, or he can assign them to team members to put in place.

If one or more of the processes applying to a team leader's team is singled out by the process architect as *must-have*, the team leader must define, document, and implement that process. Regardless, the process architect can be called upon to help in process-related areas. If the team leader identifies processes, methodologies, or tools that have or will have an impact on the successful implementation of the team's plan, but are outside of his team's direct responsibility, the team leader must initiate the steps to address this problem. The team leader must, at a minimum, work with the process architect (and project manager, if needed) to log the dependency as an action item to be assigned to someone and tracked to closure.

LESSON 8.10

The team leader is responsible to ensure that all processes, methodologies, and tools required to successfully implement the team plan are in place and appropriately used.

Q & A

Q8.1   Is it really necessary for a team leader to have her team plan reviewed by all of the following people: team members, resource manager, and project manager?

A8.1   It is imperative that all three groups review the team plan before it is approved and committed. The team plan is made up of input collected by the team leader from all available team members. (*Available* because perhaps the team has not yet been fully staffed; however, the critical mass of members should be available.) The team members must review the overall team plan after it has been constructed. It is likely that problems will be identified that should be addressed before the plan is exposed outside the team. Also, it is important that team members recognize the importance of their tasks and commitments to the overall success of the team plan.

The resource manager must review the team plan to understand the commitments being made by her direct reports. Furthermore, the resource manager needs to assess the completeness and thoroughness of the plan and will obtain the needed resources identified by the plan. Finally, the project manager must review the team plan to ensure that it is reasonable and attainable. After all, the project plan only will be as good as the team plans from which it is created.

LESSON 8.11

A team leader's team plan must be reviewed and approved by at least the team members, resource manager, and project manager.

Q8.2   Are there others that should approve the team leader's team plan besides the team members, resource manager, and project manager?

A8.2   There are other project members that might approve the plan. For example, any team leader whose plan is dependent on this team plan should have approval rights. In almost all cases, the business architect, product architect, and process architect should approve. In some cases, the client should approve. One can see that there is a great degree of interdependency across the members of most projects. The review and approval process allows these dependencies to be identified, communicated, committed, and tracked to closure.

LESSON 8.12

The review and approval process helps satisfy the widespread interdependency that is common across members of a project.

Q8.3   If a team leader is not also the technical team leader, then how do these two positions relate?

A8.3   The team leader can also be the technical team leader. However, depending on the size of the team, the complexity of the skill and technologies involved, and the interests of the team leader to also serve as the technical team leader, the team leader might not be also the technical team leader. If there is a separate technical leader, that person and the team leader would work closely to create an effective team plan. The technical leader would also spend more time with the product architect and possibly more time with the business architect than would the team leader; the team leader would likely spend more time with the process architect. However, there remains only one leader—one person ultimately accountable for the creation and performance of the team's plan: the team leader. The technical leader, however, becomes a valuable team member who will likely be working across the team in support of the team's commitments.

Q8.4   Are the business architect, product architect, and process architect also considered team leaders?

A8.4   All three *architects* perform as team leaders, each with his own position title, so he is not typically referred to as a team leader. However, all have plans for work that they must perform on a project. They can have a team of project members working under their direction. They own project documents (e.g., product requirements, product specifications, and software development process). They represent their areas of the project at project-tracking meetings—and so on.

Q8.5   When you say that a team leader needs to have approval rights over project documents that impact the success of her team's plan, how do you suggest that the approval process work?

A8.5   Let's look at two scenarios. The first scenario depicts, based on my experience, the most commonly practiced approval process embraced in most projects; however, this scenario illustrates what should *not* happen.

> Let's look in on Matt and Stephanie. Matt is the resource manager of a department with responsibility for writing and obtaining approvals for product specifications (hereafter called *specs*). Stephanie is a direct report of Matt's and is the team leader of the team that is actually writing the specs. (As discussed in the previous *Q&A* entry, the spec owner is the product architect who also can be called a team leader.) The specs are now ready to be distributed for review and approval. Matt approaches Stephanie and says, "Draft a memo for my signature that will be distributed along with the specs. The memo should be addressed to all the reviewers and approvers soliciting their comments and approval." Stephanie does so, and the memo and specs are distributed.

> Let's now look at Debi and Walt. Debi is the resource manager of a department with responsibility for testing the product to certify its readiness for the client. Walt is a direct report of Debi's and is the team leader of the team that actually performs the testing. Debi, as a resource manager, must approve the specs and therefore receives the specs and the memo that were sent from Matt. Debi says to Walt, "Please review the specs and draft a memo for my signature that states my approval or nonapproval." Walt writes a letter of nonapproval and documents ten issues with the specs that must be corrected before approval will be granted. Debi signs the memo, and it is sent to Matt.

> Debi and Matt then negotiate the ten issues. Negotiations are completed, and Debi approves the specs. Debi visits Walt and says, "Well, we just approved the specs." Walt responds, "Great! So we got all ten issues corrected?" Debi replies, "No, we had to compromise. We got five resolved to our satisfaction. We did well though. You had to be there to appreciate the negotiations."

Right now, Walt feels that his boss sold out him and his team. He said that he needed all ten issues resolved in order to meet his test plan commitments, but his boss did otherwise; she resolved only five issues. Walt is feeling less accountable for the outcome of his plan and his team's commitments. He is feeling more distant from Debi—and from the project and company. He is not so motivated to work any extra hours or work as hard as he otherwise might.

Let's now look at what *should* have happened.

Stephanie owns the specs, not her resource manager, Matt. Stephanie drafts the memo for her own signature and distributes the memo and specs to the reviewers and approvers—and copies Matt and all the resource managers of the reviewers and approvers. Walt has approval rights on the specs, not his resource manager, Debi. Walt prepares the memo for nonapproval of the specs and identifies the ten issues. Walt sends the nonapproval memo to Stephanie and copies their resource managers, Debi and Matt. Walt and Stephanie then negotiate the approval of the specs. They reach an agreement, and Walt approves. Walt visits Debi to say, "We have approved the specs." Debi says, "Great! So we got all ten issues corrected?" Walt replies, "No, I negotiated for five out of the ten, but we got the most important five issues. Even so, we can still meet our plan commitments."

Here's what just happened. Even if Walt negotiated for the same five issues on which his resource manager would have focused, the difference is that *Walt did it!* He was personally involved and exercised his judgment and authority in actively working the negotiations. Walt feels accountable and is still fully committed to his plan. The moral? Management must get out of the way, stop slowing the process, and causing accountability from the troops to wane. Let those at the lowest reasonable level be accountable for their own commitments. If they mess up along the journey, be there to help them, but don't interfere by taking on those items with which you should be holding others accountable.

LESSON 8.13
Resource managers must allow those at the lowest reasonable level to be accountable for their own commitments.

LESSON 8.14
When team leaders or team members make mistakes, their resource managers should be there to help them; however, resource managers should not personally take on responsibilities for which team leaders or team members should be held accountable.

Q8.6 This question is in reference to the previous question. If team leaders have approval rights on project documents that can impact their own plans, do their resource managers also have approval rights on these documents? If not, doesn't a resource manager lose a lot of influence over the actions of their team leaders?

A8.6 In most cases, it should be sufficient that the team leaders have approval rights; that is, the resource managers should not also have approval rights. Remember that this arrangement is all about driving accountability downward on projects and in organizations. This approach can help employees to professionally mature more quickly. It doesn't mean that the resource managers are out of the loop. After all, the resource managers are still charged with coaching and counseling the team leaders. The resource manager can say to her team leaders that she wants to review all approval memos before they are sent. This allows the resource managers to ensure that the positions being taken by the team leaders on project documents are thorough, reasonable, and professional. Resource managers can also require that they review (even if only briefly) all project documents owned by team leaders that report to them before those documents are distributed for review and approval outside the team. Here again, this allows resource managers to remain involved with their team leaders to ensure that the quality of the work that leaves the department is satisfactory.

LESSON 8.15

Resource managers are never *out of the loop* when working with their direct reports.

Q8.7 Is it okay to have contractors perform the role of a team leader?

A8.7 Whenever possible, it is prudent to have company employees serve in major leadership roles on a project; it helps develop and retain these skills within the company. However, the demand for qualified people in these positions is so high that there are many cases when a company looks toward contractors as one way to satisfy its needs.

Q8.8 Team leaders typically conduct a lot of meetings, but many meetings are poorly run and, frankly, seem mostly to be a waste of time. How should a meeting be run?

A8.8 Figure 8.2 shows a short list of guidelines that can help you run an effective meeting.

FIGURE 8.2

Meeting Guidelines

◆ Plan the meeting
◆ Reserve the meeting room
◆ Start on time
◆ Identify the meeting leader
◆ State the meeting objectives
◆ Assign a person to take the minutes
◆ Keep meeting on track; use an agenda, if appropriate
◆ Enforce common respect for all participants
◆ Summarize meeting achievements
◆ End the meeting on or before its scheduled end time
◆ Distribute meeting minutes within one workday

When planning a meeting, make sure that the attendees who are critical to the meeting's success are properly informed and have committed to attend. Reschedule the meeting if the required attendees cannot participate and the meeting cannot be sufficiently productive. Inform attendees of the meeting objectives, so they can come to the meeting with the proper mindset and prepared, if appropriate. Of course, disclose the meeting date, time, and location.

Meeting rooms should be reserved in hour or half-hour increments, beginning on the hour or half-hour. Meetings should begin, however, ten minutes after the hour (or half-hour) to allow attendees who are coming from other meetings to arrive on time. Meetings should end ten minutes before the hour (or half-hour) so that attendees can arrive at their next meeting on time.

LESSON 8.16

Meetings should begin ten minutes after the hour (or half-hour) and end ten minutes before the hour (or half hour) to accommodate attendees with multiple back-to-back meetings.

Always begin meetings on time. Do not review progress for latecomers during the meeting. At the start of a meeting, all attendees need to know who is in charge of the meeting. Everyone looks toward this person, the meeting leader, to demonstrate needed leadership throughout the meeting. The meeting leader clarifies the scope of the meeting at the start to help the meeting attendees remain focused and productive.

The meeting leader must *not* take the minutes; it would cause her to lose concentration and the ability to be fully engaged in driving the meeting. It also negatively affects the progress and pace of the meeting. The minute taker preferably is a person who is not, otherwise, an essential participant.

The meeting leader ensures that the meeting begins and remains on track to achieve its objectives using an agenda, if appropriate. Overly lengthy discussions, tangential topics, and scope creep are discouraged, and appropriate actions are taken to refocus the meeting attendees. The meeting leader creates and enforces a productive and respectful meeting environment. The meeting's success is dependent on the free flow of information and ideas, as well as the full participation of the attendees. Problems are attacked, not people.

When the meeting objectives have been met, the key points and assignments are briefly summarized. This helps the attendees to be clear on the meeting outcomes, and allows them to immediately begin taking appropriate actions while the meeting minutes are being prepared.

The meeting ends on time to accommodate other commitments of the attendees. End the meeting at least ten minutes before the room reservation time expires to accommodate attendees arriving to their next meeting on time. If the meeting requires more time than was scheduled, and the meeting cannot be continued immediately, give attendees a heads-up as to its likely rescheduled date and time.

Either the minutes-taker or the meeting leader prepares and distributes the minutes within one workday of the meeting. In either case, however, the meeting leader is ultimately responsible for the content of the minutes and ensuring their timely distribution.

The meeting leader is responsible for following these or similar guidelines. Attendees rightfully look to the meeting leader to run effective meetings. Posting these guidelines in all meeting rooms can help educate and remind meeting participants what they should expect and demand when they give up so much of their limited time to meetings. There is a direct relationship between effectively run meetings and the overall effectiveness of the related organization, project, or team.

LESSON 8.17

The best-run meetings will almost always end well before the meeting's scheduled end time.

CHAPTER 9

THE TEAM MEMBER

*A*ny person assigned to a project is called a *project member*. The project manager, business architect, product architect, process architect, and team leaders are all considered project members. Resource managers, however, are not typically thought of as direct members on a project. Why? Because they do not have any project assignments; that is, they do not *own* anything (e.g., tasks, processes, plans, and documents). However, they do provide very important support roles for a project by obtaining and assigning employees, and working with, training, coaching, tracking, and helping their employees make and meet their commitments. Because of the vital support services provided by resource managers, they are included as part of the headcount and budget and therefore are indeed project members.

But there is another group of people on a project whose members are also project members: *team members*. Team members, like everyone else on a project, report directly to a resource manager, taking career and professional direction from him. Functional and project directions primarily are taken from the team leader. As discussed in the previous chapter, the team leader typically has one or more team members on his team. In some cases, however, a team member might not work with a team leader and instead directly support the project manager, business architect, product architect, or process architect. In these cases, the team member takes functional and project direction directly from the person she supports.

Figure 9.1 lists the key roles and responsibilities of a team member. The sections that follow will discuss these items.

FIGURE 9.1

Roles and Responsibilities of the Team Member

◆ Responsible and accountable for assigned tasks
◆ Routinely informs team leader or person supporting
◆ Routinely informs resource manager
◆ Supports project members
◆ Approves project documentation
◆ Performs duties similar to the team leader if …

Responsible and Accountable for Assigned Tasks

The team member has the overall responsibility and accountability for the successful completion of her tasks. This includes estimating and planning tasks, committing to one's own work, obtaining commitments for dependencies required from others, executing and tracking tasks, delivering tasks within costs and to quality standards, and identifying and resolving problems that affect the team member's commitments. The team member should wisely choose and routinely use metrics that will aid in tracking the progress of her own tasks.

As with any project member, the team member is responsible for asking for help when it is needed. A project is only as strong as its weakest link, and every attempt should be made by the team member not to be a weak link. Team members should see that all other project members are there to support them if they are in need. After all, the project will not be successful, or as successful as it could be, without the full success of each project member. The team leader and the resource manager are the first two lines of support to help the team member be successful.

LESSON 9.1

Commitments are made to be met, not broken.

Routinely Informs Team Leader or Person Supporting

The team member must keep his team leader or the person whom he is supporting apprised of status as required. The team member is responsible for communicating progress, problems, and actions planned or taken, so the team leader can take appropriate action to help the team member when needed, as well as communicate team status to the project manager and resource manager. The team leader usually should be the first to know of problems and their status and the first to offer needed assistance.

Routinely Informs Resource Manager

The team member keeps her resource manager informed of progress, problems, and actions on a timely basis; it is not the job of the resource manager to chase after this information. Keeping the resource manager informed may be done in varying ways such as routine department meetings, team leader meetings attended by the resource manager, or one-on-one meetings with the resource manager, but it must be done. Why? So the resource manager can ensure that the team member is meeting her commitments to the project. Also, so the resource manager can be a catalyst for helping the team member when necessary. Moreover, the resource manager requires this close working relationship to be able to appropriately evaluate the performance of the team member. The resource manager works closely with the team leader and relies considerably on him to work with the team member as needed.

LESSON 9.2

Resource managers are an excellent source of support for team members.

Supports Project Members

The team member is responsible for working with other project members, as needed, to help them be successful. This means attending meetings, reviewing deliverables, participating in peer reviews, satisfying dependencies, and offering help when asked or required. Project members working together can accomplish tasks that would not be within the reach of individuals working alone. There should always be the goal of shoring up the weakest links on a project—the people and tasks that require the most help—which translates into project members helping other project members, so the project is successful, or more successful, than it might be otherwise. When the project is successful, everyone benefits.

LESSON 9.3

The most successful projects are those projects made up of project members that rally around supporting one another as needed.

Approves Project Documentation

The team member approves all project documentation on which her plan is dependent to be successfully implemented. An exception to approving the documentation might be the case when the team leader is approving project documentation on behalf of all the team members working under the direction of that team leader. In this case, the team member would review the project documentation, and pass along problems and comments to the person who has approval authority.

LESSON 9.4

A project member has approval rights—either direct or indirect—on all project documentation on which her plan is dependent.

Perform Duties Similar to the Team Leader If ...

If the team member does not work under the direction of a team leader, the team member is also responsible for similar roles and responsibilities as the team leader. For example, the team member is responsible for the processes and methodologies required to successfully implement his tasks. If the team member does not have direct control of these processes and methodologies, the team member must work with the proper personnel (e.g., process architect and/or project manager) to obtain the attention and support needed.

Q & A

Q9.1   A common complaint is that there are too many meetings to attend. What responsibility does a team member have to attend all of these meetings?

A9.1   Not just team members, but also any project member should wisely choose the meetings they will attend. Project members should, of course, attend meetings from which they receive benefit or have the expectation that they will receive benefit. Sometimes, the benefit to be derived from participating in a meeting cannot be fully known until the meeting has started. Project members should also attend meetings that have the potential for the attendee to offer value. A project member should not be so quick to avoid attending a meeting just because there is no apparent value to herself. By offering information and skills to a meeting, a project member can be a valuable participant.

   If you cannot see the benefit of your or the meeting attendees' participation, give notice that you will not attend the meeting, or excuse yourself from a meeting already under way. An exception is a project-tracking meeting; if you are a required participant, you must attend for the duration of the meeting, even after your status has been delivered. Why? Because you never know when 1) something might come up that you need to know, 2) you have information that you need to share with others, 3) you might be called upon to share information with others, or 4) you are required to discuss a matter with others.

> **LESSON 9.5**
>
> Project members should only attend meetings that offer value to the attendee, or meetings that have the potential for the attendee to offer value.

Q9.2   Many meetings are poorly run and, frankly, seem mostly to be a waste of time. How should a meeting be run?

A9.2   This question is answered in Chapter 8, The Team Leader, Section Q&A8.8.

Q9.3   Do team members attend project-tracking meetings?

A9.3   On small projects—say those of ten or less people—it is more than likely that all project members will participate in the project-tracking meetings; therefore, all team members would participate. On larger projects, it is more likely that team members do *not* regularly attend and participate in the project-tracking meetings. Instead, their team leaders participate and represent their tasks and status. This allows team members to be more productive in completing their committed tasks, as well as attend one less meeting. Having team leaders attend for their teams also can result in more effectively run project-tracking meetings.

Q9.4   Should contractors be hired as team members?

A9.4   As with company employees, contractors can make great team members. However, many teams and projects treat contractors as *second-class citizens*, which undermines the contribution potential of contractors. Contractors should be treated as fully functioning members of the teams to which they are assigned. This means making information accessible to them that they need to perform their job. It also means including them in meetings that are relevant to their duties and needs and continually providing them the education that they need to be productive. It even means rewarding them for outstanding achievements.

    Some company employees resent contractors, and it shows in their treatment of them. They might resent that the contractor often receives compensation for overtime work. They may resent that the contractor can earn more money than some of their peers in the company. They might resent that contractors don't really feel an ownership, a passion, for the work they perform. And so on. This is all highly immature and unprofessional behavior.

    If you owned a company, you would view contractors as an essential business need. You would seek them for many valid business reasons, such as you may not have people with certain skills you need, or you may only need additional skilled resources for a small period of time. Using contractors can be a good business decision for a company. They are the first to be let go when budgets tighten, and they can be the first on the scene, so companies can quickly seize new opportunities.

    If you truly believe that contractors have the best deal, then quit your job and become one. Most company employees would not want to trade positions. Furthermore, most contractors would prefer to have the job security, benefits, and career opportunities that company employees have. In summary: it's business, not personal. If you welcome contractors, and treat them with the same respect that you wish from others, you will discover hardworking, passionate people who desire to contribute and be recognized just like the rest of us.

Q9.5   A follow-up question on contractors. Isn't it wrong to spend monies to continually train contractors when they eventually will be leaving the company with their honed skills?

A9.5   Contractors, like all other project members, are trained because they need the knowledge and skills to make the project successful. However, depending on the type of training, contractors can be asked to pay for the training they will receive if the training yields skills that are viewed as being easily transferable outside the company. Or you can allow contractors to participate in the training, but not pay them for the time they spend in the classroom. Because most contractors work through a contracting corporation that offers some benefits, their own companies can pay for training time. Who will pay needs to be worked out—regardless, many contractors will need continual training.

Q9.6   My resource manager is a very busy person with over ten direct reports and a long list of responsibilities to handle. How can I make sure that my boss remains aware of my achievements?

A9.6   You are correct that your boss is very busy. You must take the approach that you are the person responsible for initiating and sustaining open communications between you and your boss—not your boss. For example, most employees have their performance evaluated once a year. When that moment arrives, the resource manager is usually straining to recall your achievements throughout the year. When the evaluation is administered to you, you may discover that your *significant* achievements were overlooked, achievements that might have improved your performance rating, had your resource manager remembered them. To compound this situation, once a resource manager has written your performance evaluation, it is rarely changed to accommodate forgotten achievements.

There is something you can do to help yourself *and* your resource manager: *written status reports*. Even if your boss is not asking for a status report regarding all of your responsibilities and achievements from you, do it anyway. These reports could be done weekly, every two weeks, or monthly; I favor monthly. The report should be as brief as possible and written as bullets or lists versus long paragraphs and wordy. A typical report should be one to three pages in length. You should list your key accomplishments since the last report, any obstacles currently facing you and your plans to mitigate them, and your key plans for the upcoming reporting period. Also include a section that addresses other areas such as praising others for their assistance or your desire to discuss a career or training opportunity. You could title this area something like "Heads Up."

Your boss will find these reports valuable not only for recalling your achievements at the end of the performance period, but also as another means to help her stay connected with you throughout the year. Of course, you have the responsibility to initiate other opportunities to communicate with your boss. If there is a training opportunity you know about or would like to initiate, meet with your boss to discuss the matter. If you are looking for a change in career direction or advancement opportunities, schedule a meeting to discuss these items. If you don't want to be surprised by your yearly performance evaluation, ask for an informal evaluation quarterly or more frequently if needed.

LESSON 9.6

Written status reports are an effective way for your boss to recall your achievements throughout the performance evaluation period.

In other words, take action! This is your career we are discussing. If you show your interest for such matters, your boss will show increased interest in working with you. If you want something to happen, you must be *bold* and take the initiative.

LESSON 9.7

You are responsible for your performance and career—not your boss, not your company, not anyone else, not anything else.

CHAPTER 10

ORGANIZING FOR LARGE PROJECTS

rojects of all sizes can benefit from the Enter*Prize* Organization. Chapter 1, Overview of the Enter*Prize* Organization, introduced the Enter*Prize* Organization by discussing a project of approximately thirty members. But how does the Enter*Prize* Organization apply to larger projects? Let's take a look.

Functional-Reporting View

Figure 10.1 shows the functional-reporting view of a project of about two hundred members. Notice that we still have the product manager (PDM) at the head of the total organization—an organization that is focused on a single project. (For a discussion on applying the Enter*Prize* Organization in an environment where multiple projects are being performed simultaneously, see Chapter 11, Organizing for Multiple Projects.) Reporting to the product manager are the same positions that were described in Chapter 1: the project manager (PM), business architect (BA), product architect (PA), process architect (PCA), and resource managers (RM). Thus far, the only change in Figure 10.1 from Figure 1.1, which shows the functional-reporting structure, is that an additional resource manager is reporting to the product manager.

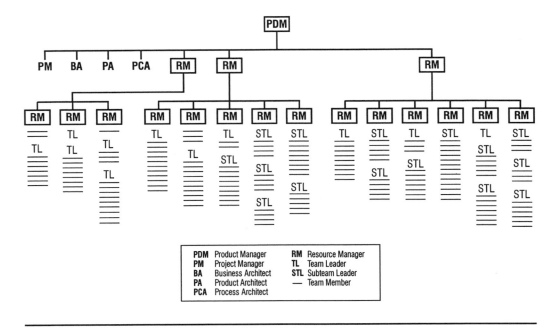

FIGURE 10.1

Functional-Reporting View for a Large-Sized Project (200 members)

PDM	Product Manager	RM	Resource Manager
PM	Project Manager	TL	Team Leader
BA	Business Architect	STL	Subteam Leader
PA	Product Architect	—	Team Member
PCA	Process Architect		

Resource Managers

Now let's go one layer deeper into the functional-reporting structure shown in Figure 10.1. Notice that multiple resource managers report to each of the resource managers at the top layer—to be specific, three, five and six resource managers, respectively. This begs the question: How many resource managers should report to a next-higher-level resource manager?

The answer is not so simple or straightforward. It depends on many factors but can be reduced to this: the number of resource managers that should report to the next higher-level resource manager depends on the demands placed on the higher-level resource manager. Demands are largely based on the needs of the reporting resource managers and their departments. For example, less experienced resource managers will require more time from their bosses. Departments employing newer technologies, or viewed by the company to be performing work that is especially high profile and important to the company, and the experience level of the top resource manager, are examples of other factors that weigh into the equation.

However, there are additional factors that can impact the time demands placed on the higher-level resource manager. For example, the higher-level resource manager may have assignments to perform that are not limited to working with their direct reports. These special assignments may include areas relating to working on cross-organizational processes and problems, setting up a cross-organizational skills inventory, performing workload and resource balancing, developing new vendor relationships, working on tactical and strategic revenue/profit planning, and going after new business opportunities.

As a general guideline, the number of resource managers reporting to a top resource manager is generally in the range of three to seven. If there are any more than seven, the top resource manager typically is not available and accessible as frequently as the reporting resource managers require.

> **LESSON 10.1**
>
> A resource manager with resource managers as direct reports typically should have a department made up of from three to seven resource managers.

Department Size

Looking again at Figure 10.1, note that each of the lower-level resource managers have departments that vary in size from ten to fifteen members. The number of department members (direct reports) assigned to report to a resource manager is largely based on the experience of the resource manager; that is, less experienced resource managers can have up to ten direct reports, and seasoned resource managers can have up to fifteen direct reports.

Resource managers temporarily can have departments of only a handful or less direct reports, as that department is expanding with new recruits. If a department has only a few direct reports for sustained periods, it may not be as cost effective as desired for the overall organization. Resource managers can have departments of far more than fifteen direct reports, but they should be in transition and eventually split to form departments of a more manageable size.

Department Skill Groups

Resource managers typically manage departments of unique skill groups. Said another way, many of these departments could be viewed as functional groups. Examples of skill groups (or functional groups) are developers, testers, writers, performance analysts, usability analysts, library build analysts, process analysts, project office support personnel, trainers, quality assurance personnel, and pre-production support personnel.

Team Leaders and Subteam Leaders

Figure 10.1 shows fourteen lower-level resource managers and their departments. Each of the fourteen shown will likely require one or more leaders within each department. They could be team leaders (TL) as defined in earlier chapters, or they could be *subteam leaders* (STL), a term introduced here. When a team leader is responsible for a team that might be considered quite large—say, more than five or ten members—additional leaders can be defined to lead various portions of the overall team. These leaders are called subteam leaders, and they can have teams that typically range from one to ten members.

LESSON 10.2

A team leader of a large team can break the team into smaller groups, each run by a subteam leader.

Team leaders attend weekly tracking meetings run by the project manager. These meetings are far more effective if the number of team leaders on the project comprise fifteen or less. On very large projects, there may be many more than fifteen teams that could be represented at the project-tracking meetings. Instead of crowding the meeting with too many representatives (team leaders), some of them are viewed as subteam leaders, who work under the project direction of another team leader. Therefore, when a team leader presents status on his plan at a project-tracking meeting, he might actually be presenting status for several different teams, each run by a subteam leader, but all of which fall under the domain of the team leader's responsibility.

LESSON 10.3

Project-tracking meetings can be run more effectively if the number of team leaders on the project is limited to fifteen or less.

Notice in Figure 10.1 that some departments have one or more team leaders, one or more subteam leaders, or a combination of both team and subteam leaders. The project depicted in Figure 10.1 has eleven team leaders and fifteen subteam leaders. Also notice that all departments have at least one team leader or subteam leader.

Because resource managers typically should not also work in the capacity of team leader or subteam leader, there should almost always be a team leader or subteam leader designated as a lead person for the department. An exception to this *rule* might be when the department members all have distinctly unique and unrelated assignments. In this case, there may be no one designated as the lead person representing the entire department. Instead, every person may be his own team leader or assigned to work under the direction of someone outside of the department.

LESSON 10.4

A resource manager typically should have one or more team leaders (and/or subteam leaders) in his department.

Support Personnel for the Project Manager and Others

The positions of project manager, business architect, product architect, and process architect could require project members assisting (supporting) each position. For example, for this approximately two hundred-member project, the project manager might have several people to help keep the overall project plan updated, run various project work meetings, help team leaders and subteam leaders with the creation and maintenance of plans, and perform other support roles to the project manager.

The project members performing in support roles should report directly to a resource manager for personnel-related items such as receiving major job assignments, coaching and counseling, performance evaluations, salary increases, promotions, awards and overall compensation issues, benefits-related issues, and the like. However, these project members would appear *dotted line* to the position they are supporting (e.g., project manager), and take project-related direction from the project member occupying that position.

Note: If an organization has a project management office (PMO), the project members supporting the project manager could come from the PMO. (See Chapter 14, The Project Management Office, for more about a PMO.)

LESSON 10.5

The positions of project manager, business architect, product architect, and process architect can require support personnel, but those support personnel report directly to resource managers.

Project-Reporting View

Figure 10.2 shows the approximately two hundred-member project from a project-reporting view, instead of the functional-reporting view shown in Figure 10.1. Notice in Figure 10.2 that the higher-level resource managers are peers to the project manager. However, the business architect, product architect, process architect, and team leaders report to the project manager from a project point-of-view. The business architect, product architect, process architect, and team leaders are the primary and required attendees at the project-tracking meeting.

LESSON 10.6

Resource managers are never shown reporting to a project manager, whether viewed from a functional or project perspective.

Because some functional areas might have a large number of project members, they can be divided into multiple small teams with a subteam leader for each team. Figure 10.2 shows how these subteam leaders work under the direction of a team leader; four groups of subteam leaders are shown. They contain six, two, two, and five subteam leaders, respectively. These four groups work under the direction of the last four team leaders shown in Figure 10.2. Look closely at them. The first team leader has two team members and six subteam leaders; the second team leader has nine team members and two subteam leaders; the third team leader has three team members and two subteam leaders; and the last team leader has no team members and five subteam leaders.

LESSON 10.7

It can be helpful for all members of a project to see the project depicted both from a functional-reporting and a project-reporting view.

FIGURE 10.2

Project-Reporting View for a Large-Sized Project (200 members)

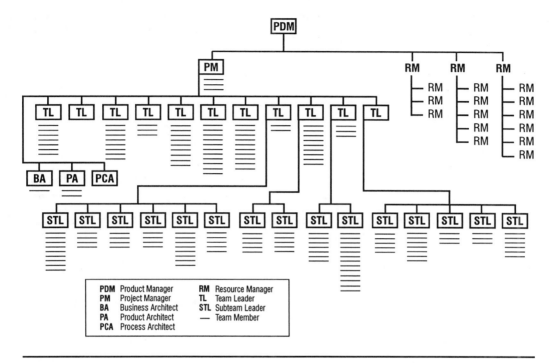

PDM	Product Manager	**RM** Resource Manager
PM	Project Manager	**TL** Team Leader
BA	Business Architect	**STL** Subteam Leader
PA	Product Architect	**—** Team Member
PCA	Process Architect	

Notice also in Figure 10.2 that the project manager, business architect, and product architect have support personnel assigned to work with them: three, one, and two project members, respectfully. These project members direct-report to resource managers. These project members were taken from the first, third, and fifth departments shown in Figure 10.1, and are depicted as lines that appear immediately under the resource manager boxes. Specifically, the two project members assigned to the product architect were taken from the first department, the one project member assigned to the business architect came from the third department, and the three project members assigned to the project manager came from the fifth department.

Figure 10.2 makes it easier to see the tremendous responsibility that the project manager has for planning, tracking, and driving a project to a successful completion. Clearly, the job of a project manager in a medium or large project is a full-time job. A project manager does not have the time, nor would it show good business sense, to take on other key roles in the project such as resource manager, product architect, or team leader. Nor should the project manager directly own many project plan tasks. To spread the project manager's responsibilities beyond defined roles and responsibilities as defined in Chapter 3, The Project Manager, will have a negative affect on the outcome of the project.

Q & A

Q10.1 Who makes the decision to break a large team into multiple small teams, each with a subteam leader?

A10.1 The team leader is expected to propose and direct this activity; however, the resource manager of the team leader must support the proposal. If the original large team consists of members who direct report to more than one resource manager, all of those resource managers will influence the final new subteam structure.

Let's look at Figure 10.2 to see how a large team can be restructured into multiple small teams. The last five subteam leaders shown all report to the last team leader. If you count the total number of team members and subteam leaders within the domain responsibility of the team leader, you will count twenty-nine project members (five subteam leaders and twenty-four team members under them). Including the team leader, that makes one large team of thirty project members—too large for one team leader to reasonably manage.

Notice in Figure 10.1 that these thirty project members direct report to the last two resource managers. In this case, the team leader, working closely with the two resource managers, proposes how to break the team into five subteams. The team leader might also propose who the subteam leaders should be; however, the resource managers must make the actual job assignments. The outcome is that one resource manager has responsibility for the team leader and two subteams, and the other resource manager has three subteams.

This is a good example for showing that the team leader is really performing as a miniproject manager for his team. That is, the team leader is responsible for the overall planning, implementation, and tracking of the team. Furthermore, the team leader is fully accountable for the team's success.

Q10.2   Do team leaders with subteam leaders within their team have routine tracking meetings with their subteam leaders?

A10.2   Yes. The team leader is leading her team much like the project manager is leading the overall project by working with the project's team leaders (and others). You could take the view that each team is a project within the larger project. If you took this to its full extent, the project manager would become the program manager, the team leaders would become project managers, and the subteam leaders would become team leaders.

Q10.3   Is Figure 10.1 the best way to organize a large project of the size shown?

A10.3   Not necessarily—there are many other ways that this project could be organized. The structure shown is one example of the application of the Enter*Prize* Organization. Another example is that there could have been four or five higher-level resource managers with three to four reporting resource managers each. The details must be left to the product manager, resource managers, and the project manager so that the most effective project organization is created. It is important to note, however, that to gain the full benefits of the Enter*Prize* Organization, the eight positions that make up the definition of the Enter*Prize* Organization (as described in chapters 2–9) must be preserved.

CHAPTER 11

ORGANIZING FOR MULTIPLE PROJECTS

$\mathcal{C}$hapter 1, Overview of the Enter*Prize* Organization, introduced many of the basic concepts behind the Enter*Prize* Organization, while focusing on a project of about thirty members. Chapter 10, Organizing for Large Projects, applied these concepts to a large project of about two hundred members. Let's now look at the organization that has multiple projects occurring simultaneously.

Functional-Reporting View of Eight Projects

Figure 11.1 shows a functional-reporting view of a multiproject organization of about 170 members. These members currently are working on eight different projects ranging in size from five to forty-six full-time-equivalent members. Table 11.1 shows the number of members in each project. The member count per project does not include resource managers or the product manager. Of course, at some point, the cost for the resource managers must be apportioned per project; however, for simplicity and illustrative purposes, resource managers are not counted in the project member count.

The first number shown in each cell of Table 11.1 represents the total number of project members, some only part time. The second number (underlined) represents the total full-time equivalent of project members. For example, Project 8 has nine different people assigned to the project, but if all of the time spent on the project by each person is cumulated, there is an equivalent of five full-time people assigned to the project.

FIGURE 11.1

Functional-Reporting View of a Multiproject Organization

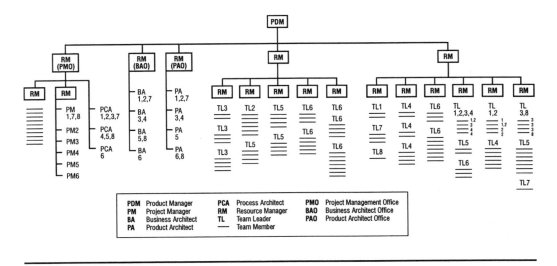

I have taken some liberty in making assumptions for determining the headcount associated with each project. Because some project members are working on more than one project, the counts are rounded to make the numbers come out whole overall. The primary purpose of Table 11.1 is to help you more readily visualize and understand the structure (Figure 11.1) that an organization comprised of multiple projects of varying sizes can adopt.

Let's now look more closely at Figure 11.1. As with other examples from earlier chapters, the product manager heads the organization and, in this case, is responsible for all eight projects. Reporting to the product manager are five resource managers.

Project Management Office

The first resource manager is the manager of the *project management office* (PMO). (The PMO will be discussed in more detail in Chapter 14, but we will briefly discuss it here.) The PMO is the home of all project managers and their support personnel. There are six project managers shown in Figure 11.1, along with their

TABLE 11.1

Number of Project Members per Project and the Number of Full-Time
Equivalents per Project (underlined)

	Project Manager	Business Architect	Product Architect	Process Architect	Team Leader	Team Member	PMO Support	Totals
Project 1	1 - .3	1 - .3	1 - .3	1 - .2	3 - 1.5	5 - 4	1 - .5	13 - 7
Project 2	1 - 1	1 - .3	1 - .3	1 - .3	3 - 1.5	10 - 9	1 - .5	18 - 13
Project 3	1 - 1	1 - .5	1 - .5	1 - .3	5 - 3.5	13 - 13	1 - 1	23 - 20
Project 4	1 - 1	1 - .5	1 - .5	1 - .4	5 - 4.5	16 - 16	1 - 1	26 - 24
Project 5	1 - 1	1 - .8	1 - 1	1 - .5	5 - 5	21 - 21	1 - 1	31 - 30
Project 6	1 - 1	1 - 1	1 - .8	1 - 1	8 - 8	32 - 32	2 - 2	46 - 46
Project 7	1 - .3	1 - .3	1 - .3	1 - .2	2 - 2	4 - 4	1 - .5	11 - 8
Project 8	1 - .3	1 - .2	1 - .2	1 - .1	2 - 1.5	2 - 2	1 - .5	9 - 5

assigned projects. Notice that the first project manager listed is the project manager for three projects (Projects 1, 7, and 8), and all other project managers have responsibility for a single project.

In this example, all the project managers report to a resource manager, who then reports to the resource manager in charge of the PMO. Also reporting to the PMO resource manager is a resource manager of a department of ten people who are primarily dedicated to support the six project managers in fulfilling their roles and responsibilities. (More about responsibilities of the PMO support personnel is described in Chapter 14, The Project Management Office.)

Notice in Figure 11.1 that there are three process architects who report to the resource manager responsible for the PMO. Only one process architect is assigned full time to work with a project (Project 6). The other two process architects spread their time working across the other seven projects. The process architects do not need to report to the PMO; however, the PMO can be a likely home for them, because they provide a great deal of support to projects and work closely with project managers.

Business Architect Office

The second resource manager reporting to the product manager is the manager of the *business architect office* (BAO). The business architects that work across all seven projects report to this resource manager. There are four business architects shown in Figure 11.1, three who perform the role of business architect on more than one project. For example, the first business architect shown is assigned to the three projects: Projects 1, 2, and 7.

Product Architect Office

The third resource manager reporting to the product manager is the manager of the *product architect office* (PAO). All product architects for the seven projects report to this resource manager. As with some instances with a project manager and several business architects, three of the four product architects also are performing in the capacity of product architect for more than one project. For example, the first product architect shown in Figure 11.1 is assigned to three projects: Projects 1, 2, and 7.

Department Skill Groups

The fourth and fifth resource managers reporting to the product manager are managers of five and six resource managers, respectfully. These eleven lower-level resource managers manage departments that provide specific functions to the overall organization. For example, a half dozen or so of the departments might design, write, and partially test the software. Several other departments might perform independent testing of the newly developed code. Another department might write the user documentation and online help screens. Yet another department or two might perform other functions such as library control and configuration management, usability analysis and testing, performance analysis and testing, and others.

Starting a New Project

When a new project is started, a project manager is assigned. Then the project manager works with the resource managers to identify the business architect, product architect, process architect, and team leaders who will be assigned to the project. The team leaders then work with their resource managers to identify which persons will have assignments on the team leaders' teams.

If the project manager requires any project management support personnel, she works with the designated resource manager within the PMO to obtain the required resource. If the business architect, product architect, or process architect require support personnel, they work with their own resource managers, as well as resource managers across the organization, to obtain required support. The support personnel for the business architects, product architects, and process architects could be direct reports into the BAO, PAO, and PMO, respectfully, if desired—similar to the PMO arrangement of support personnel for project managers. However, the BAO and PAO are depicted differently than the PMO to show an alternative approach. Any support personnel required for the process architects could come optionally from the pool of people in the PMO who are also assigned to support the project managers.

Project Example: Project 1

Of the eight projects in Figure 11.1, let's single out one project, Project 1, to examine more closely; let's see how the project members are gathered from across the organization. Figure 11.2 shows the project-reporting view of Project 1. Figure 11.3 shows, by highlighting, where the members assigned to Project 1 can be found in the functional-reporting view of the organization. Project 1 is made up of a project manager, business architect, product architect, process architect, three team leaders, five team members spread across the three team leaders, and a project support member—a total of thirteen project members. However, all of these project members are not dedicated full time to Project 1. Who is not full time on Project 1? We can determine the answers by looking closely at the highlighted areas of Figure 11.3 and also referring to Table 11.1.

Figure 11.3 shows that the project manager is working part time on Project 1; the project manager also is working on Projects 7 and 8. The business architect, product architect, and process architect are also working part time on Project 1, as well as on Projects 2 and 7; 2 and 7; and 2, 3, and 7; respectively.

Looking at Figure 11.3, we see that the first team leader and her two team members are working full time on Project 1. The second team leader is part time, as well as the one team member. (The second team leader is also working on

FIGURE 11.2

Project-Reporting View of Project 1

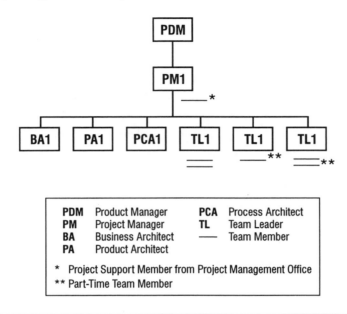

PDM	Product Manager	**PCA**	Process Architect
PM	Project Manager	**TL**	Team Leader
BA	Business Architect	——	Team Member
PA	Product Architect		

* Project Support Member from Project Management Office

** Part-Time Team Member

projects 2, 3, and 4, while the team member is also working on Project 2.) The last team leader is part time (also working on Project 2), with one full-time team member and one part-time team member (also working on Project 2). Let's assume that the project support member from the PMO is only part time.

So where are we in terms of the size of the project in full-time equivalent people? Only one team leader and three team members appear to be full time on Project 1; all others are part time. Assuming that the project manager, business architect, and product architect each spends about one-third of his time on Project 1, and that the process architect spends about one-fifth of her time on Project 1, these four project members account for 1.1 person, or the equivalent of one full-time person. If the two part-time team members combine for an equivalent of one full-time person, and we view the two part-time team leaders as adding up to one half-time person, Project 1 comprises seven full-time equivalent project members. (Don't forget the half-time person from the PMO.)

FIGURE 11.3

Functional-Reporting View of a Multiproject Organization
(with highlighting for Project 1-related areas)

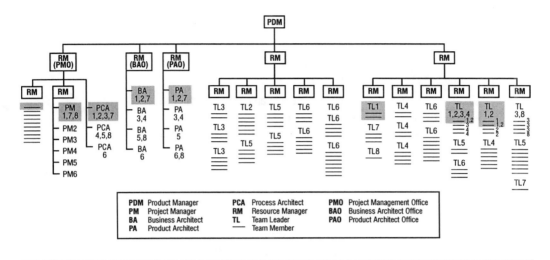

PDM	Product Manager	**PCA** Process Architect	**PMO** Project Management Office
PM	Project Manager	**RM** Resource Manager	**BAO** Business Architect Office
BA	Business Architect	**TL** Team Leader	**PAO** Product Architect Office
PA	Product Architect	—— Team Member	

Goals for a Multiproject Organization

Let's discuss, for a moment, goals that should be addressed when applying the EnterPrize Organization to an organization that has many ongoing projects. Figure 11.4 lists goals, toward which to strive, that help improve the utilization of people, and promote successful projects. Let's take a closer look at each of these goals.

Goal 1: Assign team members to only one project. It is not always possible to restrict a team member's skills to only one project. However, for purposes of obtaining the best utilization of that team member's time, every attempt should be made to limit the number of projects that a team member must work simultaneously. This helps team members achieve their best productivity by allowing them to concentrate on single tasks until they are complete.

Goal 2: Assign project managers, business architects, product architects, and process architects to work full time at their craft. Project members who perform as project managers, business architects, product architects, and process architects have a major influence on the outcome of the projects to which they are assigned. If the project does not require their skills full time, resist assigning other project duties

---

FIGURE 11.4

Goals for a Multiproject Organization

1. Assign team members to only one project.
2. Assign project managers, business architects, product architects and process architects to work full time at their craft.
3. Create departments based on functional areas.
4. Install a Project Management Office.
5. Install "offices" for business architects, product architects and process architects.
6. Maintain reasonably sized departments and teams.
7. Report key project positions as close to the product manager as possible.

---

that normally fall within the domain of responsibility of another project member. Instead, assign project members in these positions to work on *other projects* while retaining the same project position. For example, if a project manager leads a project of five members, and the demand on that position is only part time, assign that person to also be a project manager on one or more other small project(s). This allows the project manager to continue to improve her skills and increase her experiences as a project manager, thus making her much more valuable, long term, to the organization. (For an exception, see Chapter 12, Organizing for Small Projects.)

Goal 3: Create departments based on functional areas. Whenever possible, gather people of similar skills and assignments to work together. For example, create specialty departments of designers and coders, independent testers, writers of the product's documentation (both for hard copy and online purposes), training personnel, and various support groups. Collecting people of like skills to work as a group can have a great impact on all group members to more quickly improve their productivity and quality. The members of each group will work among themselves to document, implement, and continually improve their processes. The same is true for ensuring that the best tools are developed/acquired and used. Furthermore, the synergy allows members of a group to share experiences and improve their skills more quickly than would be possible had they been isolated from one other. Even if the department members are assigned to different projects, it is important that they learn and grow from one another in the pursuit of their common needs.

Goal 4: Install a PMO. A PMO can have great benefit to an organization that has many ongoing projects. It provides the care and feeding for project managers to help them be successful. Because project managers should report to the PMO, it helps them to be more objective in their decision-making by removing the strong urge to be biased toward what others on the project want versus what is best for the project. As with Goal 3, a PMO allows like-skilled people to share and continually improve common processes and tools and support one another through the sharing of their experiences.

Goal 5: Install offices for business architects, product architects, and process architects. Akin to what a PMO can do to benefit project managers, similar *offices* can benefit business architects, product architects, and process architects. These offices collect like-skilled people and allow them to leverage off one another to improve their performance and craft. Separate offices can be established for each of these skill groups, or two or more can be collected under one office. Recall in Figure 11.3 that both project managers and process architects are shown residing within the PMO.

Goal 6: Maintain reasonably sized departments and teams. If a resource manager has too many direct reports, or a team leader has too many members assigned to his team, the quality of the work produced can greatly suffer. Therefore, departments should rarely exceed fifteen members, and teams should be made up of ten or less members. Limiting the size of departments will help resource managers perform the care and feeding required for their direct reports. Attention from the resource managers can immensely help maintain a reasonable morale among the *troops*, to avert high attrition rates and ensure that each direct report is being appropriately *promoted*. Team leaders need teams that are sufficiently small in size to allow the team leader to appropriately work with the team members in helping them achieve their commitments.

Resource managers who have resource managers as direct reports should rarely exceed managing more than seven resource managers.

Goal 7: Report key project positions as close to the product manager as possible. *Referent power* is more than just a term; it's a force that a person can use to more easily drive her agendas across a project, organization, or company. In Chapter 1, Overview of the Enter*Prize* Organization, Figure 1.1, the key project positions of project manager, business architect, product architect, and process architect are shown reporting to the product manager. These are power positions—positions of large influence. By reporting to the product manager, they carry clout that can be beneficial to leaders charged with making things happen. Of course, it is not always practical to have these positions reporting directly to the product manager—

for example, if there are many ongoing projects. However, the goal is to report as close to the product manager as possible, such as reporting within a PMO which, in turn, reports to the product manager (see Figure 11.1).

Q & A

Q11.1   What if a member of an organization is committed as a project member on more than one project? Can this really work?

A11.1   It is expected that many people working in multiproject organizations will be assigned to more than one project at a time. Although not optimal, it's often necessary because of people with critical skills that are required to be stretched across more than one project. Other reasons include staffing and budget challenges and the fact that some skills are not required full time on a project.

A project member making commitments on more than one project can work fine. However, it is important to note that a project member is always held accountable for his commitments on a given project. *Don't make bad commitments!* If a project member is in trouble with meeting his commitments on one or more projects, he must alert and work with the project manager(s) and resource manager to mitigate the problem(s) as quickly as possible. The more a project member must balance his time across multiple projects, the more his demands will suffer a roller coaster of peaks and valleys.

LESSON 11.1

A project member must never make commitments that are known to be unrealistic.

Q11.2   Based on the answer to the last question, would you say that a person's overall productivity suffers if she is juggling activities across multiple projects?

A11.2   It can. Whenever anyone is working on more than one unique activity simultaneously, there is a cost to starting and stopping each activity. The more an activity is halted and restarted, the greater the negative cost to that person's productivity. A person's productivity improves when that person can dedicate all of his attention and concentration to a single activity.

Q11.3   Doesn't the answer to the last question argue that project managers, business architects, product architects, and process architects should only work on one project full time, rather than sometimes working part time on multiple projects, as championed by the Enter*Prize* Organization?

A11.3   The answer to the previous question was directed more to people in an organization that are not focusing their skill enrichment in one specialty area but are multitasking across several unrelated, or mostly unrelated, jobs. In the Enter*Prize* Organization, project managers, business architects, product architects, and process architects are not always full-time positions on small- and some medium-sized projects. In those cases, rather than have project members take on additional project tasks as a team member, for example, they should continue performing in their original positions (e.g., project manager) on one or more other projects to continue to hone their craft and skills.

Can this negatively impact their productivity? In theory, yes; but, in practice, it can have the opposite effort in the long run. The Enter*Prize* Organization encourages that project members in these four positions not dabble at their trade but become very proficient. The only way to do this is experience; the only way to get experience is by doing. If one desires to become a very good project manager or product architect, for example, he must continually be looking to improve his skills and experience base. This is accomplished by intentionally remaining focused on the appropriate tasks that continue to advance those specific skills.

Q11.4   How does a project manager decide how much to assert herself in contending for scarce resources in a multiproject organization?

A11.4   Every project manager must behave as if her project is the most important project in an organization, and drive the project to a successful completion. The project manager works constructively to help project members achieve their commitments. But a project manager should never sacrifice the successful outcome of her own project by allowing commitments made by project members to other projects to take precedence. The one exception is when the person who can make the right business decision across multiple projects (typically the product manager) has made a decision to sacrifice the outcome of one project in favor of strengthening another project.

> **LESSON 11.2**
>
> The most effective project managers behave as if her project is the most important in the organization and company.

Q11.5   As a follow-up to the last question, isn't it selfish for a project manager to behave as if her project is the most important in an organization, and proceed accordingly?

A11.5   Not at all—this is a common and erroneous misconception. Think about it. You are the owner of a software business and have ten projects ongoing at any point in time. You have ten different project managers assigned. Each project is a required business venture, or else it would never have been funded and approved by senior management. Although some projects have greater revenue and profit potential than others, all are important. Here's the key: Would you, as the business owner, want the project managers of the *lesser-priority* nine projects to yield to any request from the project manager and members working on the perceived top project?

　　The answer should be "no." If the answer is "yes," then what motivation do the lesser-priority nine project managers have for meeting their commitments? How can they be held accountable? These nine projects represent real revenue to the company and real clients that need to be satisfactorily serviced. Yes, behave as if your project is the most important. The exception, as mentioned in the previous answer, is when the product manager (or other person designated to make the business decision) says to yield; do so only then.

Q11.6   Is it possible to have more than one product manager in a multiproject organization?

A11.6   Yes, there could be several product managers. But if all the projects are versions of the same product, it is typical to have only one product manager. However, if there are multiple products being developed in an organization, and the products are uniquely different and/or target different clients, it would be typical to have multiple product managers.

Q11.7   Is it possible to have members on a project that do not all report into the chain of command of the product manager?

A11.7   It is common for project members to not all report in the same chain of command as the product manager. The examples depicted in this and other chapters represent the preferred approaches that will help an organization most easily and readily reap the benefits of adopting the concepts of the Enter*Prize* Organization. But it is not intended to relay the message that there are not other workable approaches. There are others, yet they require a greater degree of discipline to manage and effectively work—but they can be made to work.

Q11.8   Looking at Figure 11.1, the BAO and PAO departments show only four members each. Furthermore, the project managers only number six, yet they are in their own departments. Haven't you stated in earlier chapters that there should be from ten to fifteen members to a department?

A11.8   In many cases, departments of nonmanagers should typically consist of ten to fifteen members. Less experienced resource managers can have up to ten members in their departments. More seasoned resource managers can have departments of up to fifteen members. In general, it may not be cost effective to have departments of a handful of members or less. However, if a department is staffing up or trimming down, there can be times when there are other than ten to fifteen members.

    The example in Figure 11.1 could be such a case. We could, however, combine the three organizations of PMO, BAO, and PAO into one organization headed by a resource manager reporting to the product manager. The combined group can still be called the PMO, or it could have another name such as the *product office*, *project office*, or *business office*. We can then replace the four resource managers with three resource managers: 1) for support personnel, 2) to manage project managers and process architects, and 3) to manage business architects and product architects. This restructure would leave the last two departments with nine and eight members, respectfully. These departments can be considered sufficiently full, based on the significant responsibilities of the department members and resource managers.

Q11.9   When all the product architects from across an organization are gathered to report to a PAO, should there be a lead product architect?

A11.9   In almost all cases, *yes*. But it can depend on a number of factors, such as the skills and experiences of the product architects and whether or not they are working on similar products. For example, if the product architects have limited experience as product architects, and the products served by the product architects have a lot of commonality, then the answer is *yes*, there should be a lead product architect. In almost all cases, there needs to be a lead person to make the decisions that can impact all the product architects. This person may also perform as a mentor to product architects. It also should be noted that there usually needs to be a lead person over the other key Enter*Prize* Organization positions that are collected in groups: project managers, business architects, and process architects.

CHAPTER 12

ORGANIZING FOR SMALL PROJECTS

$\mathcal{E}$arlier chapters have shown how medium- and larger-sized projects can benefit from the Enter*Prize* Organization. But what about smaller projects—projects of ten or less members? They also can benefit. However, smaller projects may require an *exception* to the statement that a project member should not take on two or more of the key Enter*Prize* Organization positions of project manager, business architect, product architect, process architect, resource manager, and team leader.

If a company has a very small information systems group—say, only five persons—it is impossible for one or more project members to avoid taking on two or more of the key Enter*Prize* Organization positions. *In such a case, it is acceptable to have one project member take on more than one of these key positions.* However, every attempt should be made to avoid this.

LESSON 12.1

On small projects, a project member may have to take on some of the duties of two or more of the Enter*Prize* Organization positions.

For example, look at Chapter 11, Organizing for Multiple Projects, Figure 11.1 and Table 11.1. These charts show Project 8 to be made up of nine project members, but only five full-time equivalents (FTE). Even with a project this small, none of the project members took on more than one of the key Enter*Prize* Organization positions. Furthermore, notice that all of the positions defined by the Enter*Prize* Organization were accounted for among the project members.

TABLE 12.1

Sample Position Assignments for a Project Team of Four Members

	Product Manager	Project Manager	Business Architect	Product Architect	Process Architect	Resource Manager	Team Leader	Team Member
Project Member 1	✓	✓				✓	✓	
Project Member 2			✓	✓	✓			✓
Project Member 3								✓
Project Member 4								✓

This chapter discusses the application of the EnterPrize Organization to small projects. Two example projects are provided, one a project of four members and the other a project of ten members.

LESSON 12.2

Even on small projects, all the positions defined by the EnterPrize Organization must be accounted for among the project members.

Four-Member Project

Let's look at Table 12.1 to illustrate the point that a project member must take on more than one of the EnterPrize Organization positions. We have a project consisting of four members. Project Member 1 is fulfilling the roles and responsibilities of four of the EnterPrize Organization positions: 1) product manager, 2) project manager, 3) resource manager, and 4) team leader. Project Member 2 is taking on the positions of business architect, product architect, process architect, and team member. Project Members 3 and 4 are serving in the capacity of team members.

One might ask, "Can one project member effectively perform multiple positions, such as Project Members 1 and 2 are doing in Table 1?" The answer is "yes," if the person also possesses the multiple skills required. However, one must be careful not to take on too much work at the sacrifice of being the project member always in the critical path on the project, and therefore potentially slowing down project progress or diluting the effectiveness that the Enter*Prize* Organization can offer. Because this illustrative project is so small—only four project members—the demands on most of the Enter*Prize* Organization positions do not require full-time attention, but, collectively, the demands can become greater than any one person's time.

It is not uncommon for a project member of a smaller team to perform so many of the Enter*Prize* Organization positions that she feels pulled in too many directions, resulting in an overwhelming job. Yet the project member may wonder why she feels so overtaxed when the project is so small. Well, now you know the answer: even on small projects, all of the roles and responsibilities of each of the Enter*Prize* Organization positions must still be satisfied. To perform all of these roles and responsibilities effectively can be an arduous feat.

LESSON 12.3

Even on a small project, the demands required on a project member who takes on multiple Enter*Prize* Organization positions can be greater than that person can satisfactorily handle.

Figure 12.1 shows both the functional- and project-reporting views of the four-member project represented in Table 12.1. Both views appear the same. Notice, however, how the organization of the project loses the clarity to which we are accustomed when viewing a functional or project chart. In other words, when a project member takes on many roles—as in this example, assuming the roles of product manager, project manager, resource manager, and team leader—many of the organizational layers are lost. As a result, many of the checks and balances are lost when the same project member is the product manager, project manager, and resource manager. It becomes especially important that the person taking on multiple roles is fully capable of making appropriate decisions. However, if the person is not sufficiently trained and experienced to take on these multiple positions, it could become a serious handicap for the project.

LESSON 12.4

On small projects, where project members take on multiple Enter*Prize* Organization positions, the organizational clarity to which we are accustomed when viewing both functional and project structures can be lost. Also the checks and balances that these positions provide for one another can be lost.

FIGURE 12.1

Both Functional- and Project-Reporting Views of the Four-Member Project
Depicted in Table 12.1

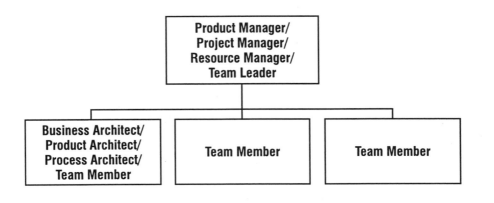

Ten-Member Project

Let's look at another example—a project of ten members. Table 12.2 shows the
Enter*Prize* Organization positions and how they might be assigned across project
members. Project Member 1 is performing the roles of both product manager
and resource manager. Project Member 2 is performing as project manager and
business architect. Project Member 3 is performing as product architect, process
architect, and team leader. All other project members are performing single roles
of either team leader or team member. Of course, many of the project members,
who are shown as other than team members, might also be taking on tasks that
team members commonly would handle. For example, team leaders in this
example should have plenty of time to also perform some of the roles that team
members perform.

Figure 12.2 shows the functional-reporting view of the ten-member project,
and Figure 12.3 shows the project-reporting view. Unlike Figure 12.1, these views
are different primarily because the product manager is not also the project
manager. The figures would look different still if the product manager was not
also the resource manager.

TABLE 12.2

Sample Position Assignments for a Project Team of Ten Members

	Product Manager	Project Manager	Business Architect	Product Architect	Process Architect	Resource Manager	Team Leader	Team Member
Project Member 1	✓					✓		
Project Member 2		✓	✓					
Project Member 3				✓	✓		✓	
Project Member 4								✓
Project Member 5								✓
Project Member 6							✓	
Project Member 7								✓
Project Member 8							✓	
Project Member 9								✓
Project Member 10								✓

Q & A

Q12.1 Are the two examples intended to show precisely how you should organize if you have a project made up of either four or ten members?

A12.1 Not at all—they are only examples of how the Enter*Prize* Organization positions might be deployed across a small project. There are other acceptable approaches.

Q12.2 How does one decide which Enter*Prize* Organization positions can be assumed by one project member?

A12.2 Which Enter*Prize* Organization positions can be taken on by one person is decided primarily by the skills of the person, but often by the availability of a project member to take on more responsibility. Caution: Each of the Enter*Prize* Organization positions requires specific skills. To assign a project member to

FIGURE 12.2

Functional-Reporting View of the Ten-Member Project Depicted in Table 12.2

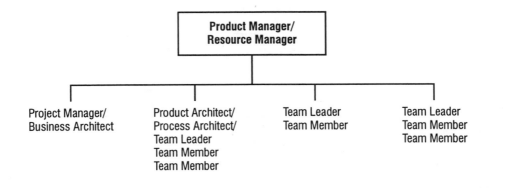

perform in a certain position without the appropriate training—or, at the least, ongoing coaching or mentoring—is performing a disservice to the project and the individual.

If at all possible, it is strongly preferred that the Enter*Prize* Organization positions of project manager, business architect, product architect, and process architect be performed full time by project members. For example, if a person is performing the roles and responsibilities of a project manager on a small team, it is highly likely that the position does not require a full-time person. However, as stated in earlier chapters, rather than have the project manager take on an additional project role of, say, team member, it is preferred that he perform in the capacity of project manager on one or more *other* small projects. Why? Because the position of project manager is so crucial to a project's success, and the effectiveness of that person is so dependent on experience that it is important to give the project manager more opportunities to learn and grow into the position. This concept also applies to the positions of business architect, product architect, and process architect.

LESSON 12.5

Every attempt should be made for the positions of project manager, business architect, product architect, and process architect to be *full-time* assignments.

FIGURE 12.3

Project-Reporting View of the Ten-Member Project Depicted in
Table 12.2

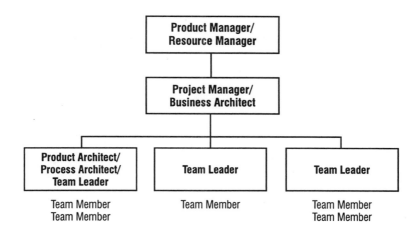

Q12.3   As a follow-up to the last question, are you saying that it is wrong to have the
project manager, business architect, product architect, and process architect
positions assumed by a project member that already is performing one of these
or another Enter*Prize* Organization position?

A12.3   No, sometimes this is necessary because of limited resources or limited skills in
an organization. Or sometimes it might be necessary because of the sense of both
importance and urgency of the project. But, if at all possible, it is in the best
interests of an organization and to the development of the people to allow them
to focus full time on these critical assigned positions. This will not only improve
morale by allowing people to develop in the areas in which they have the most
interest, but also allow people in these four key positions to accelerate their development and therefore their contribution potential.

LESSON 12.6

For an organization to benefit the most from its human resources, its people should
be encouraged to grow in the areas in which they have the most interest and
aptitude—because it is in these areas that they have the most potential to contribute.

Q12.4   I understand that one project member can take on the duties of more than one of the Enter*Prize* Organization positions, but what about a project member taking on only *some* of the duties of a position?

A12.4   This is possible but needs to be carefully considered before assigning some of the duties of a position to a project member. For example, is the project member qualified to take on the assigned duties from multiple positions? Or look at the following situation: For illustrative purposes, let's assume that each of the Enter*Prize* Organization positions is made up of ten duties (some actually have more and some less). Now let's assign a team member to half of the duties of a team leader and half of the duties of a resource manager. Who is assigned to the other half of the duties of a team leader and resource manager? Someone must own them, or there is a weak link in the project. Some things will not get done, and it can be confusing to the other project members who is actually responsible for what. Although this approach can work, it is important to deliberately look at each of the duties of each position, and ensure that they are either assigned or truly are not required on this project.

> **LESSON 12.7**
>
> All the duties of each position of the Enter*Prize* Organization must be carefully weighed before dropping any of them or splintering them across multiple project members.

Q12.5   Table 12.1 shows one person as the product manager, project manager, team leader, and resource manager. This arrangement causes some principles of the Enter*Prize* Organization to be violated, which you did not mention. For example, project managers and team leaders should not have direct reports. Another example is that resource managers should not own any activities on a project. Because the resource manager is still responsible for all of her direct reports, a problem that you cited in Chapter 7, The Resource Manager, can/will occur: the resource manager will work more diligently on, say, the project's activities at the sacrifice of performing well on her people responsibilities. Aren't you sending mixed signals? Will this really work okay?

A12.5   As mentioned earlier in this chapter, when a project member takes on multiple positions in the Enter*Prize* Organization, many of the checks and balances are lost. Yes, this situation can result in a project member performing less than exemplary in all of the positions assumed. It is a potential handicap for the project and its members on all small projects, not just those adopting the principles of the Enter*Prize* Organization.

CHAPTER 13

ORGANIZING FOR MAINTENANCE PROJECTS

*A*s discussed in earlier chapters, the Enter*Prize* Organization is well suited, by design, for software development projects and organizations. But what about maintenance organizations, also called application support, systems support, production support, and sustaining organizations? Does the concept of projects also apply to maintenance organizations? Absolutely *yes!*

Maintenance organizations are defined here as organizations that correct problems in existing products. These problems have been reported by the client or discovered by people or groups within the product's company. A *maintenance release* is defined here as an updated version of an existing product, where the updates are fixes to problems contained in earlier releases. These problems, real or perceived, can be defects in the code and/or documentation, performance problems, ease-of-use problems, or stress problems. Maintenance releases also can include enhancements; however, for purposes of this chapter, enhancements are viewed as new development work, and earlier chapters already have addressed how to organize for new software development projects.

Routine Maintenance Releases

Maintenance organizations produce maintenance releases on what should be a regular and predictable basis. For example, depending on the product, these releases can be monthly or quarterly. The client appreciates when maintenance releases are scheduled well in advance, so the client can plan accordingly; sometimes the client requires it. Moreover, if maintenance releases are not produced frequently, the client can feel neglected because reported defects are being corrected at too slow a pace. Of course, emergency defects may need to be corrected on a high-priority basis. Having regularly scheduled maintenance releases also helps to better plan the allocation of both people and computer resources in a maintenance organization.

LESSON 13.1

Maintenance releases should be produced on a regular and predictable time schedule.

Maintenance Release = Project

Each maintenance release can be viewed as a project that must be scoped, planned, and tracked until the release is completed and delivered (or placed into production). This chapter addresses the as-yet-undiscussed subject of organizing a maintenance-only project. As with other types of projects, all of the positions of the EnterPrize Organization are required for a maintenance project.

Functional- and Project-Reporting Views

Figure 13.1 shows the functional-reporting view of a maintenance project, and Figure 13.2 shows the project-related view. This project has a product manager, resource manager, project manager, business architect, product architect, process architect, three team leaders, and nine team members. Let's look closer at each of these positions.

Product Manager and Resource Manager

Figure 13.1 shows that everyone but the team leaders and the team members report directly to the product manager; team leaders and team members report to the resource manager. It is possible that the resource manager might also be the product manager. However, it is more likely that the resource manager reports to the product manager as shown in Figure 13.1. Other projects could be ongoing in parallel to this maintenance project, such as projects for new or enhanced products and maintenance release projects for other products already in use by the client.

FIGURE 13.1

Functional-Reporting View of a Fifteen-Member Maintenance Project

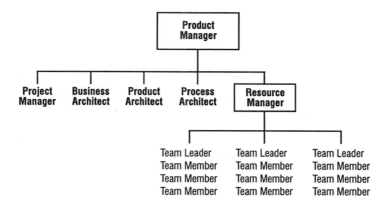

It is very likely that the product manager has so many projects going on simulta-neously that the project manager, business architect, product architect, and process architect will not report directly to the product manager, but instead to an *office* as shown in Figure 11.1, Chapter 11, Organizing for Multiple Projects. Another alternative—but not a preferred one—is that these positions report directly to the resource manager responsible for maintenance releases.

Project Manager

The project manager, sometimes called the *release manager*, is responsible for working across the team to create the scope document, which will define what problems will be fixed in this release. Then, a plan is created and tracked on a weekly or more frequent basis. The project-tracking meeting could be a formal meeting once a week, an update meeting at the start or end of each day, or some other format. However, there must be a disciplined process followed in planning, tracking, and communicating across the project team.

LESSON 13.2

Maintenance releases require disciplined planning and tracking processes.

FIGURE 13.2

Project-Reporting View of a Fifteen-Member Maintenance Project

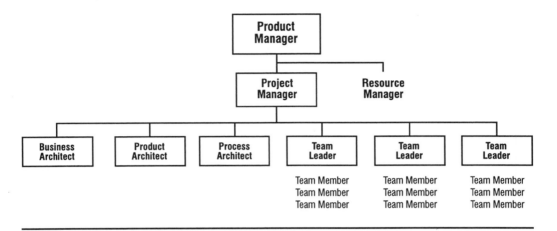

Business Architect

The business architect, as defined in Chapter 4, The Business Architect, is the client's primary advocate. Because most of the problems to be corrected have been reported by the client, the project members will likely understand many of the problems from the client's perspective. However, there will be times when the business architect will be required to communicate between the client and the project members, or to intervene on behalf of the client to ensure that the *right* problem is being corrected—and that the problem is being corrected *right*. It is not uncommon for a maintenance team to fix what turns out to be a symptom of the problem rather than correct the root cause of the problem. The business architect can offer invaluable insight on behalf of the client to ensure that the project team truly satisfies the client's needs.

Product Architect

The product architect ensures that the problems corrected do not violate the intended architecture of the product. The product architect works with the team members to help them with design and code issues, as well as application issues such as performance, data integrity, and user interface consistency. The product architect also inspects design and code changes to ensure that the intended problems are being solved properly and new problems are not being introduced. If the product architect has any free time, she might also be assigned to correct some of the problems alongside the team members. However, the preference is that the product architect performs *full time* in the capacity of a product architect, which may require that the product architect be assigned to one or more other projects.

Process Architect

Depending on cited industry statistics, up to 80 percent of the costs associated with a product are spent maintaining that product. A product defect that might have cost $50 to detect and correct at the design phase of the development of the product can cost *$5000 or more* to correct after the product has been made available to the client. Ouch! This means that a lot of money is spent repairing instead of being invested in other areas of the company that can offer a return on investment.

The process architect can perform a great service in reducing these costs. For example, the process architect examines and directs the continual improvement of the overall maintenance release process. He also works with project members to ensure the effectiveness of their own processes such as performing design and code inspections, managing code and document changes, and verifying that a fix to a problem does indeed correct the problem without harming other areas of the product. The process architect also works with the software development process and new development/enhancement projects to ensure that lessons learned from maintenance releases are benefiting future products. The process architect also proposes the metrics to be used that can help the maintenance project perform "better, cheaper, and faster."

Team Leaders and Team Members

The first two team leaders shown in Figures 13.1 and 13.2 might have maintenance teams that are involved in troubleshooting and fixing identified problems. The third team leader might lead a test group that validates that the fixes have indeed corrected the intended problems. This group might also perform regression testing of the overall product just before it is released, to ensure that the overall operation of the product has not been negatively affected in any way. (See Q13.8 later in this chapter for a definition of *regression testing*.)

FIGURE 13.3

Plan Showing a Maintenance Release Project Completing Every Month

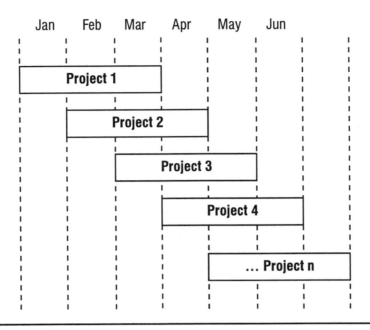

Overlapping Maintenance Releases

Figure 13.2 shows a simple view of a maintenance project, but what if there is a maintenance release every month? And what if the work for each maintenance release begins up to three months before the release is delivered, so some of the more effort-intensive problems can be fixed? Three projects could be ongoing at the same time as shown in Figure 13.3. For example, in the month of March, Project 1 is about to finish, Project 2 is midway, and Project 3 is starting. If each project is small, one project manager, one business architect, one product architect, one process architect, and one test group may be sufficient to support all three projects. Most of the team members also will likely do work on each of the projects.

Note that the greater the number of projects performed in parallel, the greater the complexity and risk in managing these projects. Also, the greater the difficulty that project members have in balancing their time across the projects. A contingency buffer must be built into each of these projects. When conflicts arise, the priority most often will be given to the project that is the closest to its release date.

> **LESSON 13.3**
>
> More than one maintenance project can be under way for the same product at any point in time.

Emergency Fixes

Anyone who has worked around maintenance organizations knows that some people resources must always be available to work on emergency fixes that can be quickly patched and sent to the client (or placed into production). The need for these people resources must be factored into project plans if the same project members also are expected to pinch-hit on emergency fixes.

Postproject Reviews

There should be a postproject review after every project. They might only be an hour or two on small projects, but they should never be more than one day on very large projects. Yet it is important to view these maintenance projects as the real projects that they are. We must continuously learn from past projects with the objective that each subsequent project will be better run and produce better results than prior projects. (See Chapter 14, The Project Management Office, for more information on postproject reviews.)

> **LESSON 13.4**
>
> Postproject reviews offer great value for subsequent maintenance projects.

Q & A

Q13.1   Should the people that develop new products or enhancements to existing products also maintain their own work after it has been delivered to the client or placed into production?

A13.1   Many organizations and companies wrestle with this question. There are a number of pros and cons either way. My experience suggests that if you have a small software or information systems group, the best approach is to combine in the same team the maintenance and new development work. This approach allows fixes to be made more quickly by the original developers, raises the developers' sensitivity to the usability and quality of their work, helps them better understand the real world where their products will be used, and offers more variation to their work, to name but a few. If you have a large software shop, it is best to separate the teams performing maintenance activities from the teams performing new development work. Otherwise, it can be too complex to manage the comingling of two groups that have very different operational demands.

> **LESSON 13.5**
>
> Maintenance work and new development work should be combined in the same team for small software shops but separated for larger shops.

Q13.2 How should the maintenance work and the new development work be parsed in a team responsible for performing both?

A13.2 There are many ways to organize a team responsible for performing both maintenance and new development work. The approach taken usually depends more on the skills and interests of the team members than on other factors. For example, let's say that the team is made up of five members. Let's also say that 20 percent of the work performed by the team is maintenance work. One approach is for each team member to plan on spending 20 percent of her time on maintenance work. Another approach is for one person on the team to spend full time on maintenance activities for the team, leaving the other team members to concentrate on new development work.

> **LESSON 13.6**
>
> The skills and interests of the team members are usually the single biggest factors in deciding how best to assign both maintenance and new development work across a team.

Q13.3 But isn't it difficult to accurately estimate the amount of time that must be spent on maintenance work?

A13.3 Although not an exact science (what is on software projects?), it is not usually difficult to estimate the amount of time needed to spend on maintenance work for products and releases that have been in use for a while. Teams supporting such products should have a set of metrics that are routinely updated and tracked. These metrics show information such as the number of defects discovered, the number of defects corrected, the severity of defects, the amount of time required to fix a defect, and the number of new problems discovered as a result of poor fixes. The metrics are required to satisfactorily plan and track the maintenance work, and ensure that the client's needs are being satisfied.

New products can be a challenge because there is no track record from which to estimate future maintenance activity. Therefore, for new products, estimates must be made in the beginning and resized as new information is made available. The estimates can be made based on defects expected per thousands of lines of code, per function point, or some other measure.

LESSON 13.7

Recording and analyzing metric results will significantly aid in planning the time necessary for maintenance work.

Q13.4   How does a maintenance team avoid overtime spikes related to unexpected problems that must be corrected immediately?

A13.4   There is no sure way to avoid occasional overtime because no one can know when problems will be reported or the severity of those problems. Members of maintenance projects must expect that overtime periods will occur, and plan accordingly by applying techniques such as assigning some members to work other than first-shift only and compensating members who work excessive overtime with periodic time off. Collecting metrics like those identified in the answer to the previous question can help in the planning process, so work effort can be better anticipated.

LESSON 13.8

Spikes of overtime work should be expected on all projects.

Q13.5   We have a hard time finding people who want to work in the maintenance area. Is this a common problem?

A13.5   It can be. There is often an air of excitement, intrigue, and adventure when building new products. Also, project members working on *new things* often seem to have an easier time in obtaining visibility across an organization and into management. However, it is important to note that project members working in maintenance organizations are (and should be) paid the same as their counterparts at the same level that build new products.

It has been my experience that project members working in a maintenance organization can actually enhance their skills more quickly than their counterparts. The reason is that a project member performing maintenance work must know more parts of a product, and must understand how those parts interrelate to the operating environment in ways that often surpass his new-product counterpart. Furthermore, working directly on client problems, often under considerable visibility and *pressure*, adds an additional dimension of reward and maturity.

One of the best-kept secrets is that some of the best talent in an organization is dedicated to maintaining products. Furthermore, there can be a more immediate sense of satisfaction from solving and fixing problems in a maintenance organization, than being subjected to the longer-term schedule pressures and potential monotony of working on the same area of a new-product project for a long time. There probably always will be a special lure for project members to work on *new stuff*; however, many of the more professionally mature organizations recognize the great value of their members working in maintenance areas. These organizations typically have members who readily volunteer and desire to work there.

LESSON 13.9

Some of the best talent in an organization is dedicated to keeping the product up and running for the client.

Q13.6 Is there any value in rotating project members who develop new code through a maintenance organization?

A13.6 Yes, it is important that the developers of new or enhanced products learn how to construct code, documentation, and test scripts that can be efficiently used, repaired, and enhanced while they are being maintained for the client. Many project members who develop new or enhanced products have not been taught how best to perform in these roles. New hires in an organization can learn a lot by first serving at least six months in a maintenance organization where they can experience firsthand the benefits of working with well-developed products and the drawbacks of working with poorly developed products. The training will help project members who rotate into jobs where they create new and enhanced products to be more effective contributors to the organization and business. But it is not only new hires that should experience maintaining products, it is also experienced project members who have developed new and enhanced code. Another benefit for rotational assignments was discussed in the previous *Q&A*; that is, a person can learn aspects (e.g., technical knowledge, sensitivity to client, and how to work under pressure) of their trade more quickly.

LESSON 13.10

Rotation assignments between development and maintenance are good business.

Q13.7   When organizing maintenance projects, how important is it to have an independent test person or independent test group?

A13.7   It not only is important, it is also *essential* that someone other than the person who corrected and tested the fix validate that the fix does indeed correct the problem, and that the fix doesn't cause additional problems. It is not only unproductive to deliver bad fixes to the client, but it also leads to business problems when the client's problems are not solved at the first opportunity to do so. In the long run, an independent tester or test group will save an organization a lot of money and problems with the client by being a check and balance, able to ensure good quality of delivered products and services.

LESSON 13. 11

Using an independent test person or test group on a project reflects good business judgment.

Q13.8   What is regression testing? Is it a good practice?

A13.8   *Regression testing*, as used in this book, is the final series of tests performed after a major test has occurred (e.g., function test, system test) and/or the final test of a product. The test typically comprises a selected set of test scripts taken from prior tests that are run as final verification that the product works as it was intended. Regression testing verifies that the product function that used to work still does.

Regression testing is not only a good practice; it is also an essential practice for many software organizations to survive. It is alarmingly common, for example, for product-related problems to be fixed but to also cause or reveal additional problems. Without performing a regression test, these problems can surface after the client has begun to use the product.

LESSON 13.12

Regression testing is an essential activity on all projects.

CHAPTER 14

THE PROJECT MANAGEMENT OFFICE

The Enter*Prize* Organization does not require a *project management office* (PMO) in order to be effective. However, a PMO can offer great benefits, the larger the overall organization and the larger the number of projects within that organization.

A PMO is a group of people with a mission to support project managers in the successful launch, implementation, and completion of projects. It includes performing any tasks that can benefit current or future projects. This mission can be interpreted narrowly or broadly, depending on the budget and overall objectives of a PMO.

This chapter addresses the following PMO-related topics:

◆ examples of tasks for which a PMO might be responsible

◆ how to organize a PMO

◆ dangers of having no PMO

◆ creating a PMO that is respected across the organization it serves

◆ answers to commonly asked questions.

Figure 14.1 lists examples of tasks for which a PMO might be responsible. Let's examine each of these tasks.

FIGURE 14.1

Examples of Project Management Office Tasks

◆ Providing qualified project managers
◆ Providing project management consulting
◆ Providing project management mentoring
◆ Creating and maintaining project management processes
◆ Providing project management tools and support
◆ Conducting project orientation and culture training
◆ Providing project planning and tracking support
◆ Creating and maintaining project command centers
◆ Supporting project meetings
◆ Facilitating project meetings
◆ Preparing project status reports
◆ Performing project reviews
◆ Performing postproject reviews and follow-ups
◆ Filing/summarizing postproject reviews
◆ Ensuring that new projects apply lessons learned
◆ Performing product reviews and follow-ups
◆ Providing contract proposal support
◆ Sponsoring project management education
◆ Archiving/retrieving project records

Providing Qualified Project Managers

The single most important service that the PMO provides is making available qualified project managers for launching and running projects. The expectation is that these projects will meet quality goals, be delivered on time and within budget, satisfy the client, and meet maintenance objectives, which are often, but erroneously, overlooked. Maintenance costs can bring an organization to its knees if it invests too heavily in supporting existing products, and doesn't invest sufficiently in the development of new and enhanced products.

LESSON 14.1

The most important service of a PMO is to provide qualified project managers to an organization.

Ideally, all project managers in an organization should report to a PMO-like organization. It allows project managers to pool their skills and knowledge, share project management best practices, and support one another as needed. What it really means is an opportunity for project managers to develop professionally much more quickly than most could ever hope, if they were working isolated from one another.

LESSON 14.2

Organizations that have many project managers should also have a PMO.

Providing Project Management Consulting

Project management consulting is providing project management services and products to an organization as needed. These services and products may take on many forms such as providing project management-related training, documenting processes and procedures (including templates), assisting in project planning and tracking activities, performing project reviews, and running an entire project from start to finish.

The PMO provides consulting-type services and products to its immediate constituency, but it could also be expanded to serve a *market audience* of other organizations internal to the company. Although outside the objectives of this chapter, a PMO could be further expanded to address project management consulting opportunities that are *external* to the company and could become a source of revenue and profit.

A challenge for the PMO—particularly a start-up PMO—is determining how to deploy its limited resources across an organization that is starving for project management help. Obviously, the priority must go to the areas where the greatest positive impact to the organization and company can be made.

> ### LESSON 14.3
>
> A PMO should deploy its limited resources to the areas where the greatest benefit to the organization and company can be felt.

Providing Project Management Mentoring

Mentoring is different from consulting. *Mentoring* is working with a person to help develop his skills and increase his effectiveness in a specific area of interest. Mentoring should be personal and confidential. It is best performed by a person who is not your boss or in your direct management chain of command. Why? Because you will learn more quickly, be more attentive, and ask more intimate questions about how you should conduct yourself as a project manager if you know that none of the conversation will be used in a later performance evaluation or related to a salary increase, award, or promotion. Mentors must be trusted to keep private the intimate conversations regarding your professional development. Mentors and the mentoring process are most effective when the person being mentored trusts the relationship and views it as a risk-free environment.

Your boss probably has the skills to be a good mentor but typically is not the best mentor for you. She is responsible for coaching and counseling your performance, and it is beneficial to have a good working bond between you and your boss. But, if you reveal your inner weaknesses and misgivings, most bosses, being human, may reflect some of those conversations and insights into your next performance evaluation. It's akin to a judge telling a jury to disregard what it just heard. Most of us cannot, although our intentions are honorable at the time. Therefore, the best mentors typically are outside your management chain, so there is no potential conflict of interest between what a mentor hears you say and his position to potentially use that information *against* you.

If project managers are to grow at the rate their potential allows, they must have mentors—and competent and trusting ones at that. Mentors are typically senior project managers who have had firsthand experience in project battles and lived through and learned from their own mistakes. These mentors are people who truly have your best interests at heart and with whom you are free to develop a good and trusting working relationship.

LESSON 14.4

Mentoring should be personal and confidential.

Creating and Maintaining Project Management Processes

The PMO maintains a repository of documented project management processes for all projects to follow as needed. These processes—also called standards and procedures—include those for defining the organizational structure of projects (including defining the roles and responsibilities of key project positions, ala the Enter*Prize* Organization), planning projects, tracking projects, escalating issues to higher levels of project leadership, performing project reviews, and performing postproject reviews. Many of these processes include templates to aid in the implementation of the process.

Providing Project Management Tools and Support

The PMO should decide on the project management tools that will be used and supported across the organization. Once the tools have been selected and approved, compliance is essential. Having a standardized set of tools reduces costs for purchasing tools, reduces training costs, and increases the long-term productivity of the users of the tools and the benefits from sharing templates.

The PMO could be the liaison for purchasing tools and ensuring that users have the latest releases. The PMO also could be responsible for working with tool vendors in reporting problems and receiving fixes or workarounds. The PMO has a responsibility for ensuring that tool users are receiving satisfactory training. The users of the tools also must have an interface to call and with which to work when questions or problems arise. The PMO could provide this interface or ensure that an interface is available from somewhere else across the organization.

LESSON 14.5

Project management tools should be standardized across an organization.

Occasionally, one or more of the selected project management tools will not meet the needs of a project, or will actually add unnecessary overhead time and costs to a project. It is important that good business judgment is used when determining the tools that a project must use. Remember that project management tools are meant to serve the users of the tools, not the other way around.

LESSON 14.6

Users of project management tools must be helped by the tools, not hindered.

Conducting Project Orientation and Culture Training

When a new project is started, it is strongly recommended that *project orientation* and *culture training* (hereafter, referred to as culture training) occur for all project members. Culture training is the formal training of all project members—usually at the start of a project—in key hard skills, soft skills, and processes essential for ensuring a successful project. Culture training provides all project members with a common understanding of how the project will be run and the role that each project member is expected to play. The PMO is the likely organization to conduct these culture-training classes, or find suitable instructors to do so. The project manager can teach a portion or all of the class, if desired.

LESSON 14.7

Culture training classes not only can give a new project a jumpstart, but they also can help power a project through to a successful completion.

Culture-training classes typically are one to two days in length, depending on the size and duration of the project and the *culture maturity* of the project members. Very small projects of five or less members may require classes that are only a half-day long. Figure 14.2 lists topics that are among those to be addressed in a culture-training class. Let's look a bit closer at each of these topics.

Roles and responsibilities of key project positions. Key project positions such as those described in this book for the EnterPrize Organization are described and discussed.

FIGURE 14.2

Examples of Topics to Be Addressed in a Culture Training Class

◆ Roles and Responsibilities of Key Project Positions
◆ Project Planning Process
◆ Project Tracking Process
◆ Escalation Process
◆ Project Reviews
◆ Postproject Review
◆ People Communications
◆ Soft Skills
◆ Lessons Learned

Project planning process. The process to be followed in planning the project is described and discussed. This includes discussion of the development process to be followed and how the plan will be maintained.

Project tracking process. The process to be followed in tracking the progress of the project plan is described and discussed. Discussed topics include the frequency of project-tracking meetings, meeting agenda, tracking meeting ground rules, role of project-tracking participants, identifying high-risk/high-priority problems and their mitigations, recording and closing project action items, metrics to be tracked, when to create a problem recovery plan, and what a problem recovery plan should contain.

Escalation process. The process to be followed when an escalation is required to resolve an issue is described and discussed. An *issue* is defined as a problem that, if not resolved, is believed to have a significant harmful effect on the outcome of the project. An *escalation* is when two affected parties are unable to agree on the resolution of an issue, and a sincere attempt to negotiate a resolution has occurred; then higher levels of the project's leadership must be called upon to help resolve the issue. (For more information on the escalation process, see Chapter 16, The Escalation Process.)

Project reviews. The process to be followed in conducting project reviews and the frequency and timing of project reviews. (For more information on project reviews, see an upcoming section in this chapter, *Performing Project Reviews*.)

Postproject review. The process to be followed in conducting the postproject review at the end of the project. (For more information on postproject reviews, see an upcoming section in this chapter, *Performing Postproject Reviews and Follow-Ups*.)

People communications. A discussion of common interpersonal communications problems that can arise on a project and how to avoid or deal with them. Examples include admitting when you are wrong, giving praise and showing appreciation, asking for help, being willing to help others, considering the impact of your words, attacking problems and not people, eliminating surprises, being willing to break with tradition, and asking questions rather than assuming.

Soft skills. A discussion of attributes and behaviors that one can adopt to become a more effective project member. Discussion topics include how to deal with criticism, risk taking, fear of failure, the importance of perseverance, setting goals, managing time, how to make and meet commitments, being accountable for one's own actions, challenging conventional thinking, recovering from setbacks, and believing in yourself.

Lessons learned. A discussion of the lessons learned from the most recent postproject reviews, and how this project will apply the most significant lessons.

Culture training classes, although not yet in common use, provide uncommonly great benefits to starting a project and its members on a productive footing toward launching and implementing an effective project.

Providing Project Planning and Tracking Support

The PMO support personnel, at the direction of a project manager, should be willing and able to assist any and all members of a project in the development of individual or team plans. For example, after a project manager has a project plan kick-off meeting, and the team leaders are directed to put their detailed plans in place, the PMO support personnel stand ready. The PMO can give instruction on how best to develop a plan, show what a plan might look like, and perform early reviews of the team leaders' plans. When each of the team leaders' plans is ready for the project manager to review, the PMO support personnel assist in the review process by helping to identify plan problems, documenting problems, assigning owners to those problems, and tracking the problems to closure.

After each of the team leaders' plans are reviewed and accepted by the project manager, all the individual plans are collected, and the overall project plan is created. The project plan usually includes a subset of the tasks from each team leader's plan. For smaller projects, the project plan might consist of all of the tasks (not a subset of tasks) from all the team leaders' plans, or it might consist of all the tasks owned by the project members if the project is so small that there are no designated team leaders.

The project plan is owned by the project manager and administered by the PMO support personnel. The project manager must first approve changes to an approved project plan, and then the PMO support personnel update the project plan accordingly. Except for very small projects, the project manager should not personally be making change updates to a project plan. It can become quite time consuming, and take the project manager away from more important daily issues requiring her attention.

LESSON 14.8

On other than small projects, the project manager should not invest her limited time directly interfacing with project management tools.

Creating and Maintaining Project Command Centers

PMO support personnel, under the direction of the project manager, can create a designated space or room for tracking a project. This area can be called the *project command center*, the war room, or simply the project room. It contains the most current status on the project and can be used to track the project. It also can be useful in briefing senior management or the client on the project. The room can have many charts, graphs, and lists that show the high-risk items and their mitigations, the critical path activities of the project, the schedule and budget data, the assigned action items, and many other exhibits of value when running and tracking a project.

Small projects of a few months or less duration typically would gain little benefit from a project command center. However, larger projects can gain great benefit by raising the overall visibility of the progress being achieved on the project. Of particular benefit is the heightened focus that the most important project problems can receive—helping them get the attention that their urgency demands.

A project command center can be effective in creating an image that says, "We are serious about this project and doing what is necessary to ensure its success."

Supporting Project Meetings

The project manager conducts the project-tracking meetings, which typically are performed weekly. The minutes of the meeting are captured by PMO support personnel, so the project manager can fully focus on running the meeting. After the meeting, the assigned PMO support person prepares the meeting's minutes and passes them by the project manager for review and approval. Once approved, the minutes—as well as information for next week's project-tracking meeting (e.g., meeting agenda, updated project plan, updated action items, and other items, as needed)—are distributed to the project-tracking meeting members and to management and the client, as needed.

Facilitating Project Meetings

For medium- to larger-sized projects, the project manager will require some help in running or facilitating project meetings other than the weekly project-tracking meeting. There is too much going on for a project manager to personally be involved in all happenings that could benefit from her attention. These *happenings* usually take the form of work, escalation, and information meetings, and they can be quite time consuming. PMO support personnel facilitate or participate in these meetings on behalf of the project manager. In all cases, the support personnel keeps the project manager fully informed of the latest information and actions.

PMO support personnel can help free a project manager so she can concentrate on the most important meetings and work on the most important problems.

Preparing Project Status Reports

Depending on the size of the project and the number of senior management (including those for the client) that must be kept apprised of project status, the preparation of project status reports can consume a lot of time. Graphics-type charts are essential for conveying major messages focusing on presenting status that is reasonably easy to understand. These charts take time to create and then subsequently update for each project status-reporting period. It is not a good use of a project manager's limited time to be overly absorbed in performing this task. PMO support personnel perform the execution of such administrative tasks. However, the project manager is fully responsible for the accuracy and completeness of the data displayed, as well as for all the text that accompanies the status charts. This means that the project manager must direct the creation and approve the content of all project status that is formally presented across the organization and beyond.

Performing Project Reviews

A *project review* is an independent review performed at selected points along the software development process for a project still under way. It allows an active project to be examined to determine its overall health; actions are then recommended to immediately address any significant problems that are identified.

Project reviews are typically performed every three to four months on projects that are six months or longer. They are best performed near major milestones, especially prior to releasing additional funding for a project. Project reviews should be scheduled in advance and appear as tracked activities in the project plan.

Project reviews should be arranged by someone not directly on the project that is being reviewed. The PMO is a likely organization to administer project reviews. It selects the members of the review team, typically comprising one to five *experts* from *outside* the project. Depending on the project to be reviewed, the review team members might have skills in areas such as the technical aspects of the product being developed, project management, quality, marketing, business management, and legal.

LESSON 14.11

Project reviews should be conducted every three to four months for projects that are of six months duration or longer.

The PMO prepares a list of topics that selected project members must address during the project review. The project members typically called to present before the project review team are members assigned to the key EnterPrize Organization positions of product manager, project manager, business architect, product architect, process architect, team leaders, and selected resource managers and team members. On small projects, all project members may be asked to participate in the project review. The topics list is approved by the project review team and then provided to the appropriate project members to aid in their project review preparation.

The review team conducts the project review; its goal is to identify only significant project problems. The selected project members present the requested information to the review team and respond to the questions asked by it. A project review might take anywhere from two hours to three days, depending on the size and complexity of the project. For most projects—those consisting of twenty-five to one hundred members—a full day should be sufficient. By contrast, a project of five members may require only two hours.

After the project review, the review team prepares summary charts and presents its assessment informally to the project manager, then to management, the project members, and, optionally, the client. Out of professional courtesy, the project manager is permitted to see the findings first. Many times the project manager will identify inaccuracies in the findings or items taken out of context. Such comments from the project manager can help ensure the integrity and usefulness of the findings. The problems identified must be logged as *action items* and tracked to closure via the project's tracking process.

The PMO performs an administrative role before, during, and after the project review to ensure that all parties perform their duties when, where, and how required. The PMO also ensures that problems identified are properly addressed and closed.

Performing Postproject Reviews and Follow-Ups

A *postproject review* is the review of a completed project by a selected group of project members who represents all of the major organizations that participated in the project. For a small project, all project members should participate. The group identifies those things that went right, those things that went wrong, and those areas where improvement can be made. The objective is to learn from project experiences, so future projects can benefit.

Postproject reviews should be scheduled in advance and appear in the project plan as the last, or one of the last, activities to be performed. Preferably, post-project reviews should *not* be conducted by a member of the project being reviewed, especially the project manager. Instead, a person outside the project, someone completely objective and neutral, should conduct them. The PMO is the preferred organization to provide such a facilitator, who might be a project manager from another project, a trained facilitator, or both. The PMO also provides administrative support in planning and scheduling the postproject review.

After the postproject review is conducted, the facilitator must prepare a presentation that summarizes the findings from the review for management, the project members, and, optionally, the client. Key problems identified are logged as *action items* that are assigned to the appropriate groups or people across the organization and tracked to closure. It is intended that these problems will be addressed by correcting the processes that allowed the problems to occur. A report also is written to archive the findings, so future projects can study and learn from this postproject review.

LESSON 14.12

Postproject reviews should be mandatory, so future projects can benefit from lessons learned on prior projects.

Filing/Summarizing Postproject Reviews

Performing postproject reviews yields little benefit unless those reviews are communicated and studied at the start of new projects, so future projects learn from prior projects' mistakes and successes. A repository needs to be created, where these reports can be filed, then retrieved for later reference. The PMO can provide this service.

In addition, as these postproject review reports are collected and filed, the PMO should periodically—say, after every five to ten reports received—summarize the most important findings, and make a *postproject review summary report* available for quick and easy retrieval and study. This summary report should reflect the latest findings, so it can offer great time savings to project members who wish to learn from experience.

LESSON 14.13

Maintaining a postproject review summary report can be invaluable for project members to save time obtaining ideas to apply to future projects.

Ensuring That New Projects Apply Lessons Learned

When a new project is started, the project manager and other leaders of the project defined by the Enter*Prize* Organization should review the most recent postproject review reports. The planning and implementation of the new project should reflect key lessons learned from prior projects. To ensure that key lessons are being used, the project manager—and, optionally, other project members in lead project positions—must present what is being done on the new project that is different from prior projects as a result of lessons learned. The project manager should present this information to the product manager, the manager of project managers, or a small review panel that exists wholly for this purpose. This exercise, called the *project improvement activity*, is included as an activity in the project plan and tracked accordingly. If a review panel is used (the preferred approach), the creation and administration of this panel should be performed by the PMO.

LESSON 14.14

A three-member review panel with sign off authority can have a profound positive impact on ensuring that the planning and implementation of new projects reflect the lessons learned from prior projects.

Warning: Experience suggests that projects will not improve at the rate possible unless two events happen. The first is that an activity for this exercise be included in the project plan. The second is that a sign-off by a third party (e.g., a review panel) occurs to certify that sufficient attention to learning from previous postproject reviews is being made.

Performing Product Reviews and Follow-Ups

A *product review* is a review performed independently at selected points *after* the product has been delivered to the client. It allows a product in *production* to be examined for meeting key business parameters including customer satisfaction, return on investment, and quality goals. A product review also provides valuable feedback to the development and support groups, so they can continue to improve their processes and the results of key measurements.

Product reviews should be performed at least every three to six months, maybe monthly at the launch of some critical products. The PMO is a candidate organization to examine after-delivery issues, so the development and support of current and future products can benefit from the key findings. It is also important to ensure that appropriate action is taken, immediately if needed, to ensure the success of the delivered products.

Similar to project reviews, the PMO selects the members of the product review team, which may comprise from one to five *experts*. These reviewers should not be directly associated with the product; however, they should possess a broad range of skills and interests, including marketing, product support, customer relations, and business management.

In preparation for the first product review, the PMO prepares a starter set of topics and metrics that those people associated with the launch, support, customer satisfaction, and revenue/profit issues of the product can address in a formal product-review meeting. Many of the metrics should have been decided well beforehand, and reflect target objectives that are expected to improve over time (e.g., customer satisfaction, product support costs, warranty costs, and time required to fix product problems). The list of topics and metrics is reviewed, updated as needed, and approved by the product review team. These topics and metrics are then provided to appropriate people to aid in their preparation for the product review.

The product review team conducts the product review. The selected people to present do so and then respond to questions asked by the review team. After the review, the team prepares summary charts and presents its assessment to management, others as appropriate, and, optionally, the client. Key issues identified must be logged as *action items* and tracked to closure by the PMO.

LESSON 14.15

One of the many benefits of a product review is that it can provide valuable feedback to the development and support groups, so they can continue to improve their processes and the results of key measurements.

The PMO performs an administrative role before, during, and after the product review to ensure that all parties perform their duties when, where, and how required. The PMO also ensures that issues identified are properly addressed and closed.

Providing Contract Proposal Support

Who is verifying the reasonableness of proposed contracts going out to other areas of the company or outside the company? What about proposals coming into the organization from vendors? Perhaps several vendors have bid on a project, and the best candidate must be selected. The PMO is a likely group to administrate or lead the review of these proposals for completeness, accuracy, realism, and good business arrangements. The PMO might assemble a review team comprising experts from across the organization. They might represent technology, testing, project management, legal, sales, marketing, and any other areas that can add value to reviewing and evaluating the proposal.

Sponsoring Project Management Education

The PMO champions the proliferation and benefits of good project management. Project management education is one method of spreading project management knowledge and skills. The PMO is responsible for identifying a series of training classes, seminars, and other events needed to institutionalize sound project management practices within its serving organization. Even if an education organization already exists within the organization or company, the PMO is accountable for ensuring that the right attention is focused on project management training.

Classes are targeted for many different audiences interested in project management such as project managers, team leaders, team members, resource managers, product managers, business and product architects, process architects, clients, and others. The classes focus on fundamentals such as using project management tools, planning and tracking projects, and organizing projects—to the more advanced topics of earned value, risk management, and learning from previous postproject reviews—to further advanced topics incorporating project reviews as part of classroom instruction. Classes on leadership, the soft skills, and people communications are also included in the required curriculum.

The PMO is accountable for the professional development of project managers, including developing the curriculum, ensuring that project managers spend sufficient time on professional development, and ensuring that each project manager is meeting professional standards, be it certification or otherwise. This includes the PMO identifying the knowledge, classes, and experience that must be completed or attained for a project manager to become certified. The certification can take the form of a company or university certification or a diploma or certification by a leading project management association such as the Project Management Institute (PMI®). For information on becoming a member of PMI, to learn about the many products and services of PMI, or to learn about becoming a certified project management professional (PMP®), visit PMI's web site: www.pmi.org.

Archiving/Retrieving Project Records

The PMO provides a repository for archiving project documents and retrieving those documents when requested. This service provides many benefits to an organization and its projects, including:

◆ a trail of proof to verify that sign-off on key documents has occurred
◆ access to documents that might be used as templates for documents of future projects
◆ historical information that can help with the planning of future projects
◆ valuable information that might be crucial should litigation result on a project.

How to Organize a Project Management Office

Theoretically, a PMO can be formed with only one project under way. In this case, there would be only one project manager and perhaps one or more PMO support personnel. But, it is likely that benefits will be more apparent if there are several projects in progress. Figure 14.3 shows an example of a more typical starting point for a PMO. There is only one department in the figure, and it comprises three project managers, a team leader, and five team members (also called PMO support personnel).

Support personnel can provide a wide range of services that have been discussed earlier in this chapter. These services focus upon assisting project managers in their everyday duties, such as:

◆ creating and maintaining project plans
◆ providing support and training on project management tools for project team leaders and members
◆ creating, teaching, and maintaining project management processes
◆ assisting in the preparation of project-tracking reports
◆ administering project reviews
◆ filing/summarizing postproject reviews
◆ archiving/retrieving project records.

FIGURE 14.3

Functional-Reporting View of a Small Project Management Office

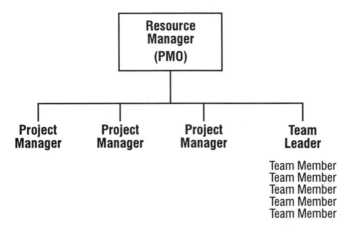

It is important to understand that the primary purpose of the PMO support personnel is to assist a project manager in any way necessary to help ensure his project's success. Off-loading work from the project manager—particularly administrative-type work—frees the project manager to focus on actively working with project members, the client, and senior management in moving the project forward.

The team leader shown in Figure 14.3 interfaces with both the project managers and the support personnel. She helps balance across her team incoming workload requests from the three project managers. The team leader also provides direction to the support personnel and reviews their work output as needed.

As the number of projects served by the PMO increases, and the duties that the PMO takes on increases, the size of the PMO can grow to two or more departments. Figure 11.1 in Chapter 11, Organizing for Multiple Projects, shows another example of organizing a PMO. It shows two departments and three process architects reporting to the resource manager of the PMO; one department consists of project managers and the other department consists of PMO support personnel. The PMO support personnel could be led by one or more team leaders (not shown in Figure 11.1).

Dangers of Having No Project Management Office

If an organization has several projects under way and no PMO, the project managers are probably not learning from one another. They are probably not sharing project management best practices or being challenged to incrementally and continuously improve their skills and knowledge in managing projects. Furthermore, there is a strong temptation for project managers to be overtly influenced by the product managers to whom they directly report, and make emotionally or politically driven decisions rather than the best business decisions.

Project managers, like all professionals, cannot truly understand how best to perform their jobs unless they have been properly trained, and are then coached and mentored while performing as project managers on active projects. The benefits of assembling project managers across an organization into a single department that focuses on the needs and nurturing of project managers can have a profound positive impact on the success of projects and the professional maturing of project managers. Project managers must continuously learn from lessons of prior projects, as well as learn from the latest thinking in good project management. The likelihood that project managers can steadfastly and objectively grow to master the profession of project management is slim to nonexistent if they are reporting to many different areas scattered across an organization.

LESSON 14.17

Project managers that are scattered across an organization with no common bond, such as a PMO, are significantly handicapped in consistently improving their performance from project to project.

Is Your PMO Respected?

Many PMOs are not well received or well respected across an organization. A PMO might be viewed by the organization it serves as simply being organizational overhead that adds too little value to justify. *Many times this is an earned reputation!* But the reputation can be turned around and made quite positive.

When a PMO provides services that have a direct benefit to an organization and its projects, a good reputation is inevitable. For example, look at the following starter list of services that a PMO can provide, and ask yourself if such a PMO would be welcomed in your organization:

◆ Provide well-trained and competent project managers to run key projects.

◆ Periodically provide project management consulting as requested.

◆ Review contract proposals from vendors or from within the home organization.

◆ Sponsor project management education seminars and classes.

◆ Develop, document, and maintain project management best practices.

◆ Conduct project culture training.

◆ Perform project reviews.

◆ Perform postproject reviews.

◆ Ensure that new projects are applying lessons learned.

The PMO has responsibility for educating the organization it serves about the benefits it brings to projects, as well as the benefits it brings to the overall enterprise. A PMO must be able to defend its existence; it must create and track metrics that can show the results of its positive contributions. For example, a PMO should survey its customers, both internal and external, on a routine basis to verify that it truly is adding value, and the value is measurable and consistently improving.

The strength and reputation of a PMO rests first with the effectiveness of its project managers. For example, if the project managers are not receiving the proper training, coaching, and mentoring, they will likely be ineffective. If the project managers have a weak mastery of the needed soft skills, they will likely be too soft to be sufficiently effective. (See Chapter 15, Are You *Too Soft?*) The effectiveness of project managers can be influenced by the support that they receive from mentors, one another, and the PMO support personnel. Be aggressive in defining a PMO that boldly seeks to improve the overall success of the projects and organizations it serves.

LESSON 14.18

Project managers' reputations will directly reflect upon the reputation of the PMO.

Q & A

Q14.1 Is a project management mentor really of any great benefit? Or is it just another fad or way to burn a budget?

A14.1 Project management mentors are, by far, the best way to develop effective project managers. Mentors must be seasoned project managers who have "been there, done that," messed up, and lived to learn from the experience. Mentors must be accessible to work with project managers, while the project managers perform their basic tasks such as planning, tracking, and performing problem management. Mentors especially must be available during times of crises.

For those of you with years of project management experience, think back to how a project management mentor—the *right* mentor under the *right* circumstances—would have helped you accelerate your learning of both the hard and soft project management skills, avoid some hefty mistakes, and—as a side benefit—might have moved your career ahead sooner.

The project manager, in the position of being the most influential person on a project, can have a profound impact on a project's outcome. With projects commonly costing or impacting many thousands, even millions, of dollars, doesn't it make good business sense for a project manager to be provided with mentoring help in the quest for success of both the project manager and the project?

LESSON 14.19

There is no better apprenticeship for budding project managers than to have strong project management mentors working alongside them.

Q14.2   Are there some guidelines for mentors that you can share?

A14.2   Figure 14.4 is a short list of example guidelines that a mentor may follow to help the *mentee* develop his potential.

A strong measure of the effectiveness of a mentor is seen through the success of the mentee and his project. However, it is important to note that the mentor's objective is not promotions for the mentee; any expectations in that direction can interfere with the great learning opportunity available. The focus must be on performance and achieving results; however, promotions might be a byproduct for the mentee who consistently exceeds expectations.

To be most effective, trust must be developed between the mentor and the mentee. Discussions need to be relaxed and candid from both sides. The mentee must be encouraged to be inquisitive without concern for asking *dumb* questions or confiding about mistakes made. The dialogue between the two must be held in confidence and should *not* be used in performance evaluations. For this reason, the mentee's manager—or any manager in the mentee's chain of command—usually is not the best mentoring choice.

The mentor needs to help the mentee recognize his strengths, interests, and areas for improvement. The mentor will recommend classes, conferences, workshops, books, articles, and even other *experts* to help with the mentee's personal growth.

FIGURE 14.4

Guidelines for an Effective Mentor

◆ Helps enhance performance
◆ Provides a penalty-free relationship and never betrays confidences
◆ Helps identify and develops strengths, interests and specific skill areas for improvement
◆ Assists in the creation of a "Development Plan"
◆ Meets at least monthly

The mentee has the responsibility for creating, with the mentor's help, an individualized development plan that includes the identification of needed knowledge, skills, and experiences and a plan to acquire or achieve them. This plan should complement any related aid offered by the mentee's company.

The mentor needs to be accessible to the mentee during crucial periods such as the development of new plans, establishing a project-tracking process, replanning exercises, and crises. In most cases, face-to-face contact of one to three days per month should be adequate, as long as telephone access is available within twenty-four hours.

The most effective project managers are developed day by day, not year by year or project mistake by project mistake. Mistakes will happen, even with the best mentoring. However, project managers with strong mentors should find their effectiveness continually improving. The company and everyone connected with the project will share in those gains.

LESSON 14.20

The time and cost invested in acquiring a mentor is small compared to the benefits that can be gained.

Q14.3   You mentioned that one's boss typically is not the best mentor. Then should a person avoid an employee-mentor relationship with her boss?

A14.3   Bosses (resource managers) typically have good mentoring skills. The danger is when the information that the boss obtains through mentoring an employee (direct report) is used later in the employee's performance evaluations and when determining salary increases or when selecting candidates to receive performance awards and assigning new job opportunities, to name a few. It's not that the boss is lying or making up false information; the boss is using factual information. It's that the boss is privy to more information than he necessarily needs to know, and that information can influence decisions that must be made related to the employee. For some employees, having a mentoring relationship with their bosses can work fine, but, for many others, it can be less than desirable. You have to decide for yourself. However, whatever you decide, it is important for both you and your boss to have a good working relationship.

LESSON 14.21

Regardless of whether there is a mentoring relationship between a direct report and her resource manager, it is important that both parties maintain a good working relationship with each other.

Q14.4   How should an employee go about finding a mentor?

A14.4   Before looking for a mentor, first decide on what you want to be mentored. For example, do you want someone to work with you to improve your project management hard skills (e.g., planning, tracking, risk management, and others) or your soft skills and ability to work well with others, or help you find the career most suitable to your interests and aptitude? Once you can be specific, your resource manager is usually the right choice for a first stop. Your boss typically has contacts beyond yours and may find a suitable mentor, or she might suggest areas for you to search. Mentors can come from anywhere—e.g., work, family, church, social contacts, university faculty, and business people in the community.

If your boss knows you are interested in finding a mentor, she also knows that you care about your career and will likely work more closely with you on professional development. It is important to know that it is the employee's responsibility to initiate seeking a mentor, not the resource manager's. However, it is the resource manager's responsibility to help the employee meet his professional development needs.

LESSON 14.22

The employee is responsible for seeking out a mentor, not his resource manager.

Q14.5   Are relationships with mentors long term?

A14.5   Not necessarily—a new project manager might have a mentor assigned to get her oriented to project management processes. This could be a relatively short-term arrangement, whereas a reasonably experienced project manager might have a mentor to infrequently call upon for unusual crises, which could require long-term mentoring.

Q14.6   If I attended a culture-training class on my last project, do I need to attend the culture-training class on the new project?

A14.6   The answer is almost always, *yes*. Culture training classes are necessary, so the project members know what is expected of them and how to interrelate with other members on the project. Project members cannot know what is expected of them unless they are told. We all come from different backgrounds and experiences. The culture desired on our new project is not something we all learn through some sort of osmosis. Furthermore, project managers can conduct their projects differently and these differences—along with new lessons to learn—need to be communicated.

Participating in a culture-training class is a lot like trying to get JELL-O to stick to a wall. If you fill a bowl full of JELL-O, and throw it against a wall, only a fraction of the JELL-O will stick. If you refill the bowl with the JELL-O that did not stick to the wall but fell to the floor, and rethrow the bowl against the wall, more JELL-O sticks, but not all. The more the process is repeated, the more the culture-training lessons will stick. (JELL-O is a registered trademark of Kraft Foods, Inc.)

> **LESSON 14.23**
>
> The more you participate in culture-training classes, the more you mentally retain the important lessons.

Q14.7   After a project review has been conducted, to whom does the review team present the findings first: management or the project members?

A14.7   As stated in the section, *Performing Project Reviews*, earlier in the chapter, the findings should first be shown privately to the project manager; it is an act of professional courtesy. Because the project manager wields such an influential position on a project, all problems can be either directly or indirectly viewed as a reflection of the project manager's performance. This act of courtesy benefits both the review team and the project manager, because the project manager can help ensure that the review team did not jump to any improper conclusions, taken out of context or misunderstood. The private review with the project manager is not intended to allow the project manager to weaken the impact of legitimate findings.

On small projects, the findings then can be presented to all interested parties at the same time. However, for other than small projects, management sees the findings next, then the project members. Unfortunately, it is common for project review teams to ignore presenting the findings to project members. This not only is an act of arrogance, but it also misses an important benefit of the project review: allowing the project members to view their perceived performance, what they are doing right, and what could be done better. Whether the client sees the results with the management team, afterward, or never, is based on the relationship that the company has with the client. It is desirable for the client relationship to support sharing the findings from the project review with the client.

LESSON 14.24

The findings from the project review should first be privately shown to the project manager.

LESSON 14.25

Do not overlook sharing the project review findings with all members of the project.

Q14.8 It was mentioned earlier in the section, *Performing Postproject Reviews and Follow-Ups*, that the project manager should not conduct the postproject review? Why not?

A14.8 Most project managers likely have the skills to conduct a postproject review; the problem is that the project manager is too close to the project. Because most problems can be either directly or indirectly associated with the project manager, she could behave defensively as problems are identified. Although some project managers are able to rise above this behavior, it is best to avoid putting anyone in such an awkward position in the first place. Note, however, that the project manager should participate in the postproject review.

Q14.9 In the Introduction for this book, you reference a book for more information on conducting postproject reviews. The book is quite methodical about preparing for the postproject review. Is all this preparation really necessary?

A14.9 After the book was published, I stumbled upon another approach that requires much less preparation, but is arguably just as effective. The approach is for the postproject review participants, other than the facilitator, to *not* prepare at all. Instead, the facilitator walks through the development cycle, activity by activity, from the beginning to the end, and asks for feedback on what went right and what could have been better during the implementation of each activity. My experience shows that all significant problems and achievements still will be identified by following this simpler, less time-consuming approach.

LESSON 14.26

Postproject reviews do not require preparation by anyone other than the facilitator.

Q14.10 Do you recommend that a review of a vendor or in-house contract occur at the end of the contract period?

A14.10 Absolutely *yes*! Many organizations not only do not perform reviews of contracts after the work has completed, but also they make the same mistakes on future contracts—thus costing their companies hundreds of thousands of dollars, sometimes millions of dollars, in lost time, low quality, cost overruns, and low customer satisfaction. The PMO can add discipline to the contract proposal process, so an organization is learning from contract to contract.

LESSON 14.27

Your organization should be learning from contract to contract.

Q14.11 In Chapter 7, The Resource Manager, the section entitled *Performs Resource Planning and Allocation*, it was stated that the resource manager is responsible for balancing people resources across multiple projects and anticipating future demands for their skilled resources. Who, if anyone, is responsible for performing this role across all projects in an organization?

A14.11 This is a likely task for the PMO. Obviously, this task can have great benefit in helping the product manager or the leaders of an organization decide the capacity of an organization to take on new projects. A caution: In most cases, it is sufficient to gather and update this information monthly or even quarterly. Updating too frequently requires a level of detailed discipline beyond that which most organizations have instituted. Furthermore, performing the task too frequently can become too costly for an organization. Use good judgment when performing this task, and only perform it if the information gathered is used.

Q14.12 Why is it that most projects repeat the sins of predecessor projects, especially when many of the project leaders know better?

A14.12 This is an age-old question but one with an answer. There are many reasons that contribute to project leaders not learning from past project mistakes. However, I believe that the major factor is that many project leaders do not demonstrate the *leadership* and *boldness* to deliberately drive the necessary changes in their own projects.

Isn't it interesting that we expect professionals in *other* professions to continually improve, but we don't expect the same from ourselves, our organizations, or our *projects*. For example, we expect an athlete to continually improve his skills and *stats*. We expect a sports team to study the mistakes and successes of the last game, and review the performance and weaknesses of the upcoming opponent. We expect NASA to learn from every space launch and mission. We expect airlines—you get the idea.

We are paid professionals. We need to exercise leadership and boldness to insist on organizations that perpetuate self-improvement. For example, don't merely add an activity to a new project plan that says the project manager must "review lessons learned from the most recent postproject reviews." Reviewing something, by itself, usually yields little improvement. However, having to convince a review panel of three members that you have appropriately applied the most significant lessons learned to your new project can yield marked improvement. If you cannot convince the review panel, you must replan and reconfront the review panel until you can demonstrate the application of these lessons.

LESSON 14.28

Project managers must demonstrate the leadership and boldness necessary to make the needed changes happen.

CHAPTER 15

ARE YOU TOO SOFT?

The Enter*Prize* Organization is not only about effectively organizing software projects with clearly defined roles and responsibilities appropriately spread across the project members. The Enter*Prize* Organization also is about driving *accountability* across members of a project with the intent of optimizing their performance to yield a successful project.

To be most effective, project members must not only understand their responsibilities but also which behavior to adopt to effectively accomplish their commitments. This chapter describes the necessary behaviors to demonstrate the full measure of accountability that is so critical to a project's success.

Being *too soft* is the number-one reason why project managers and project members are ineffective in performing their duties and meeting their commitments. What do I mean by too soft? If your behavior results in being consistently less effective than possible to accomplish your responsibilities, you are too soft.

LESSON 15.1
A project can be only as successful as the commitments upon which it is based.

Project members frequently behave too softly. Whether you have a large role or a relatively small role on a project, being too soft can have a damaging impact on achieving your portion of the project, and therefore can cause harm to the overall project.

LESSON 15.2

Most of us are *too soft* most of the time.

This chapter mostly will focus on project managers rather than on other project members. I have chosen project managers because of the overwhelming influence they have on positively (or negatively) affecting the successful outcome of a project. The messages in this chapter, however, do apply to all project members—be they leaders or not. This chapter will:

◆ show examples of too-soft behavior (behaviors to avoid)
◆ discuss why we frequently exhibit too-soft behavior
◆ identify the behaviors we should adopt to become more effective in meeting our commitments and making things happen.

Examples of Too-Soft Behavior

It is my experience that most project managers are not willing to make tough and unpopular project-related decisions, even though their instincts warn them that they are not taking the most effective action. These project managers are not leading their project teams to quickly resolve their projects' most important problems. They allow the project team frequently to operate on consensus and what seems to please the most people or please the most vocal, influential people. In order to avoid or reduce conflict, they tend to make decisions that often are not in the best overall interest of the project. In other words, the best *business* decisions are not always made because of behavior that is *too soft*.

LESSON 15.3

Your instincts alert you when you don't make the best business decision.

Figure 15.1 lists examples of project manager actions (or inactions) that are indicative of too-soft behavior. If you find that you occasionally exhibit this behavior, that's okay. We all do. However, if you find yourself frequently demonstrating this behavior, then you are too soft as a project manager. Let's look at each of these examples.

Holds back from providing constructive criticism to project members. As a project manager, your job is to lead the project to successful completion. Others should be able to learn at times from your knowledge and experiences. It is hoped that you will impart your wisdom in time to help avoid negative situations from

---

FIGURE 15.1

Examples of Too-Soft Behavior for a Project Manager

Behaviors to Avoid

◆ Holds back from providing constructive criticism to project members

◆ Avoids escalating to higher levels of management project-related problems that are at an apparent impasse for resolution

◆ Unwilling to passionately defend the right project plan to the product manager, to executives, or to the client

◆ Behaves as if there is little or no authority to support his or her responsibility

◆ Puts off insisting on and driving project management best practices throughout the project

◆ Avoids or delays asking for help when needed

◆ Lax in holding project members accountable for their commitments and actions

◆ Complains rather than constructively works issues to closure

◆ Takes on too much work instead of assigning tasks to the appropriate project members

◆ Remiss in seeking out and obtaining needed project management training of both hard and soft skills

◆ Evades taking a position on an issue rather than alienating project members

◆ Avoids or excessively delays making key decisions

◆ Predominately focuses on other than the top three problems

---

occurring. Your constructive criticism is invaluable throughout the project such as when project plans are being created and reviewed, during the routine project-tracking meetings, during work and escalation meetings, and other opportunities when you are working alongside your project members.

Avoids escalating to higher levels of management project-related problems that are at an apparent impasse for resolution. When two parties are unable to resolve a problem that, if left unresolved, can have a serious negative impact on the project, then an escalation likely will be required. The escalation is to higher levels of the project's leadership (usually management), and should be initiated within two working days of recognizing that the problem cannot be expediently resolved. As the project manager, you should ensure that these problems are getting needed swift attention to ensure their complete resolution. You should insist that the required escalations occur, no matter how high in your (or another) company the escalation may take you.

LESSON 15.4

Provide timely, constructive criticism to project members.

Unwilling to passionately defend the right project plan to the product manager, executives, or the client. The project manager directs the creation of the project plan, which includes defining the operating ground rules that will be used in the creation of the plan such as: accounting for holidays and vacations, the skill level of project members, education/training needs, and realistic projections of personnel staffing; basing estimates on defensible productivity rates; and including x percent contingency buffer for all activities. The project manager is expected—and has the duty—to defend the right plan; both the project members and the higher-ups expect it.

LESSON 15.5

Initiate an escalation to higher levels of management—within two workdays—of any project-related problems that are at an apparent impasse for resolution.

The project manager must creatively and passionately insist on a realistic, achievable plan. If the project manager is unable to sell the higher-ups on an acceptable plan, special tracking metrics must be defined and instituted as early-warning signals, should the plan begin to fail. There also should be resizing activities added to the project plan to be performed just prior to major phases completing and before the release of additional funding. Another action is to plan for project reviews every three to four months on projects of six months' duration or longer. In other words, if the project manager is not able to sell the right plan, steps must be taken by the project manager to more closely monitor the plan's execution.

LESSON 15.6

Passionately defend the *right* project plan to the product manager, executives, and client.

Behaves as if there is little or no authority to support his responsibility. The project manager must never adopt the self-fulfilling prophecy of "I have all the responsibility, but without the appropriate authority." As a project manager, when was the last time your boss called you on the carpet for exceeding your authority? For most of us, we cannot remember a time *throughout our entire careers.* (If you can remember a time, and you did nothing illegal or unethical, then I applaud you! You are in a minority group.) The message here is that we have the authority—*we just don't take it!* The most effective project managers practice the mantra, "it is better to beg for forgiveness than to ask for permission," as they deliberately and steadfastly "make things happen."

LESSON 15.7

If an unrealistic plan is committed, institute early-warning signals, and plan for project resizings.

Puts off insisting on and driving project management best practices throughout the project. The project manager is responsible for bringing project management best practices to the project and insisting on their adoption. Management is not responsible for this; nor is anyone else. As the *owner* of the project, the project manager must insist that the appropriate project environment be created to best ensure the successful outcome of the project. If the project manager is not sure what these best practices should be, she must solicit help.

LESSON 15.8

Behave as if you have the authority to match your responsibility.

Avoids or delays asking for help when needed. Remnants of what I call the "John Wayne mentality"—asking for help is a sign of weakness, but going it alone is a sign of strength and virtue—remain strong in our culture. Perhaps this mentality was required for survival in the Wild West. But today, as people come together as a team to pool their talents and skills to create achievements far more complex and superior than any one person could hope to accomplish, asking for help is a sign of strength. *Not* asking for help is a sign of weakness and can undermine the success of the project.

LESSON 15.9

Drive project management best practices throughout the project.

In today's fast-paced, highly competitive, global economy, it is more important than ever to ask for help when it is needed. No one person knows it all. In fact, increasingly, knowledge is less concentrated in one person or a small number of people; instead, an array of specializations among project and organizational members is evolving. The project manager must not only ask for and obtain any needed help; he also must encourage project members to adopt the same good sense.

LESSON 15.10

Ask for help when needed.

Lax in holding project members accountable for their commitments and actions. The project manager must give project members an opportunity to estimate effort, and commit to their portion of the overall project plan. If the estimations and commitments are questionable, project members must defend their positions. Once the committed plans have been agreed, progress must be tracked against them. Should problems arise, the project members must be held accountable to appropriately address the problems. The project manager is there to help any and all project members be successful with their portion of the plan. It is not about punishment or blame. It's about creating a winning environment where everyone behaves professionally in meeting their commitments and, when the need arises, provides help for one another.

LESSON 15.11

Hold project members accountable for their commitments and actions.

Complains rather than constructively works issues to closure. Complaining is talking *at* a problem rather than constructively working to correct a problem. The project manager must practice the behavior that she expects from others and not ever get caught up in complaining about *anything*. Instead, the project manager must encourage legitimate project problems to be logged, assigned, and tracked to closure.

LESSON 15.12

Constructively work issues to closure; don't complain—ever!

Takes on too much work instead of assigning tasks to appropriate project members. Project managers have responsibility for ensuring that project-related tasks and action items are being assigned to the appropriate project members and that members are *not* taking on these tasks themselves. The project manager must take care not to become a critical path on the project. If this happens, it can cause grave harm to the project, because the project manager is no longer available to perform his duties of focusing on the assignments and problems across the entire project.

LESSON 15.13

Assign tasks to appropriate project members rather than taking on unnecessary burdens; if necessary, provide appropriate help.

If some project members are overloaded and cannot take on more work, even though there is remaining work to be assigned in their area of the project, they should nevertheless be assigned the work. However, the project manager and the associated resource managers must work to help these project members obtain the resources and aid they require. Other than in isolated cases, it is wrong for a project manager to take on someone else's work. It only serves to weaken the ownership and accountability ethic that project members must be taught to demonstrate.

Remiss in seeking out and obtaining needed project management training of both hard and soft skills. The project manager must continually seek to improve her project management skills, requiring attending classes, seminars, reading the latest literature, and networking, to name a few. Nobody is—or ever will be—so good or so knowledgeable at being a project manager that she can forego any future training or learning. The continual educational investment that you make will pay back many times over throughout your career. Continuing education is mandatory, not optional. A benefit from attending training sessions that is often overlooked is networking with other professionals. These professionals may be a future source of knowledge, advice, or *lessons learned*.

LESSON 15.14

Routinely seek out and obtain needed project management training of both hard and soft skills.

Evades taking a position on an issue rather than alienating project members. The project manager is the only project member steadfastly looking out for what's best for the project. All other project members predominantly are looking out for what's best from their own project perspectives—as they should be. Therefore, the project manager must not hesitate to assert his position of power to influence the direction and outcome of project issues that are drifting or might begin to drift.

LESSON 15.15

Take timely positions on issues.

As a leader, it is common to find yourself in a position where one or more of the parties involved do not like a particular action or decision you have made or chosen to support; yet this is a crucial part of your job. Everyone associated with the project wants you—*needs you*—to make these decisions, so the project will continue to progress in the most effective manner possible. If you believe you will be more popular and effective by not making these decisions, try backing off, and watch your overall popularity dive, not to mention your effectiveness.

Avoids or excessively delays making key decisions. As Thomas J. Watson Jr., former chairman of IBM, had been known to say, "Better to make a decision and occasionally be wrong, than make no decisions." I will add, "or excessively delay in making a decision." None of us makes the best decisions all of the time, but if you wait to make your decisions when you have all possible information to ensure that the best decisions are being made, you will lose all competitiveness. Holding back from making key decisions also holds a project hostage from achieving the required forward progress that everyone expects.

LESSON 15.16

Make decisions as they are needed—don't delay or abstain.

Predominately focuses on other than the top three problems. I stated in an earlier chapter that the number-one reason why projects fail is because project members do not focus on identifying and then solving the top three project problems. Consequently, serious problems are allowed to linger until they erode the project's schedules and commitments.

LESSON 15.17

Focus daily on the top three problems and their corresponding solutions.

A project manager must always know the project's top three problems that must be driven to closure. Furthermore, these three problems should consume most of the project manager's attention each and every day of the project. Unfortunately, there is a strong tendency to focus on the problems that appear to bark the loudest or are the easiest to solve. But the best project managers know that by always focusing on solving the top three problems, the project will receive the care and feeding needed to manage it to successful completion.

Why We Are Too Soft

Being too soft is not good—for you, your team, or your project. It's not good for your upcoming performance evaluation either, along with your job security or attaining your true potential. So why are most of us consistently too soft? Let's look at some reasons.

- ◆ We don't know how not to be too soft—how to change our behavior. We've had too little instruction or mentoring on the skills (mostly the soft skills versus the hard skills) that can improve our effectiveness.
- ◆ We are afraid of alienating others—concerned that people will not like us. We are uncomfortable with taking an unpopular or unconventional position. We can't deal with any form of rejection. What others think of us is more important than what we think about ourselves.
- ◆ We are uncomfortable with getting too much attention and having to defend our actions. We may feel ill equipped to defend ourselves publicly, particularly against those who are the most outspoken.
- ◆ We are concerned that we might hurt somebody's feelings. We go out of our way to show our compassion for others. We would rather be too soft than risk someone misunderstanding our actions—even though our criticism or actions are needed and are constructively given.
- ◆ We are afraid of losing control. We fear being a leader that has insubordinate or rebellious followers. We fear our requests will be rejected, and we will be powerless, alone, and miserable.
- ◆ We do not feel that we are getting compensated enough to demonstrate tougher behavior. We believe the compensation must be greater to justify driving others and pursuing commitments with greater passion. We feel the rewards don't outweigh the drawbacks.
- ◆ We are concerned that tougher behavior will burn bridges—be career limiting. We fear doing the right thing may require doing the politically incorrect thing. We are not willing to "rock the boat" and potentially risk our salary, jobs, or careers.
- ◆ We don't like our job and don't care enough about the outcome of our actions. We believe that the job is just not worth dealing with any additional hassles or annoyances.
- ◆ We are afraid of acquiring too much work or too much responsibility. We fear that passionately driving to pursue our commitments may result in more work and responsibility than we care to take on.

- We don't understand our job. We come across too soft because we don't understand our job well enough to have confidence to deliberately drive it to its successful completion. Nor do we fully understand the need for us to be a catalyst in order for things to happen in a timely, complete, costly, and quality manner.
- We are uncomfortable asking for help. We believe that we will lose respect and future career opportunities if we admit that we need help and seek that help.
- We are easily intimidated by others. We cannot deal with losing face in front of others—nor have we the fortitude, the backbone, to defend what we believe to be right.
- We believe what we are holding others up to achieve is not realistic. We don't drive harder to make things happen because we are opposed to the overall commitment to which we are being held, and we personally don't feel the ownership or commitment ourselves.
- We procrastinate to another moment. We put off actions and justify to ourselves that it's okay because we will eventually face up to the obstacles or our responsibilities later—when it will be easier and more comfortable.
- We are concerned about being viewed as rude, insensitive, arrogant, or a bully. Here again, we are more concerned about what others think of us than we think of ourselves.

These are but some of the reasons we might use as excuses for being too soft. The bottom line, however, is that, by being too soft, we are being less effective—probably ineffective—in achieving our responsibilities and commitments.

LESSON 15.18
There are no benefits to practicing too-soft behavior.

It Is About Results, Not Effort

The effective project manager adopts the *results*-oriented mantra, "I'm involved. I'm doing. I'm achieving," rather than the *efforts*-oriented mantra, "I'm trying. I'm trying. I'm trying." Project success is about *results*, not just effort.

Consider this scenario. Say you have a child of grade-school age. Your child participates in sports at the local community park. There are fifteen teams competing. How many teams will receive trophies when the season completes? One? Three? Four? For most communities, *all* of the players on *all* fifteen teams will receive a trophy! But only one team is the *champion*.

What's happening here? We are being trained at a young age to believe that *success* is all about effort, not results. We are, in effect, sending the message, "You show up for most practices and games, and when the season is over, you will be a winner; you will achieve success." I'm not saying that this scenario shows improper behavior or guidance. Young people have fragile, developing self-esteem systems. We need to encourage them to come out of their shells, express themselves, participate, and explore the great potential that is bounded within them. But many of us, as we entered the work force, never switched hats from focusing on *effort* to focusing on *results*. The business world has no problem choosing a hat: it is *results* that count—*delivering a product that satisfies the customer and offers the organization an appropriate return on investment.*

LESSON 15.19

It is important to focus on *results*, not effort.

It is the project manager's job to lead the project's members in the important pursuit of a successful project and product—anything else can be viewed as failing. In most cases, a project's success is directly related to the impact (results versus effort) that the project manager had on the project team throughout the project.

LESSON 15.20

In most cases, there is a direct relationship between a project's success and the effectiveness of the project manager.

Behave as You Would If *You* Owned the Business

The most effective project managers behave as if they are running their own businesses. They believe—and their actions demonstrate—that *the buck stops here*; they are fully accountable for the project. They see their project (not their company) as their business. There are many decisions they must make, for which they will be accountable, and they frequently and respectfully draw upon the knowledge, experiences, and insights of those around them, so they can make the most informed decisions. But they are careful not to be overreliant on consensus management; they recognize their duty to be fully accountable for the outcome of the project. This can mean that, at times, the most effective project managers will stand alone with what they believe to be the right decision.

Demonstrate Behavior for Others to Model

As noted in an earlier section, *Why We Are Too Soft*, to avoid being too soft does not mean you have to be rude, insensitive, arrogant, or a bully. None of these attributes are acceptable—ever! On the contrary, an effective project manager must strive to demonstrate behavior for others to model. For example, make yourself available and approachable to coach and support others through their problems and setbacks, be a constructive catalyst when change or a given action is required, and demonstrate respect and dignity for all project members. It is not about finding fault or making someone feel uncomfortable. It's about helping the project's members and encouraging them to help each other, so the prevailing project attitude is: *we all are successful together.*

If you believe that *too-soft behavior* will win you friends and influence others, it won't! It will have the opposite long-term effect. Those around you will lose respect for you as a leader, your project's outcome will be negatively impacted, and your career can become stagnant—or even shortened.

> **LESSON 15.21**
>
> The attitude to permeate throughout the project is that *we are all successful together*.

Are You Up to Becoming an Effective Project Manager?

If you have difficulty making unpopular decisions—if you allow what others think about you to be more important than what you think about yourself—if you follow the "squeaky wheels" around you rather than your own inner compass—then you might not be ready to be an effective and successful project manager. But, don't despair. All project managers who perform their roles effectively today had these challenges to overcome yesterday. You too can persevere if it is important to you.

> **LESSON 15.22**
>
> You can learn to become an effective project manager if it is important to you.

Q & A

Q15.1 I would be more inclined to constructively criticize my team members if I were more perfect in my own actions. Comments?

A15.1 All of us make mistakes, and all of us will continue to make mistakes, although some more than others. It's not about *your* mistakes, it's about your responsibilities as a leader in helping others to learn, grow, and contribute to the team's success. By the way, the best leaders passionately work at being role models for others to follow. This includes admitting when you make a mistake.

LESSON 15.23

If you are not coaching, directing, and teaching others, then you cannot be an effective leader.

Q15.2 If I escalate an issue too high up the management chain, won't this make me look bad because I need help? Won't I likely burn relationship bridges in the process?

A15.2 If an issue is unable to be resolved in the lower ranks, then it must be taken up the management chain, so it can be resolved. This is good business judgment, and it's what you would want your employees to do if you owned the company. As for burning bridges, escalating to resolve an issue is performed for business reasons; it is not to be taken personally. The parties involved on both sides of an escalation are expected to behave professionally at all times. It doesn't mean that anyone has done anything bad. It means that you want to influence the outcome of an event or decision, which is your right or the other party's right; it may also be your duty.

LESSON 15.24

Escalating doesn't mean that anyone has done anything bad.

Q15.3 I don't have a problem asking for help when it is from a peer or even a team leader, but I have difficulty asking for help when it is from someone in management. Any suggestions?

A15.3 Yes, when you find yourself in trouble and at risk of not meeting your commitments, you must seek help, no matter where it leads you. The approach to follow in asking for help, particularly as you go up the corporate hierarchy, is to be prepared with the following three pieces of information:

1. Clearly define the problem for which you need help. A problem that is incompletely or vaguely defined wastes valuable time, energy, and funds.

2. Describe the proposed solution. If more than one plausible solution exists, list them; but be accountable, and take a position on the solution you favor.

3. Be specific about what you are asking. A vague request may get a vague response. Telling an executive, for example, *exactly* what you need, as clearly and precisely as possible, increases the likelihood that the executive will satisfy the request. Being specific has the added benefit of helping the executive to feel that she is really helping.

Let's look at an example.

> You are the team leader of an independent test team. It appears that the development shop will be about three weeks late delivering their code to your test. You believe that you have sufficient time in your test plan to do an effective test, but you cannot *eat* the three-week delay. You ask for $50,000 so you can reduce your twelve-week test cycle to nine weeks. The $50,000 will be spent on acquiring a software test program ($20,000) that automates the testing process and hiring college co-ops ($30,000) to convert the test scripts to run on the software test program. These actions are expected to accelerate the testing process and improve its reliability, thus shaving three weeks from the original planned test cycle and delivering the product on schedule.

If you question whether or not asking for help is the right thing to do, then ask yourself this: If this were my own business, and an employee was faced with the same situation as I am today, would I want my employee to ask for my help? Or continue on the current project path that will not lead to a successful outcome? This can become an easy question to answer when you think of it in terms of owning the business.

By the way, an interesting side effect occurs when you ask for help. By showing your human side and also sending signals that you take pride in your work and care about the success of the project, the respect others have for you typically increases over the level of respect you experienced at the outset of the project. Of course, not asking for help and endangering the success of a portion of or the entire project is a quick method for losing respect and trust from others.

We all need help from time to time. Everyone wins—beginning with you—when needed help is sought. Do what you know is right, not what you might observe happening around you or what you might be accustomed to. Don't become part of the problem!

LESSON 15.25
You become part of the problem if you don't ask for help when you need it.

Q15.4   You say to focus on the top three problems. Many times there are more than three. What then?

A15.4   In Chapter 3, The Project Manager, in the section, *Manages to Project Priorities*, there is mention of managing to the top three to five priorities. The message is that the number of top priorities with which to focus can vary from time to time, but focusing on anything more than five top priorities can handicap a project from making reasonable progress. If the members of a project are spread too thin on working too many problems at once, project *churning* occurs, and little gets accomplished. Discipline is needed to not only isolate the top three to five priorities, but to also ensure that the project members assigned to solve the problems spend most of their time each day solving the problems. (I often use the sound bite "top three problems" because it is easier to say and remember as an important concept, rather than "top three to five problems.")

Q15.5   You list examples of too-soft behavior in a chart (Figure 15.1). Can you provide the list in a manner that shows behaviors to adopt rather than avoid?

A15.5   Yes, Figure 15.2 has been included for that purpose. You may notice that many of these items are also listed as lessons within this chapter.

Q15.6   The concept of a *benevolent dictator* was introduced in Chapter 5, The Product Architect. Can you expand on this concept? Did you mean it to apply only to the product architect, or does it apply to all project leaders?

A15.6   The benevolent-dictator concept applies to all project leaders. Let's look more closely at it and how it is beneficial to the person using it, as well as to a project.

In running a country, democracy is the best thing going to date. However, in running a business or project, my experience has shown that the benevolent-dictator concept is the most effective style. A benevolent dictator leads by actively soliciting information and opinions from project members and others—listens, then demonstrates the leadership, courage, and boldness to personally make the right decision. The benevolent dictator then stands accountable for that decision. He also holds his subordinates accountable for their decisions, and they in turn hold their subordinates accountable for their decisions, and so on. In other words, everyone is encouraged and expected to make the decisions that affect their own domain of responsibility.

FIGURE 15.2

Examples of Behaviors of an Effective Project Manager

Behaviors to Adopt

◆ Provide timely, constructive criticism to project members

◆ Escalate to higher levels of management within two work days project-related problems that are at an apparent impasse for resolution

◆ Passionately defend the *right* project plan to the product manager, to executives, and to the client

◆ Behave as if you have the authority to match your responsibility

◆ Drive project management best practices throughout the project

◆ Ask for help when needed

◆ Hold project members accountable for their commitments and actions

◆ Constructively work issues to closure; don t complain ever!

◆ Assign tasks to the appropriate project members instead of taking on unnecessary burdens; if necessary, provide appropriate help

◆ Routinely seek out and obtain needed project management training of both hard and soft skills

◆ Take timely positions on issues

◆ Make decisions as needed; don t delay or abstain

◆ Focus daily on the *top 3* project problems and their corresponding solutions

LESSON 15.26

A *benevolent dictator* is a leader who actively and sincerely solicits information and opinions from project members and others, then demonstrates the leadership, courage, and boldness to personally make the *right* decision and stands accountable for that decision.

Now, I am not talking about *micromanaging*. Micromanaging occurs when a leader chooses to make decisions for anyone and everyone within her influence. The micromanaging leadership style is highly offensive; it neither teaches the importance of nor capitalizes on the promise of accountability.

LESSON 15.27

The micromanaging *leadership* style should only be used in rare instances, if at all, and for very short periods of time.

Many organizations and projects attempt to operate on either consensus or democratic rule. Consensus, which has been overhyped for years, is mostly an ineffective tool for managing teams and projects. *Consensus* is obtaining the buy-in from a team or group by adjusting the final decision to a position with which everyone can live. In an attempt to satisfy all team members buying into the team's decision, the solution is almost always nonoptimal and, frankly, is often without vision and personal commitment.

LESSON 15.28

For other than the most trained teams, consensus causes the most important decisions to be compromised, to be watered down.

What's that? You say there *is* personal commitment because everyone had a say in the decision? Yes, everyone had an *opportunity* to speak his mind, but my experience shows that many don't speak up, or they are quick to compromise or live with someone else's proposal—even if they feel it is weak. Many members of a group consensus don't feel personally committed; they hide behind the facade of the team or group. What do I mean by *personal commitment*? Personal commitment is when *you*, personally, are charged with making a decision, and then *you* are held accountable for the outcome of that decision. Teams cannot feel this level of accountability; only individuals can.

What about using the democratic voting process? Organizations or projects that consistently reach decisions by democratic rule frequently can be more *ineffective* than reaching decisions through consensus. Why? Because the majority vote is usually enough to lock in a decision. Unfortunately, everyone with a vote to cast is looking out after her own personal interests or the personal interests of the team that she represents. Consequently, the *right* business decision can easily be overlooked or dismissed.

You might be asking now, "If the benevolent-dictator concept is so effective, why don't more leaders adopt this style of leading?" Two big reasons—the first is that in the free world, many of us shy away from any association with the word *dictator*. Even with the adjective *benevolent* (e.g., good, kind, charitable) added, we still feel uneasy. The other big reason—the biggest one—is that to be a benevolent dictator means that we have to make decisions that will, at times, be unpopular. Many of us have a hard time making decisions that will be criticized by others. In fact, the primary reason why project managers fail, as this chapter reveals, is because they are too soft and have difficulty making the tougher decisions.

I often hear project managers and resource managers say that they cannot effectively adopt the benevolent-dictator concept, because they have a serious shortage of project members and employees with the good business sense—the leadership skills—to make the tough decisions expected of a benevolent dictator. I strongly disagree! For most of us, I believe that we *do* have the people we need; they just haven't been trained properly. After all, they watch how *we* manage and copy our styles.

All of us need to be trained, coached, and mentored in the skills and behaviors that make the most effective leaders. Nearly everyone will rise to the expectations that we set for them—providing that we constructively nurture them along the way. If you want a project to be run like a business, where decisions are made based on what's best for it, and you want project members to consistently be accountable for their own actions, teach and encourage the powerful benevolent-dictator concept at all levels of a project and organization. It's good business!

Q15.7 The advice in this chapter and elsewhere in the book is certainly helpful and makes good sense. However, it's not easy to practice all of these lessons. There is a great force that seems to pull at me to go back to old habits. What can I do?

A15.7 There are many people and places that may be accessible to whom you can turn for encouragement and direction—including your boss, a mentor, a friend, a family member, books, and schools. But ultimately we are all on our own to pursue change to both our own behavior and those areas that we can influence around us.

It might be helpful to remind yourself of three things. The first is that if something is important enough for you, you almost always can find a way to make it happen. The second is that it is not reasonable to expect to achieve everything at once. Learning, experiencing, and growing are lifelong events. We achieve our dreams and desires by taking forward steps, often one at a time, knowing that we occasionally must take a step or two backwards.

Third, there are many, many people who have been faced with hardships equal to or greater than our own and yet were able to overcome the obstacles. I leave you with the thought that *if they can do it, so can you*. Now go make it happen!

LESSON 15.29

We achieve our goals a step at a time but should expect occasional steps backward.

LESSON 15.30

If others can persevere and achieve their goals, this is proof that it can be done—for you as well!

CHAPTER 16

THE ESCALATION PROCESS

*O*ne of the most difficult but common situations we face in our jobs is how we resolve critical problems when we must depend on someone else—someone who chooses not to accommodate our needs. What can we do?

I am often requested to perform project reviews on projects that are *in trouble*. *In every case,* the top problem I identify is that the most critical problems are not receiving—and have not received—adequate attention. I am talking about problems that, if not solved quickly, will cause significant harm such as missed schedules, compromised quality, cost overruns, and lost customers.

If untimely attention to these critical problems has such a significant negative impact on an organization's success, why aren't we better at wrestling them to closure? The following list reveals many of the common reasons why we avoid addressing critical problems:

- We are afraid of conflict.
- We are afraid we will "burn bridges" with those with whom we must work.
- We think we will lose on the matter anyway.
- We don't want someone to look bad.
- We aren't convinced that our position is correct.
- We don't want to expend the time and energy.
- We don't know how to resolve such conflicts professionally.
- We aren't sure what is acceptable behavior in our organization.

In all cases, we need to appropriately deal with the reason, so critical problems receive the immediate attention they require. This chapter will discuss a valuable tool to employ when an *issue* arises that, if not resolved, can cause harm to a project; the tool is escalation. This chapter addresses the following escalation-related topics:

◆ definitions of issue and escalation
◆ guidelines to follow when pursuing an escalation
◆ why escalations are good business
◆ two examples of applying the escalation process
◆ answers to commonly asked questions.

What Is an Issue? An Escalation?

What causes a problem to become critical, to become an issue? When two parties are unable to agree on the resolution of a problem and that problem, if left unresolved, can have a significant harmful impact on the project, it becomes an *issue*.

What does one do when an issue arises? After an earnest attempt by the two parties to negotiate a resolution without success, higher levels of the project leadership must be called upon for help. This is called an *escalation*.

Escalation Guidelines

Escalations are a powerful tool for resolving conflicts and moving a project forward. But there are guidelines to follow in order for project members to achieve the full benefit that this tool can provide. Figure 16.1 lists these guidelines.

Escalate only after a sincere attempt has been made to resolve the issue. Escalations are not an excuse to ignore working with the other party to resolve a conflict. A reasonable attempt to resolve the issue should first occur. Look at the other party's point of view, and be creative in reaching a compromise from your original position, a compromise with which you can live that does not undermine the basic needs you have that must be satisfied.

The objector is responsible for escalating the issue, unless the objector is an approver. This means that if you are the one who needs the other party to come around, you must initiate the escalation. There is an exception: if you are an *approver*, the other party must initiate the escalation in order to win *your* approval. Let's look at an example.

FIGURE 16.1

Escalation Guidelines

◆ Escalate only after a sincere attempt has been made to resolve the issue

◆ The objector is responsible for escalating the issue, unless the objector is an "approver"

◆ Initiate the escalation within two work days

◆ Escalate the problem, not the person

◆ Always inform your management (your resource manager) prior to initiating an escalation and obtain his or her approval to proceed

◆ Always inform involved parties before beginning the escalation

◆ When an escalation is underway, do not stop working the plan-of-record

Miguel is a team leader who also owns a document that must be reviewed and approved by several other people, each representing a team, organization or, perhaps, only representing themselves. The document is distributed both to reviewers and approvers. Reviewers are people who have an interest in the document, but the document's content does not necessarily impact their own work and commitments. Approvers are people who have a dependency on the content of the document in order to perform their work and meet their commitments.

Responses from the reviewers and approvers are returned to the owner of the document, Miguel. All but two of the responders, Barbara and Jen, have approved the document. Barbara is an approver, and Jen is a reviewer. Because Barbara is an approver, Miguel must obtain his approval on the document before Miguel can declare that the task of receiving approval on the document has been completed. Therefore, Miguel and Barbara must negotiate the problems that Barbara has identified with the document. If they are unable to agree on the resolutions to the problems, Miguel must initiate the escalation to the next position level over Barbara, which is typically Barbara's resource manager.

Because Jen is a reviewer, Miguel does not require Jen's approval of the document. However, as a professional, Miguel should have an interest in understanding Jen's problems with the document, and determine whether or not he should resolve them. If Miguel and Jen cannot agree on the resolution of the problems, Jen must initiate the escalation to the next position level over Miguel, typically his resource manager.

Initiate the escalation within two workdays. The party responsible for initiating the escalation should do so within two workdays of knowing that the problem is unresolvable at its current level; usually the escalation meeting can occur within those two days. However, if you are escalating to high levels of management, you will find it more difficult to schedule meetings that can happen within two workdays. In these cases, you *initiate* the escalation within two workdays in order to quickly place your meeting on the calendars of the people involved.

Escalate the problem, not the person. Do not make the disagreement personal; escalations are not ever intended to be personal. You are escalating because the issue is a business matter that must be resolved, not because of the person. In fact, neither party is usually wrong. They both are likely doing the right thing from their points of view, based on their assignments and commitments.

LESSON 16.1

A person's professional maturity is on display during an escalation.

Always inform your management (your resource manager) prior to initiating an escalation, and obtain her approval to proceed. It is important that your resource manager be aware of your intent, because you will need her support. Your resource manager has three options from which to choose and can say:

1. "I support your position. Go for it. Let me know if you want or need any help from me."

2. "I support your position. Go for it, but I want to participate with you."

3. "I do not support your position. I do not want this issue to be escalated (or escalated further). Do what you must to resolve the issue at its current level, even if that means giving in to the other party's demands."

LESSON 16.2

Resource managers typically decide the fate of escalations.

Always inform involved parties before beginning the escalation. The escalation meeting should be productive and focused on facts; therefore, all parties should be well prepared. Time may be required for one or more of the parties to properly prepare or for the parties to come up with other creative ideas to help resolve the issue. Avoid surprising anyone in an escalation. Although the surprise *might* give you an advantage in the escalation meeting, there can be resulting personal collateral damage that can be far worse for the people involved than if either lost the escalation. Furthermore, if you surprise the other party and win the escalation, you may be the cause of a decision being made that is not in the best business interests of the project.

> ### LESSON 16.3
>
> Surprising the other party in an escalation is not only unprofessional, but it can be a waste of time if the meeting must be rescheduled to continue when all parties can be better prepared.

When an escalation is under way, do not stop working the plan-of-record. If some aspect of the project plan is being escalated or might be affected by the outcome, don't wait for the issue to be resolved before continuing work on the plan. A disastrous happening would be for people to sit idle or work an unapproved plan while the approved plan is being escalated. No one can know for certain the outcome of the escalation; therefore, keep everyone marching together, working the designated plan-of-record, until officially decided otherwise.

Escalate Is Not a Dirty Word

Escalations are a healthy and essential part of a business environment; they:

- provide a check-and-balance mechanism to help ensure that proper actions are taken
- resolve problems early
- help reduce frustration among project members
- improve overall productivity by reducing rework that can result from implementing the wrong plan of record
- help prioritize work activities
- encourage employee participation and ownership of problems.

An escalation provides a member of a project with an expedient and professional method to resolve conflict. We all have our assignments and agendas to accomplish. Frequently, while on the course of achieving our missions, we face obstacles that impede our progress. Many of these obstacles are outside of our realm of direct control and require intervention from higher levels of a project's leadership. This intervention is required to help clarify and manage priorities to ensure that conflicts are being resolved in favor of what is in the best business interests of the project.

An escalation is a way of clarifying priorities.

There are many different approaches to conducting an escalation. For example, some organizations insist that the next levels of management on *both* sides of an issue be present. Yet, other organizations allow the objector to take the issue up the other chain of management with optional presence of the objector's management. This latter approach is preferred and will be shown in an upcoming example. Ensure that you understand the approach followed in your organization.

When two parties do not agree on the resolution of an issue, usually neither party is wrong. Both parties are correct from their own points of view and missions. Often a person with broader responsibility for the project is required to resolve the issue and is able to weigh the options more objectively, related to the overall impact to the project.

Usually, neither party is *wrong* in an escalation.

An escalation continues until one of the following occurs:

◆ the person initiating the escalation is satisfied with the outcome of the escalation
◆ the final management point of escalation has occurred, and a decision has been made
◆ your resource manager has directed the escalation process to stop.

After an issue is resolved, both parties should abide by the decision made. Only if significant new information becomes available that could reverse the decision should the escalation be revisited. Otherwise, the issue should be considered closed.

Escalation Example 1

We are now ready to apply the escalation guidelines to an example. Figure 16.2 depicts a simple functional-reporting view of the EnterPrize Organization for a project made up of approximately sixty members. The functional-reporting view is the project perspective to use when performing an escalation.

There are eight team leaders shown as TL1 through TL8 (see Figure 16.2). There also are six resource managers shown as RM1 through RM6. RM1 and RM2 each have two resource managers reporting to them. (This is less than the "usually from three to seven" that we discussed in Chapter 7, The Resource

FIGURE 16.2

Escalation Example 1

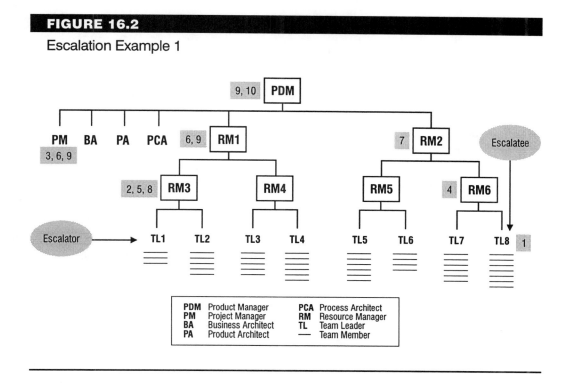

Manager.) Only two resource managers are reporting to RM1 and RM2, strictly for illustrative purposes to help simplify the points to be made in this example. The product manager, PDM, also is a resource manager.

Figure 16.2 shows TL1 as the *escalator* and TL8 as the *escalatee*. The escalator is the person initiating the escalation, and the escalatee is the person whose position on an issue is being challenged by the escalator. For purposes of illustration, the issue being escalated doesn't matter. However, we will assume that the escalator, TL1, owns a project document—say, a test plan—that was distributed for review and approval to several project members. TL8, a team leader, has approval rights on the test plan and believes that the plan needs more work before TL8 will approve it. TL8 has identified eight specific items that must be tested that are either missing or incomplete in the test plan.

Looking again at Figure 16.2, the numbers 1 through 10, which appear alongside some of the members of the project, represent the steps to be followed in driving an escalation to its possible full course. Let's now look closely at each of these steps.

Step 1. TL1, the escalator, does not receive the required approval on his test plan from TL8. TL1 discusses with TL8 the eight problems that resulted in the nonapproval and attempts to resolve them. They are able to negotiate and agree on resolving four of the problems, but, without all eight problems resolved, the test plan still is not approved by TL8. Both parties do their best to resolve the differences but are unable to do so. They both believe that they are doing the right thing from their own points of view. TL1 then informs TL8 that it is his intention to escalate the issue (nonapproval of the test plan) to TL8's resource manager, RM6.

Step 2. TL1 informs his resource manager, RM3, of his intent to escalate the issue to RM6. RM3 must decide which of the three options to take. (The three choices are listed earlier in this chapter under *Escalation Guidelines*.) RM3 decides, "I support your position. Go for it. Let me know if you want or need any help from me." With the support from RM3, TL1 continues the escalation.

Step 3. TL1 informs the project manager and appropriate others, if applicable, of the impending escalation. These people may want to be involved in the escalation. Let's say, for this example, that the project manager is the only one to notify, and the project manager chooses not to attend the escalation.

Step 4. TL1 schedules a meeting with TL8 and his resource manager, RM6. After discussing the issue, RM6 chooses to support TL8's position on the issue, and the test plan is still not approved. TL1 informs RM6 of his intention to escalate the issue to RM6's resource manager, RM2.

Step 5. TL1 informs his resource manager, RM3, that the issue has not yet been resolved to obtain an approved test plan. He recounts the discussions in the escalation meeting with RM6 and TL8. TL1 informs RM3 that it is his intent to escalate the issue to RM2. RM3 again must decide which of the three options to take. RM3 declares, "I support your positions. Go for it. Let me know if you want or need any help from me." With the support from RM3, TL1 continues the escalation.

Step 6. Again, TL1 informs the project manager (and appropriate others, if applicable) of the impending escalation, and again the project manager chooses not to attend the escalation. This time, however, RM3 must inform his resource manager, RM1, of the impending escalation. RM1 is viewed as a peer to RM2 and therefore may want to be involved, or at least informed, of the escalation. Just as RM3 had to decide which of the three options to take, so too must RM1. RM1 says, "I support your position. Go for it. Let me know if you want or need any help from me." The escalation continues.

Step 7. TL1 schedules a meeting with RM2, RM6, and TL8. After discussing the issue, RM2 chooses to support TL8's position on the issue, and the test plan remains unapproved. TL1 informs RM2 of his intention to escalate the issue to RM2's resource manager, PDM.

Step 8. Once again, TL1 informs his resource manager, RM3, that the issue has not yet been resolved to obtain an approved test plan. He recounts the discussions in the escalation meeting with RM2, RM6, and TL8. TL1 informs RM3 that it is his intent to escalate the issue to the big boss: the product manager (PDM). RM3 again must decide which of the three options to take. RM3 states, "I support your position. Go for it, but I want to participate with you." Again, with the support from RM3, TL1 continues the escalation.

Step 9. Once again, TL1 informs the project manager (and appropriate others, if applicable) of the impending escalation. This time, however, the project manager chooses to attend the escalation with PDM. RM3 must again inform his resource manager, RM1, of the impending escalation because of the high level within the organization toward which it is heading. RM1 must inform PDM as well and obtain a decision from PDM, if the escalation should be brought to the PDM's level. It is possible that the PDM might decide that he is paying RM1 and RM2 big bucks to resolve such issues and that "these types of issues should not have to reach me." For purposes of illustration, PDM gives the go-ahead for the escalation to proceed. This time, all the resource managers want to attend. After all, the big boss will be there, and there may be precedence setting (and reputations to defend). The escalation continues.

Step 10. TL1 schedules a meeting with PDM, RM1, RM2, RM3. RM6, TL8, and PM. After discussing the issue, PDM chooses to support TL8's position on the issue. What now? Should TL1 state his intention to escalate the issue to the PDM's boss? No! TL1 can read an organization chart; TL1 backs off and relinquishes to TL8's demands. The test plan is changed to accommodate TL8's remaining problems, is approved, and the issue is finally closed.

You may ask if we have escalated this far, why stop now? We stop because the person who can make the final business decision did. That person in this example is the product manager. The PDM has the authority to make the final decision, because both sets of parties involved in the escalation process work under the direction of the PDM.

There is one other option that could be played but should *rarely* be used. Many companies call it the *open door*. Companies with an *open-door* policy tell employees that if they believe that they are being treated unfairly, or they believe that an unjust decision has been made, there is recourse. They can appeal that decision to a higher authority in the company, even if it means going over their boss' head, a higher boss in the same chain of command, or a special executive designated for such a purpose. An open-door policy is a safety valve for employees to professionally and maturely resolve issues, usually personal ones, which were not resolved satisfactorily, using the standard and usual means.

LESSON 16.6

The *open door* should be used only as a last resort and very infrequently, if ever.

Escalation Example 2

Let's look at another escalation example—this time, a simpler example. Figure 16.3 shows the same project that we saw in Figure 16.2, with the difference that the escalator and the escalatee report to the *same* resource manager, RM3. Let's assume that we are dealing with the same test plan owned by TL1, as we discussed in the previous example, but in this example it must be approved by TL2. TL2 chooses not to approve the test plan. Let's look at the escalation steps to take.

Step 1. TL1, the escalator, does not receive the required approval on his test plan from TL2. TL1 discusses with TL2 the problems that resulted in the non-approval and attempts to resolve them. They are able to negotiate and agree on resolving some of the problems but not all. Therefore, the test plan still is not approved by TL2. Both parties do their best to resolve the differences but are unable. They both believe that they are doing the right thing from their own points of view. TL1 then informs TL2 that he plans to escalate the issue (nonapproval of the test plan) to their resource manager, RM3.

Step 2. TL1 schedules a meeting with TL2 and their resource manager, RM3. After discussing the issue, RM3 chooses to support TL2's position on the issue. Now what? Should TL1 escalate the issue to his boss' boss, RM1? No! As with the previous example, TL1 backs off and relinquishes to TL2's demands. The test plan is changed to accommodate TL2's remaining problems, is approved, and the issue is closed.

The issue was not escalated higher than RM3 because both parties, TL1 and TL2, report to RM3; therefore, RM3 has authority to make the final decision. Here again, the open-door policy could be exercised, but I do not encourage employees to buck their bosses' decisions. Going open door over your boss' head is a highly personal decision that must be carefully thought through. What should happen, however, is Step 3.

FIGURE 16.3

Escalation Example 2

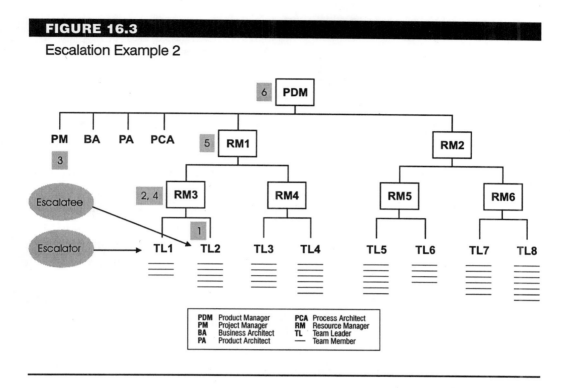

PDM	Product Manager	PCA	Process Architect
PM	Project Manager	RM	Resource Manager
BA	Business Architect	TL	Team Leader
PA	Product Architect	—	Team Member

Step 3. TL1 must inform the project manager of the outcome of the escalation if that outcome has any impact on the project, such as schedules, budget, quality, or customer satisfaction. In this case, the changes that TL1 must make to the test plan—even if they are the right things to do—could impact the project's schedules and budget. If the project manager chooses to reopen the escalation to reverse or change the decision, the project manager has that right and proceeds with Step 4. Otherwise, the issue remains closed.

Step 4. The project manager approaches RM3 and discusses reopening the issue. If RM3 agrees, TL1, TL2, and RM3 meet again, but this time with the project manager to discuss altering the prior resolution of the issue. If RM3 continues to take a position that the project manager finds to be outside the best interests of the project, the project manager will continue the escalation. The escalation will proceed up the management chain one resource manager level at a time (see steps 5 and 6 in Figure 16.3) until either the issue is resolved to the project manager's satisfaction, or the PDM makes the final decision.

LESSON 16.7

The project manager has the right to reopen a closed issue if the resolution to that issue impacts the project unfavorably.

Q & A

Q16.1   The examples discussed were a bit too tidy to reflect my organization. All project members and resource managers do not report to our product manager. How then should escalations proceed? And who is the final point of escalation?

A16.1   The escalation path begins simply enough. Each project member reports to a resource manager, whether permanently or temporarily, for the duration of the project. If an issue arises, the escalator takes the issue up the resource-manager path of the project member who is the escalatee. The key question is who is the final point of escalation. More often than not, it is usually an executive, who is funding the project. After the first escalation to the *top*, it will become apparent just who occupies the top post.

The project manager of a project should always ensure that there is an escalation process defined for her project. The process should state the escalation guidelines to follow, similar to those in this chapter. The escalation process should also show the positions and names of people in those positions where the escalation can proceed. And, of course, the escalation process must state who is the final point of escalation. Don't overlook providing several example escalation scenarios so project members have something to follow.

LESSON 16.8

The project manager is responsible, near the start of her project, to ensure that an escalation process is defined and approved for the project.

Q16.2   How does the escalation process proceed if the issue being escalated causes the escalation path to go to an external client or external vendor?

A16.2   Again, the project manager must have the escalation process defined and approved near the start of the project. This way, there are no surprises to any group related to the project. The project members must initiate escalations when there is an issue not being resolved, regardless of where the escalation takes them. Whether the escalation is in the client or vendor's territory has no bearing on the need to pursue it to a swift closure.

Q16.3 Why do resource managers decide the outcome of an escalation instead of the project manager?

A16.3 Resource managers commit the resources needed for a project. They work with their team leaders and team members in committing to their pieces of the project plan. If a project manager had the authority to, at will, decide the outcome of the project's issues—issues which usually impact use of resources to resolve—resource managers would feel helpless, a loss of control, and frustrated when continually committing their limited resources to a moving target. After a while, resource managers can feel less committed overall, and their future commitments can be weak and without conviction. Also, they can lose interest in the project.

But with resource managers deciding the outcome of these issues, they are still tightly involved with the project and their direct reports; this is good and intended. They are more likely to feel reasonable control and accountability for decisions affecting their resources. The Enter*Prize* Organization is largely built on checks and balances. The resource managers provide a check and balance for many of the decisions made by a project manager, because the resource managers work closely with the project from their own domain's (department) perspective. Occasionally, resource managers might decide an issue that is contrary to the health of the project. When this happens, the project manager can step in and intervene as shown in *Escalation Example 2* described earlier in the chapter.

LESSON 16.9

Resource managers need to be principle players in escalations to help ensure that they maintain a sense of ownership and commitment for the contributions of their direct reports.

Q16.4 One of the escalation guidelines states that project members should continue to work the plan-of-record until an escalation has concluded. If a project member believes that the escalation has a very high chance of altering the plan-of-record, shouldn't he take the small risk, and begin working what likely will become the altered plan?

A16.4 This is difficult to discuss without specific examples of issues being escalated and attempting to articulate the probability that the escalation will alter the plan-of-record. In general, do *not* stop working the plan-of-record until the escalation has concluded. If the product manager, project manager, or other project leader with good information or business sense directs the project's members to stop working the plan-of-record before the escalation has ended, that is their right, and you should stop. However, in a case like this, no matter what the project members do, the issue in question must be closed as soon as possible to avoid confusion, delays, and possible rework.

Q16.5 It's hard *not* to take an escalation personally when someone is disagreeing with a position you are taking on an issue. Is there ever a time when all parties welcome an escalation?

A16.5 Absolutely yes—in fact, the more you practice escalations in a professional manner, as this chapter describes, the more they will become a welcome part of your project culture and less associated with personal attacks. For example, when you escalate an issue that seeks to redirect a project member's priorities, that project member usually doesn't care what her priorities are, just that she is doing the right thing. The project member might even believe that your priorities are the correct ones but feels caught between that which you are asking and what she is being told to do. Escalations are not personal; they support a good business environment. If you owned the company, you would want—even encourage—your employees to use escalations as a tool to resolve issues that are not proceeding to closure with the sense of urgency they require.

LESSON 16.10

Escalations are not personal. They are an essential part of a healthy business environment.

Q16.6 Why doesn't a resource manager take the issue away from the project member and personally work it to closure, thus freeing the project member to work more productively on other things?

A16.6 Resource managers in many organizations and projects do just that, but it is a very *bad* thing to do. It teaches project members not to be accountable for problems that are really theirs to solve. It also encourages them to transfer responsibility and accountability for their commitments to their resource managers. Furthermore, it is not teaching them to be leaders, make good decisions, and learn to work with their project members to resolve conflicts. Although a resource manager has authority to personally work to resolve them, it should be done selectively and infrequently.

LESSON 16.11

Project members must own their issues until they have personally driven them to closure.

Q16.7 In the first escalation example described in the section, *Escalation Example 1*, why did RM3 inform RM1 instead of TL1 informing RM1? I thought you wanted to drive accountability onto TL1.

A16.7   I do; TL1 is driving the issue toward closure. RM3 is informing RM1 for two reasons. The first is to give a show of support to TL1. The second reason is that RM3 is better connected to RM1 and can almost always personally get through to speak with and influence RM1 easier and faster than TL1.

Q16.8   Referring again to *Escalation Example 1*, if the issue being escalated had any impact on the client, shouldn't the business architect be involved in the escalation process?

A16.8   Yes, but the product architect and process architect also may need to be involved. As the example states, the escalator must inform "appropriate others."

Q16.9   In *Escalation Example 2*, no mention is made of the project manager conferring with his resource manager, the product manager, before performing escalations. Does the project manager need to obtain his boss' approval?

A16.9   The project manager has a unique position within a project and does not need to obtain his boss' support before initiating an escalation; the support is already there. The project manager's resource manager *expects* the project manager to escalate issues when needed. The exception is when the project manager is escalating to a resource manager, who is at an equivalent level or higher to the product manager, whether that person is within or outside the project manager's company. When this is the case, the project manager must inform the product manager of the project manager's intentions to escalate. The product manager then chooses one of the three options that we discussed in the section, *Escalation Guidelines*.

Q16.10   I'm concerned that teaching these escalation skills will bring my organization to its knees. Everyone will be encouraged to escalate instead of trying to work things out. The resource managers and executives will become immobilized from working these escalations. What is your experience with this?

A16.10   Most organizations believe your concern will be realized. I also thought this would be the case many years ago; instead, my experience has shown the opposite. The vast majority of issues are worked at the initial level where they are identified and never become part of an escalation. When escalations do occur, they mostly are resolved at the first escalation level. It is rare for an issue to go the distance, but, when they do, it's the right business step to take. When taught properly, project members will rise to the expectations placed upon them and not abuse a tool like escalations.

LESSON 16.12

When taught properly, experience has shown that project members can be trusted to not overuse or abuse the use of escalations.

CHAPTER 17

ADDITIONAL QUESTIONS AND ANSWERS

This chapter addresses questions and answers regarding the Enter*Prize* Organization that do not necessarily fit in the context of earlier chapters. Some questions address the Enter*Prize* Organization in general, and some address a specific aspect of the Enter*Prize* Organization. These questions have been asked at workshops and consulting engagements; they are included here because of their general interest.

Q17.1 This book addresses the Enter*Prize* Organization as it relates to projects. Does the Enter*Prize* Organization also apply to programs?

A17.1 Yes, a program is defined as a group of related projects managed in a coordinated way. (This definition was extracted from *A Guide to the Project Management Body of Knowledge*, by the Project Management Institute, 1996.) Most of the concepts that make up the Enter*Prize* organization also apply to programs. For example, just as defined roles and responsibilities are required for the project members that make up a project, so too are they required for the members that interface across the projects at the program level. These program members include the program manager, a *program business architect*, a *program product architect*, a *program process architect*, and *program team leaders*. (Program team leaders are the project managers.) These roles are very similar to those defined in this book; the primary differences are that the domain of responsibility is broader for program-level positions.

The information in Chapter 14, The Project Management Office, is especially relevant because there can be many projects that make up a program. Chapter 15, Are You *Too Soft?*, is dedicated to overcoming too-soft behavior and is directly applicable to the members of a program, particularly those members in leadership positions. And Chapter 16, The Escalation Process, also applies to programs.

This book focuses on projects because that is where the basic concepts discussed in this book must first be applied. In other words, whether projects are standalone or in related groups to make up programs, these concepts must be practiced.

Q17.2   Do I have to follow the concepts in this book to have a successful software project?

A17.2   No, there are many successful projects that do not follow all or even most of the concepts of the EnterPrize Organization. But there are many, many more unsuccessful projects that also do not follow these concepts. In my opinion, the EnterPrize Organization is the *most effective method* to follow to organize a software project and appropriately drive and balance responsibility, personal accountability, and authority across the project members to optimize their performance and yield a successful project.

Q17.3   If an organization already feels it has successful projects, should the EnterPrize Organization be of any interest to it?

A17.3   Every organization should be open, even hungry, to considering new ideas. The EnterPrize Organization concepts did not come together in the first sitting. The collection of concepts documented in this book represent many years of personal experience and observation on hundreds of projects with thousands of people. No doubt, the EnterPrize Organization will continue to evolve based on feedback, new concepts, technology, and a host of other factors.

Q17.4   Is the EnterPrize Organization similar to the Software Engineering Institute's capability maturity model in that it must be implemented one level at a time?

A17.4   No, the EnterPrize Organization does not have levels. It immediately can be fully implemented across a project or organization.

Q17.5   Isn't the EnterPrize Organization, if implemented as defined in this book, going to cause additional overhead to my organization and projects with so many positions of such specific focus? In my organization, we have numerous cases where one person is assuming the roles and responsibilities of several positions as defined in the EnterPrize Organization.

A17.5   If you think that your project cannot afford the additional overhead of keeping the key positions of the Enter*Prize* Organization separate, I have startling news for you: *there is no overhead.* This is the resource required to satisfactorily organize and implement a successful project and organization that is sensitive to its continuing commitments to people, projects, products, and clients. If your project is compromising some of the roles and responsibilities of the people who hold these key positions, you likely are paying the price in cost overruns, slipped schedules, low quality, low morale, high employee turnover, and/or low client satisfaction, to name a few. For a case where it is acceptable for a project member to take on more than one of the key positions of the Enter*Prize* Organization, see Chapter 12, Organizing for Small Projects.

> ### LESSON 17.1
> It has been the author's experience that the Enter*Prize* Organization does not require additional cost and schedule overhead to that which is required to run an effective project and to invest in the people and the future.

Q17.6   If I only implement a portion of the Enter*Prize* Organization, which concept(s) is the most important to adopt?

A17.6   If all of the Enter*Prize* Organization concepts are not implemented together, you lose significant benefit. It would be analogous to a puzzle with missing pieces; the puzzle's value is greatly diminished. The Enter*Prize* Organization is well balanced in that all of its primary roles and responsibilities are assigned across project members in reasonable and achievable portions. Having said this, if you were to choose only one of the major concepts to adopt, adopt the roles and responsibilities of the project manager. Why? Because the project manager has such a great position of influence on a project that if you adopt the roles and responsibilities, as defined in Chapter 3, The Project Manager, many of the other concepts will come together because of the actions of the project manager.

> ### LESSON 17.2
> For best results, the Enter*Prize* Organization is designed to be adopted in its entirety, not piecemeal.

Q17.7   Is it a good idea to implement the Enter*Prize* Organization on only a portion of a project before rolling it out across the entire project?

A17.7   No, do not implement the Enter*Prize* Organization on only a portion of a project. It is far better to teach and implement its concepts across all of a project, so everyone is communicating at the same level and with the same expectations.

LESSON 17.3

The Enter*Prize* Organization should be implemented across an entire project rather than only in some areas of a project.

Q17.8 Should I pilot the Enter*Prize* Organization on a project before adopting its concepts across an organization made up of many projects?

A17.8 Piloting the Enter*Prize* Organization can be helpful, particularly for large organizations. It can allow the concepts to be better understood by the people charged with rolling them out across the organization. Furthermore, the feedback that is received likely will help sell the concepts to other projects in the organization.

If you have a relatively small organization made up of only a handful of small- to medium-sized projects, you could fully implement the Enter*Prize* Organization across the organization at the same time.

Q17.9 Should I implement the Enter*Prize* Organization only on new projects, or should I also implement it on projects that already are under way in their development cycle?

A17.9 As a general rule, it is best to begin these concepts at the start of a new project. However, if a project is in trouble or at high risk for not being successful, the Enter*Prize* Organization should be implemented as soon as possible.

LESSON 17.4

It is best to *roll out* the concepts of the Enter*Prize* Organization at the start of new projects or on projects in serious *trouble*.

Q17.10 Does it matter what software development model an organization is following before the Enter*Prize* Organization can be adopted?

A17.10 No, this is one of the great features of the Enter*Prize* Organization. No matter what software development model you follow or plan to follow—iterative, incremental, spiral, waterfall, cleanroom, UML, or other—the concepts of the Enter*Prize* Organization can be applied. You do not have to tip your development process upside down or even sideways to adopt the Enter*Prize* Organization concepts.

Q17.11   What is the relationship, if any, between a work breakdown structure (WBS) and the Enter*Prize* Organization?

A17.11   Let's first look at a definition of WBS: "a deliverable-oriented grouping of project elements which organizes and defines the total scope of the project. Each descending level represents an increasingly detailed definition of a project component. Project components may be products or services." (This definition was extracted from *A Guide to the Project Management Body of Knowledge*, by the Project Management Institute, 1996.)

   A project plan should include a detailed WBS for the work that must be performed. The major phases of the software development process (e.g., requirements, definition, design, construction, test, packaging, and so on) may be used as the first level of decomposition for the WBS. The next level may define the project deliverables associated with each phase. Subsequent levels break the deliverables into smaller components in sufficient detail to define individual activities (e.g., tasks) that are performed by project members. The Enter*Prize* Organization fully supports the use of a WBS that is derived from the software development process which in turn is derived from a software development model. The actual activities defined in a WBS are not affected by the use of the Enter*Prize* Organization. However, because the Enter*Prize* Organization defines the roles and responsibilities of the project leaders and team members, which project members own the activities may be affected. For example, the business architect owns the product-requirements document, and the product architect owns the product-specifications document.

Q17.12   Does the Enter*Prize* Organization influence the prioritization and selection of projects?

A17.12   The Enter*Prize* Organization mostly focuses on successful planning, implementation, and delivery of business-approved projects. Prior to a project being funded, an organization must have a process that includes a *review board* evaluating the business opportunities, the capabilities of the development organization, and other factors to ensure that the right projects are launched and completed to meet the organization's business objectives. Once a project is under way, its project manager must run the project as if it is the most important project in the organization. If one or more funded projects are contending for the same resources, people or otherwise, an escalation may be needed to determine if one project has priority over another for the stated resources.

Q17.13   In the Enter*Prize* Organization, who is responsible for ensuring that the people often viewed as *outside* the project are appropriately involved? These *outsiders* may include, for example, people who must train others in the use of the product, or people who must operate/support the product in the production environment? Moreover, who is responsible for ensuring that the product is not too costly to operate or too difficult to enhance?

A17.13   Multiple project members are involved in addressing these questions. For example, the process architect defines the software development process to be followed, so there are adequate *checks and balances* across the project from persons both within and outside the project. This includes ensuring that all of the appropriate people are included at the appropriate points in the development process. As an example, the production support people have approval rights over the product specifications and test plans. This ensures that the appropriate maintenance and support services are included in the definition of the product, the product will be sufficiently easy to operate, the product is well tested, and operations costs are within acceptable boundaries. The product architect is responsible for defining and architecting the product, so it will be conducive to later enhancements. If a maintenance organization performs enhancements, that organization has approval rights over the architecture of the new product. The Enter*Prize* Organization ensures that roles and responsibilities across the project are sufficiently defined so that all parties are communicating, and everyone understands who is accountable for what.

Q17.14   My company's products are not limited to software. Do the concepts of the Enter*Prize* Organization also apply to nonsoftware projects?

A17.14   From my experience, the Enter*Prize* Organization concepts may apply to projects in general, whether they yield products or provide services. These products and services need not be limited to software, but I want to be careful here. I am not promoting the Enter*Prize* Organization as a for-all, fits-all. Although it may have broad applicability, it has been primarily focused on software projects. Use of the Enter*Prize* Organization concepts beyond software projects is left strictly to the discretion, imagination, and resourcefulness of the reader.

Q17.15   I work in an organization where the use of effective project management practices is minimal, and projects are almost always in trouble. The overall work environment is not very desirable. We continue to make the same mistakes from project to project.

Personnel attrition appears higher than that of other companies. Overtime is high for many people, and morale is fairly constantly *low*. Should I leave and look for a company that practices concepts of the Enter*Prize* Organization or something similar?

A17.15   From the question, I cannot know precisely the causes of the undesirable work environment and therefore give you advice with surgical precision for your situation. However, as a general statement, *the grass is not greener on the other side*. It has been my experience that if people are unhappy with their work environments, and hop to another company to get away from the disarray and unwillingness to improve what exists in their current settings, they eventually experience the same problems at new companies. The reason for this is because, for most of us, if we are unwilling to do something about it, then *we are the problem*. If we are unwilling to dig in our heels, and be a catalyst for change in our current place of employment, we are likely to follow the same behavior elsewhere. Therefore, everywhere we go, we will see the same problems. We need to become accountable for our own actions, and drive the needed changes—which leads us into the next Q&A.

LESSON 17.5

Contrary to common perception, "the grass is *not* greener on the other side."

Q17.16   How do I sell top management on project management best practices, such as the Enter*Prize* Organization?

A17.16   I converse with thousands of people each year. One of the most asked questions by project managers is: "How can I get buy-in for *project management best practices* where I work?"

This standard answer is the *wrong* answer: "You must sell your ideas to top management. Once they buy in to your proposal, they will lead the charge for reform; this reform includes directing their staffs to comply. Then the next level of management will direct their staffs to comply, and so on, until the *word* has traveled down to the troops on the front lines, and the changes are embraced by all. *If they don't support you, then you cannot substantially influence the practices accepted in your projects or across your organization. Therefore, you must keep working to sell top management.*"

In most cases, this approach does not work. In the few instances when this approach does work in driving and institutionalizing project management best practices, it is a welcomed experience. It would be great if this approach worked all the time, but it is wishful thinking.

So, what's the solution? Think, for a moment, as if you were top management. Ask yourself what you would expect of someone who is coming to you for support to solve a problem. What would you expect that person to communicate to you? You would expect to be made to fully understand 1) the problem, 2) the solution (that will be owned and led by someone other than you), and 3) *precisely* what is expected of you—what your role is—to help bring about the solution. These are the issues you address.

If you have done these things, then you almost always will get support from top management and from the management below them. However, if, after an earnest attempt, you still are ineffective in selling change to top management—for whatever reason—don't resort to common behaviors: withdrawing, complaining, and whining yourself exhausted. If you do behave this way, the problem will now be *you!*—if it wasn't already.

Instead, you should *fix the problem as it relates to your domain of responsibility*—that is, in those areas that fall within your job assignment. For example, if you are a project manager, it is your job to ensure that project management best practices are defined and enforced on *your* project—*not* across your organization made up of many projects. Defining project management best practices for *your* project is *not* management's responsibility, it is yours (unless best projects have already been defined and institutionalized in your overall organization).

LESSON 17.6

Be accountable for correcting those problems that relate to your domain of responsibility.

As a project manager, you have more influence in changing the way your project is planned, tracked, controlled, and run day to day than anyone in top management could possibly ever have. Your project will be planned according to how you lead the planning activities. It will be tracked based on your direction of when, where, how, and what—and so on.

If you are successful in selling top management on change, and obtain its support, this is the most effective method to change an organization's culture. However, in absence of management's full support, you must take responsibility, accountability, and authority to drive the needed change in those areas that define your domain. Don't wait for someone else to do it for you. If everyone focused on solving the major obstacles that prohibit her from achieving her commitments, the entire organization would experience a giant leap forward in improving its performance. Don't become part of the problem. Be a part of the solution in those areas that impact your performance and success.

GLOSSARY

Note: Bold terms within a definition also are defined within this glossary.

accountable. Being answerable for results of one's own acts and commitments.

accountability. Synonym for **accountable**.

action item. A **project** problem that is logged, assigned to an owner to resolve, and then tracked until it is closed.

application support organization. See **maintenance organization**.

approver. A person who must personally give his approval on an item (e.g., a document, plan, or action) before that item can be considered *approved*. Approvers frequently have a dependency on the item to perform their work and meet their commitments. See **reviewer**.

architect. See **product architect**.

architecture. See **product architecture**.

BAO. See **business architect office**.

benevolent dictator. A leader who actively and sincerely solicits information and opinions from project members and others, then demonstrates the leadership, courage, and boldness to personally make the *right* decision, and stands **accountable** for that decision.

business architect. The person who performs as the **client's** advocate. The business architect owns the **product requirements**, manages client expectations, is charged with ensuring that the *right* **product** is built, and ensures that the client is appropriately represented throughout the development process.

business architect office (BAO). A **department** or group that can serve as a home base for **business architects**.

change-control board. Typically a group of people who meet as needed to follow the agreed-to process when a change to a controlled document is proposed. A typical use is to control changes proposed to documents such as the **product requirements** and the **product specifications** after these documents have been approved.

client. The person, **organization**, or company that typically pays for and uses the **product** or service being developed or deployed.

closet plan. The creation and collection of lower-priority small **projects** that develop function deemed nonessential, yet desirable, to a sanctioned project plan. If the function is satisfactorily developed from any of these nonessential projects by a predetermined date or point in the sanctioned project plan, that function can be added to the sanctioned project plan and included in the **product**.

command center. See **project command center**.

complaining. Behavior of talking *at* a problem rather than constructively working to correct the problem.

component. A major design piece of a **product**. The collection of components comprises the programming portion of a product. A component is usually comprised of one or more modules or objects.

culture training. The formal training of all **project members**—usually at the start of a **project**—in key hard skills, soft skills, and processes that are essential in helping to ensure a successful project.

customer. See **client**.

department. A group of people typically comprised of two or more teams, each having a distinct mission and headed by a **resource manager**. A department of non-managers typically consists of up to fifteen people. A department of resource managers typically consists of up to seven resource managers.

dictator. See **benevolent dictator**.

direct report. A person who reports to a **resource manager**. Only resource managers have direct reports. Having direct reports means that you have *personnel* or *administrative* responsibilities for employees, performing such duties as hiring and firing; evaluating performance; providing salary increases, promotions, and awards; and that you look out for their professional development and careers. Another way to say this is that resource managers address what is typically called *manager-employee issues*.

domain of responsibility. Includes all responsibilities and commitments that fall within the scope of a person's assignment.

earned value. A method for measuring **project** performance. It compares the amount of work that was planned with what was actually accomplished to determine if cost and schedule performance is as planned. (This definition was extracted from *A Guide to the Project Management Body of Knowledge*, by the Project Management Institute, 1996.)

empowerment. The act of understanding your job, taking ownership of your job, and doing whatever is necessary to accomplish that job, providing that it is within legal and ethical parameters.

Enter*Prize* **Organization**. A method to organize software **projects** to appropriately drive and balance responsibility, personal **accountability**, and authority across the members of a project with the intention of optimizing their performance and producing a successful project.

escalatee. The person whose position on an issue is being challenged by the **escalator**.

escalation. The act of calling upon higher levels of a **project's** leadership to resolve an **issue**. When two affected parties are unable to agree on the resolution of an issue, after a sincere attempt to negotiate a resolution has occurred, an escalation is pursued to resolve the issue.

escalator. The person who initiates an **escalation**.

issue. A problem that, if not resolved, is believed will have a significant harmful effect on the outcome of the **project**.

John Wayne mentality. The mistaken belief that asking for help is a sign of weakness, but going it alone is a sign of strength and virtue.

lessons learned. See **postproject review**.

maintenance organization. An **organization** that corrects problems in existing **products**. Also called application support, systems support, production support, and sustaining organization.

maintenance release. An updated version of an existing **product**, where the updates are fixes to problems that earlier **releases** contained. A maintenance release can also contain minor enhancements to the product.

management. One or more **resource managers** whose primary role is to support the nonmanagers as they perform their day-to-day work.

management reserve. Contingency of time and/or funds, which have been set aside after a **project** has been planned. The time and/or funds usually are used at the discretion of the **project manager**, should the need arise.

meets minimum requirements. Providing the **client** with a **product** that satisfies her needs, so she can be successful; not committing to provide unessential function. Unessential function, if it is to be included as part of the product, is developed by way of a **closet plan**.

mentoring. Working with a person to help develop his skills and increase his effectiveness in a specific area of interest. Mentoring should be personal and confidential and is best performed by a person that is not your boss or in your direct line of command.

objectives. See **product objectives**.

open door. An open invitation for an employee of a company to appeal a decision that affects the employee, which she believes is unfair or unjust. The appeal can be taken over the boss' head to higher levels of **management** or to a special position or executive designated for that purpose. The open door is a safety valve for employees to professionally and maturely resolve issues, usually personal ones, which cannot be satisfactorily resolved using the standard and usual means. The open door only should be used as a last resort and very infrequently, if ever.

organization. A group of people typically divided into two or more departments. Multiple projects are typically under way and are, wholly or in part, staffed by the people comprising the organization.

PAO. See **product architect office.**

PMO. See **project management office.**

post mortem. See **postproject review.**

postproject review. The review of a completed **project** by a selected group of **project members** who represent all the major organizations that participated on the project. For a small project, all project members should participate. The group identifies those things that went right, that went wrong, and where improvement can be made. The objective is to learn from project experiences, so future projects can benefit.

postproject review summary report. A report identifying the most significant findings from **postproject reviews.** The report is updated routinely—say after every five to ten postproject reviews—and is used as a quick and easy method for **project members** to review the most important lessons learned from postproject reviews.

process architect. The person who serves as the process champion for the **project.** The process architect is charged with ensuring that the appropriate processes are defined, documented, and followed, so high productivity, high quality, and minimal cycle times are achieved.

product. A software package, consisting of at least code and publications, eventually put into a production environment or delivered to a **client.** In a broader sense, the definition of product also includes the product support materials that are required for activities such as marketing and maintenance. A *software package* can be a product that must be developed, or it can be an already-packaged or partially-packaged application.

product architect. The person **accountable** for the technical solution to the **client's** problems. The product architect owns the **product specifications,** the overall design (**architecture**) of the **product,** and ensures that the product is built *right.*

product architect office (PAO). A **department** or group that can serve as a home base for product architects.

product architecture. The level of design required for defining how the **components** of the **product** technically work 1) with one another, 2) with the surrounding hardware and software environment in which they must operate, and 3) internally. This design identifies the components that make up the product, defines the functional mission for each component, and defines, at a high level, the internal design of each component. (In some development shops, product architecture is synonymous with high-level design.)

production support organization. See **maintenance organization.**

product manager. The person with overall responsibility—from cradle to grave—for the success of a **product.**

product objectives. A document that defines the solution to the problem (or set of problems) defined in the **product-requirements** document. This document defines, at a high level, a **product** that will satisfy a marketing opportunity and focuses on the perceived needs of the targeted **client(s)**. The product-objectives document is intentionally approximately one-tenth the size of the **product-specifications** document.

product requirements. A document that describes the **client** and market problems that need to be solved. This document focuses exclusively on the problems that need to be solved, not the solutions to those problems.

product review. An independent review that is performed at selected points after the **product** has been delivered to the **client**. A product review allows a product in *production* to be examined for meeting key business parameters including customer satisfaction, return on investment, and quality goals.

product specifications. A document that describes, in detail, precisely what the **client** will receive and use when the completed **product** is made available. Every function, command, screen, prompt, and other user interface-related items are documented, so all the participants involved in the software development process (including the client) know the product they are to build, document, test, use, and support.

program. A group of related **projects** managed in a coordinated way. (This definition was extracted from *A Guide to the Project Management Body of Knowledge*, by the Project Management Institute, 1996.)

program manager. The person who directs the planning and execution of a **program** and is held personally **accountable** for the success of the program.

project. A temporary endeavor undertaken to create a unique **product** or service. (This definition was extracted from *A Guide to the Project Management Body of Knowledge*, by the Project Management Institute, 1996.)

project command center. A designated space or room that contains the most current status about the **project** and is used to track the project. This area also is called the *war* room or simply the project room.

project improvement activity. An activity included in a project plan that requires the **project manager** to convince a review panel of three members (or a designated person) that the project manager has appropriately applied the most significant lessons learned from recent **projects** to the new project.

project manager. The person who directs the planning and execution of a **project** and is held personally **accountable** for the success of the project—sometimes referred to as *release manager*.

project management. The planning, implementing, and controlling of a **project** with the specific goals of building and delivering a **product** or performing a service within the scope, schedule, cost, and quality that satisfies the **client**.

241

project management consulting. The act of providing **project management** services and **products**. These services and products may take on many forms such as providing project management-related training, documenting processes and procedures (including templates), assisting in project planning and tracking activities, performing **project reviews**, and running an entire **project** from start to finish.

project management office (PMO). A group of people whose mission is to support **project managers** in the successful launch, implementation, and completion of their **projects**. This includes performing any tasks that can benefit current or future projects.

project member. A person assigned to a **project** such as the **project manager, business architect, product architect, process architect, team leader,** and **team member**. **Resource managers** are not typically thought of as being direct members of a project, because they usually do not have any project-related assignments. However, they do provide very important support roles for a project by working with, tracking, coaching, and helping their employees make and meet their commitments. Because of the vital support services provided by resource managers, they are included as part of the headcount and budget for a project and therefore are project members.

project office. See **project management office**.

project review. An independent review that is performed at selected points along the software development process for an active **project**. A project review allows an active project to be examined to determine its overall health. Actions are then recommended to immediately address any significant problems that are identified.

project support office. See **project management office**.

regression testing. The final series of tests performed after a major test has occurred (e.g., function test, system test) and/or the final test of a **product**. The test typically comprises a selected set of test scripts, taken from prior tests, that are run as final verification that the product works as it was intended. Regression testing verifies that the product function that used to work still does.

release. See **version** and **maintenance release**.

release manager. See **project manager**.

requirements. See **product requirements**.

resize project. An activity included in a project plan that appears at the end of major phases. The **project**, or a portion thereof, is resized if this activity is judged by the **project manager** as being required.

resource manager. The person who hires, fires, makes job assignments, coaches, counsels, evaluates, awards, promotes, and secures future work opportunities for her direct reports.

responsibility domain. See **domain of responsibility**.

reviewer. A person who has an interest in an item (e.g., a document, plan, or action), but the item does not necessarily impact his own work and commitments. The item should be made available for review to reviewers but can be considered *approved* without the agreement of the reviewers. See **approver**.

SEPG. See **software engineering process group**.

soft behavior. See **too-soft behavior**.

software engineering process group (SEPG). Typically a group of people who serve as representatives from the varied functional groups across an **organization**. The primary roles of the group are to define, document, maintain, and improve the subprocesses that are the underpinnings of the software development process used across an organization and its **projects**.

specifications. See **product specifications**.

subteam leader. The person who directs the planning and execution of a team and is held personally **accountable** for the success of the team. The team referred to here is a portion of a larger team that is led by a **team leader**.

sustaining organization. See **maintenance organization**.

systems support organization. See **maintenance organization**.

team leader. The person who directs the planning and execution of a team and is held personally **accountable** for the success of the team.

team member. A **project member** who typically works under the technical direction of a **team leader** or someone else within the team leader's team. However, a team member can work independently of a team leader, and take technical direction from a project member such as the **project manager, business architect, product architect, process architect,** or her **resource manager**.

too-soft behavior. Behavior that results in being consistently less effective than what is otherwise possible in accomplishing responsibilities.

version. The first offering of a new **product** or follow-up offerings with significant enhancements added.

WBS. See **work breakdown structure**.

work breakdown structure (WBS). "A deliverable-oriented grouping of **project** elements which organizes and defines the total scope of the project. Each descending level represents an increasingly detailed definition of a project component. Project components may be products or services." (This definition was extracted from *A Guide to the Project Management Body of Knowledge*, by the Project Management Institute, 1996.)

UPGRADE YOUR
PROJECT MANAGEMENT KNOWLEDGE
WITH FIRST-CLASS
PUBLICATIONS FROM PMI

A FRAMEWORK FOR PROJECT MANAGEMENT

This complete project management seminar course provides experienced project managers with an easy-to-use set of educational tools to help them deliver a seminar on basic project management concepts, tools and techniques. *A Framework for Project Management* was developed and designed for seminar leaders by a team of experts within the PMI® membership and reviewed extensively during its development and piloting stage by a team of PMPs. It serves as a first step for individual attendees who wish to obtain their Project Management Professional (PMP®) certification.
ISBN: 1-880410-82-6 (Facilitator's Manual Set), ISBN: 1-880410-80-X (Participant's Manual Set)

THE PMI PROJECT MANAGEMENT FACT BOOK

A comprehensive resource of information about PMI and the profession it serves. Professionals working in project management require information and resources to function in today's global business environment. Knowledge along with data collection and interpretation are often key to determining success in the marketplace. The Project Management Institute (PMI®) anticipates the needs of the profession with *The PMI Project Management Fact Book*.
ISBN: 1-880410-62-1 (paperback)

PROJECT MANAGEMENT SOFTWARE SURVEY

The PMI® *Project Management Software Survey* offers an efficient way to compare and contrast the capabilities of a wide variety of project management tools. More than two hundred software tools are listed with comprehensive information on systems features, how they perform time analysis, resource analysis, cost analysis, performance analysis, and cost reporting, and how they handle multiple projects, project tracking, charting, and much more. The survey is a valuable tool to help narrow the field when selecting the best project management tools.
ISBN: 1-880410-52-4 (paperback), ISBN: 1-880410-59-1 (CD-ROM)

THE JUGGLER'S GUIDE TO MANAGING MULTIPLE PROJECTS

This comprehensive book introduces and explains task-oriented, independent, and interdependent levels of project portfolios. It says that you must first have a strong foundation in time management and priority setting, then introduces the concept of Portfolio Management to timeline multiple projects, determine their resource requirements, and handle emergencies, putting you in charge for possibly the first time in your life!
ISBN: 1-880410-65-6 (paperback)

RECIPES FOR PROJECT SUCCESS

This book is destined to become "the" reference book for beginning project managers, particularly those who like to cook! Practical, logically developed project management concepts are offered in easily understood terms in a lighthearted manner. They are applied to the everyday task of cooking—from simple, single dishes, such as homemade tomato sauce for pasta, made from the bottom up, to increasingly complex dishes or meals for groups that in turn require an understanding of more complex project management terms and techniques. The transition between cooking and project management discussions is smooth, and tidbits of information provided with the recipes are interesting and humorous.
ISBN: 1-880410-58-3 (paperback)

TOOLS AND TIPS FOR TODAY'S PROJECT MANAGER

This guide book is valuable for understanding project management and performing to quality standards. Includes project management concepts and terms—old and new—that are not only defined but also are explained in much greater detail than you would find in a typical glossary. Also included are tips on handling such seemingly simple everyday tasks as how to say "No" and how to avoid telephone tag. It's a reference you'll want to keep close at hand.
ISBN: 1-880410-61-3 (paperback)

THE FUTURE OF PROJECT MANAGEMENT

The project management profession is going through tremendous change—both evolutionary and revolutionary. Some of these changes are internally driven while many are externally driven. Here, for the first time, is a composite view of some major trends occurring throughout the world and the implication of them on the profession of project management and on the Project Management Institute. Read the views of the 1998 PMI Research Program Team, a well-respected futurist firm, and other authors. This book represents the beginning of a journey and, through inputs from readers and others, it will continue as a work in progress.
ISBN: 1-880410-71-0 (paperback)

NEW RESOURCES FOR PMP CANDIDATES

The following publications are resources that certification candidates can use to gain information on project management theory, principles, techniques, and procedures.

PMP RESOURCE PACKAGE

Earned Value Project Management by Quentin W. Fleming and Joel M. Koppelman

Effective Project Management: How to Plan, Manage, and Deliver Projects on Time and Within Budget
    by Robert K. Wysocki, et al.

A Guide to the Project Management Body of Knowledge (PMBOK® Guide) by the PMI Standards Committee

Human Resource Skills for the Project Manager by Vijay K. Verma

The New Project Management by J. Davidson Frame

Organizing Projects for Success by Vijay K. Verma

Principles of Project Management by John Adams, et al.

Project & Program Risk Management by R. Max Wideman, Editor

Project Management Casebook edited by David I. Cleland, et al.

Project Management: A Managerial Approach, Third Edition by Jack R. Meredith and Samuel J. Mantel Jr.

Project Management: A Systems Approach to Planning, Scheduling, and Controlling, Sixth Edition by Harold Kerzner

A GUIDE TO THE PROJECT MANAGEMENT BODY OF KNOWLEDGE (PMBOK® GUIDE)

The basic management reference for everyone who works on projects. Serves as a tool for learning about the generally accepted knowledge and practices of the profession. As "management by projects" becomes more and more a recommended business practice worldwide, the *PMBOK® Guide* becomes an essential source of information that should be on every manager's bookshelf. Available in hardcover or paperback, the *PMBOK® Guide* is an official standards document of the Project Management Institute.
ISBN: 1-880410-12-5 (paperback), ISBN: 1-880410-13-3 (hardcover)

INTERACTIVE PMBOK® GUIDE

This CD-ROM makes it easy for you to access the valuable information in PMI's *PMBOK® Guide*. Features hypertext links for easy reference—simply click on underlined words in the text, and the software will take you to that particular section in the *PMBOK® Guide*. Minimum system requirements: 486 PC; 8MB RAM; 10MB free disk space; CD-ROM drive, mouse, or other pointing device; and Windows 3.1 or greater.

MANAGING PROJECTS STEP-BY-STEP™

Follow the steps, standards, and procedures used and proven by thousands of professional project managers and leading corporations. This interactive multimedia CD-ROM based on PMI's *PMBOK® Guide* will enable you to customize, standardize, and distribute your project plan standards, procedures, and methodology across your entire organization. Multimedia illustrations using 3-D animations and audio make this perfect for both self-paced training or for use by a facilitator.

PMBOK® Q&A

Use this handy pocket-sized question-and-answer study guide to learn more about the key themes and concepts presented in PMI's international standard, *PMBOK® Guide*. More than 160 multiple-choice questions with answers (referenced to the *PMBOK® Guide*) help you with the breadth of knowledge needed to understand key project management concepts.

ISBN: 1-880410-21-4 (paperback)

PMI PROCEEDINGS LIBRARY CD-ROM

This interactive guide to PMI's annual Seminars & Symposium proceedings offers a powerful new option to the traditional methods of document storage and retrieval, research, training, and technical writing. Contains complete paper presentations from PMI '92–PMI '97 with full-text search capability, convenient onscreen readability, and PC/Mac compatibility.

PMI PUBLICATIONS LIBRARY CD-ROM

Using state-of-the-art technology, PMI offers complete articles and information from its major publications on one CD-ROM, including *PM Network* (1990–97), *Project Management Journal* (1990–97), and *A Guide to the Project Management Body of Knowledge*. Offers full-text search capability and indexing by *PMBOK® Guide* knowledge areas. Electronic indexing schemes and sophisticated search engines help to find and retrieve articles quickly that are relevant to your topic or research area.

Also Available from PMI

Project Management for Managers
Mihály Görög, Nigel J. Smith
ISBN: 1-880410-54-0 (paperback)

Project Leadership: From Theory to Practice
Jeffery K. Pinto, Peg Thoms, Jeffrey Trailer, Todd Palmer, Michele Govekar
ISBN: 1-880410-10-9 (paperback)

Annotated Bibliography of Project and Team Management
David I. Cleland, Gary Rafe, Jeffrey Mosher
ISBN: 1-880410-47-8 (paperback),
ISBN: 1-880410-57-5 (CD-ROM)

How to Turn Computer Problems into Competitive Advantage
Tom Ingram
ISBN: 1-880410-08-7 (paperback)

Achieving the Promise of Information Technology
Ralph B. Sackman
ISBN: 1-880410-03-6 (paperback)

Leadership Skills for Project Managers
Editors' Choice Series
Edited by Jeffrey K. Pinto, Jeffrey W. Trailer
ISBN: 1-880410-49-4 (paperback)

The Virtual Edge
Margery Mayer
ISBN: 1-880410-16-8 (paperback)

ABCs of DPC
Edited by PMI's Design-Procurement-Construction Specific Interest Group
ISBN: 1-880410-07-9 (paperback)

Project Management Casebook
Edited by David I. Cleland, Karen M. Bursic, Richard Puerzer, A. Yaroslav Vlasak
ISBN: 1-880410-45-1 (paperback)

Project Management Casebook Instructor's Manual
Edited by David I. Cleland, Karen M. Bursic, Richard Puerzer, A. Yaroslav Vlasak
ISBN: 1-880410-18-4 (paperback)

PMI Book of Project Management Forms
ISBN: 1-880410-31-1 (paperback)
ISBN: 1-880410-50-8 (diskette version 1.0)

Principles of Project Management
John Adams et al.
ISBN: 1-880410-30-3 (paperback)

Organizing Projects for Success
Human Aspects of Project Management Series,
Volume 1
Vijay K. Verma
ISBN: 1-880410-40-0 (paperback)

**Human Resource Skills for the
Project Manager**
Human Aspects of Project Management Series,
Volume 2, Vijay K. Verma
ISBN: 1-880410-41-9 (paperback)

Managing the Project Team
Human Aspects of Project Management Series,
Volume 3, Vijay K. Verma
ISBN: 1-880410-42-7 (paperback)

Earned Value Project Management
Quentin W. Fleming, Joel M. Koppelman
ISBN: 1-880410-38-9 (paperback)

Value Management Practice
Michel Thiry
ISBN: 1-880410-14-1 (paperback)

Decision Analysis in Projects
John R. Schuyler
ISBN: 1-880410-39-7 (paperback)

The World's Greatest Project
Russell W. Darnall
ISBN: 1-880410-46-X (paperback)

Power & Politics in Project Management
Jeffrey K. Pinto
ISBN: 1-880410-43-5 (paperback)

**Best Practices of Project Management
Groups in Large Functional Organizations**
Frank Toney, Ray Powers
ISBN: 1-880410-05-2 (paperback)

Project Management in Russia
Vladimir I. Voropajev
ISBN: 1-880410-02-8 (paperback)

**A Framework for Project and Program
Management Integration**
R. Max Wideman
ISBN: 1-880410-01-X (paperback)

**Quality Management for Projects
& Programs**
Lewis R. Ireland
ISBN: 1-880410-11-7 (paperback)

Project & Program Risk Management
Edited by R. Max Wideman
ISBN: 1-880410-06-0 (paperback)

ORDER ONLINE AT
WWW.PMIBOOKSTORE.ORG

Book Ordering Information
Phone: 412.741.6206
Fax: 412.741.0609
Email: pmiorders@abdintl.com
Mail: PMI Publications Fulfillment Center
 PO Box 1020
 Sewickley, Pennsylvania 15143-1020 USA